Dear
Wh

Azor

Environment of Hate:

The New Normal for Muslims in the UK

Saied Reza Ameli
Arzu Merali

Islamic Human Rights Commission

www.ihrc.org.uk

First published in Great Britain in 2015
by Islamic Human Rights Commission
PO Box 598,Wembley, HA9 7XH
© 2015 Islamic Human Rights Commission
Design & Typeset: Ibrahim Sadikovic

ISBN 978-1-909853-00-3

Cover image: Photo by Joel Goodman/LNP/REX Shutterstock.
EDL demonstration in Dudley where approximately 500 EDL supporters
protested the building of a new mosque in the town. English Defence League
demonstration in Dudley, West Midlands, Britain - 07 Feb 2015. Conservative
Party candidate for Dudley North, Afzal Amin, has resigned after it was
revealed he plotted with EDL to organise a fake race demonstration in the town
in a bit for votes.

Contents

List of Tables

List of figures

Acknowledgements

The following have contributed immensely to this project:

Afroze Zaidi-Jivraj, Ahmed Uddin, Aini Ghafoor, Ali Akbar Abidi, Ali Zaidi, Anjum Riaz, Anjum Abbas Shah, Arham Haideri, Asgher Abbas, Asif Raza, Aun Naqvi, Banin Rizvi, Bob Pitt, Ebrahim Mohseni Ahoei, Ehsan Shahghasemi, Fahim Sinn, Fawad Hussain, Hikmah Muhammad, Kamal Khan,Kanwal Fatima, Massoud Shadjareh, Maqsood Anwar, Mohammod Choudhury, Mohsin Ali Raza, Mojtaba Hajijafari, Mustafa Virani, Musthak Ahmed, Nadia Rasheed, Raza Abbas Shah,Raza Kazim, Salman Hussain, Seerat Fatima, Syed Naveed Naqvi, Syed Zulqarnain Haider Rizvi,Thania Uddin, Ummul Banin Rizwi, Wajahat Hussain and Zainab Rizvi.

To Abed Choudhury and Lena Mohamed, many thanks for the specialist advice and contribution. Likewise thanks to the following for their insights over the period of this project: Marie Breen-Smyth, Kwame Nimako, Sandew Hira, Ramon Grosfoguel, Houria Bouteldja, Katy Sian, Salman Sayyid and Hatem Bazian.

A special mention to Faisal Bodi, Adam Majeed and Ibrahim Sadikovic for all the unsocial hours' work. A very special mention to Ashiya Mendheria for the same but an acknowledgement that without her this work would not have come together in any shape or form.

Finally, thanks to Sayid Hussain Ali, Sumayyah Sadat and Sayid Ali Akbar, for all their patience.

May Allah swt reward you all.

Preface

It is with great regret that the authors find themselves writing up this research. This project, now named the Domination Hate Model of Intercultural Relations (DHMIR), started out in 2009, as a way of collecting data on the experiences of hatred and hostility faced (in this case) by Muslims.

Six years on, the second survey to be conducted in the UK shows that the project was not only timely but sadly also prescient. The first set of results showed that there were serious problems in the way structural reproduction of the idea of 'Muslim', 'Islam' and something like 'Muslimness', and that the experiences of Muslims testified to this phenomena. In the current study, the situation is clearly worse.

The authors have tried to overview changes, significant cultural and paradigmatic shifts, events etc. for the intervening period. However our charge is the same. The moral responsibility for changing this state of affairs lies with institutions of power – governmental, media, legal et al.

At the time of writing Britain is seeing a huge political shift, with marginalised people from the majority community, as well as minorities, organising in response to governmental programmes that are causing massive social and legal upheaval and exclusion. This organisation is vociferous yet unprecedented in this generation. This movement is hopeful at a time when many felt hopeless, and the authors hope that this work, though distressing in content, may help this or any other movement that sincerely seeks to transform society for the better. The question remains as to what, if anything, those who retain power will do in response? The fact that the authors and many others wonder whether further punitive sanctions against political and social mobilisation are likely, sums up the negative state of affairs, and the negative state that they write about.

That negativity permeates the environment, which the authors will argue, is an environment of hate – one that has become the normal experience and expectation of Muslims in the UK.

Islamic Human Rights Commission

Chapter 1

A Background

Summarising key issues that affect Muslims in the UK is not a simple task given the rapid and measurable shift in climate in the United Kingdom with regard to so-called minority issues. This sea change, if compared with the work of IHRC from the previous decade and indeed with key race relations organisations and relevant academics writing through the 1980s until now, marks key cultural shifts and policy changes.

For the purposes of contextualising the findings of the 2014 IHRC survey, the following issues will be discussed in this chapter to outline the authors' arguments that the cultural, legal and political landscape has changed not only drastically but for the worse: the concept of the end of structural racism and the post-racial society; the idea of NGOs, civil society and the Victorian model of social responsibility; anti-democratisation and the (other) outcomes of subalternisation; militarisation and subhumanisation, and securitisation; and grassroots backlash.

From structural racism to the post-racial

An understanding of structural racism, counter-intuitively, was recognised by the British state through its interaction with communities from the end of the 1950s through to the late 1990s. The immediate post-war period saw immigrants from Commonwealth countries, encouraged by the British state, come and take jobs in the low wage economy that those from the majority community did not want to take. Those arriving, as subjects of the Commonwealth, had long term residence rights and the possibility of becoming fully-fledged citizens (Lea, 2003).

'Disturbances' in 1958, when 'gangs of white youth attacked members of the small and newly arrived West Indian community in west London focused the minds of the political elite on the need for a 'race relations' strategy' (Lea, 2003). The two-pronged strategy involved restricting long term settlement from the Commonwealth, and working out an integration strategy, which included outlawing discrimination and creating new bodies to foster ethnic integration. These latter can be seen as fulfilled in part by the introduction of race relations laws, notably the Race Relations Act 1976, as well as institutions such as the now defunct Commission for Racial Equality. Even if seen as cynically motivated by successive governments, these developments were a de facto acknowledgement that institutions (schools, workplaces and by extension all institutions of the state) are obliged to protect ethnic minorities from discrimination. The operation of racism within structures is acknowledged at the very least. The drive for integration, whilst focusing on the need to socialise immigrant cultures to the state, acknowledged that the state's relations with its ethnic communities was problematic and in need of change.

Even the Scarman report, undertaken by a Conservative peer under the auspices of a Conservative government which looked into the riots of 1981 by largely black youth, expressed sentiment that would be crystallised in the term 'institutional racism' by Macpherson nearly two decades later. Scarman wrote of practices which are 'unwittingly discriminatory against black people.' (Scarman 1981 para 2.22) and 'police attitudes and methods have not yet sufficiently responded to the problem of policing our multi-racial society." (Scarman 1981 para 4.70) (both cited in Lea, 2003). Scarman saw the riots as an expression of 'a demand for inclusion in social citizenship rights by those who had become marginalised through a combination of racial discrimination and economic decay. His proposed reforms were directed to this end.' (Lea, 2003)

Despite the foregoing, official narratives focused on the idea of a British way of 'doing race relations' that is markedly different from both its US and European counterparts, i.e. multiculturalism, a term coined in UK political parlance by the then Home Secretary Roy Jenkins in 1966, who said that:

> "I do not regard [integration] as meaning the loss, by immigrants, of their own national characteristics and culture. I do not think that we need in this country a 'melting pot', which will turn everybody out in a common mould, as one of a series of carbon copies of someone's misplaced vision of the stereotyped Englishman… I define integration, therefore, not as a flattening process of assimilation but as equal opportunity, accompanied by cultural diversity, in an atmosphere of mutual tolerance". (Lester, 2009)

This view - setting out a supposedly anti-assimilationist agenda - has for a long time characterised a view of British race relations. Its supporters claim that it has fostered a sense of belonging amongst ethnic communities, and lately religious communities, see e.g. Ameli and Merali (2004a), and Comres (2015) who put the figure of Muslims feeling loyalty to the UK at 95%. Its detractors claim it has fostered separateness (see e.g. Cameron, 5 February 2011 and Phillips quoted in Baldwin and Sherman, 10 April 2004), and more vocal detractors have claimed that it has created a sense of entitlement to difference that undermines 'Britishness'. These two strands of critique will be dealt with later. This attack on multiculturalism has escalated over the last decade since the introduction of the PREVENT programme as part of the former New Labour government's CONTEST strategy. What is pertinent to understand at this stage of the discussion is that this undermining of multiculturalism detracts from the idea of any sort of structural identity of the state. This reproduces the idea of the state as simultaneously 'neutral' and embodying 'Britishness'. To do so and in doing so it reinforces the idea of a monolithic and powerful 'otherness' that detracts from 'Britishness'. This otherness is clearly racialised, firstly by colour and latterly by culture and religion (Grosfoguel and Mielants, 2006).

Where racism is acknowledged, it comes from the idea that racism is perpetrated by individuals - or as Scarman described, the knowingly prejudiced police officer, the 'bad apples'. This is the epitome of the post-racial society, as Sayyid et al (2013) explain:

> "This denial of the significance of racism and its unique trajectory feeds into the contemporary 'post-racial', liberal logic which attempts to mask, hide and dismiss the prominence of racism which is constructed as a thing of the past, no longer important or relevant. The relationship between race and power and how racism operates structurally throughout society is instead overshadowed by a cloud of (neo-) liberalism which suppresses race to the extent that European societies are able to state that they are not racist..."

This trend can be identified in the late 1990s as a backlash amongst the right wing commentariat (Sayyid et al, 2013) to the Macpherson enquiry (1999) which clearly forced the idea of 'institutional racism' to the fore. Whilst Macpherson stated the police to be thus, it forced other public institutions to acknowledge the existence of the phenomenon. In particular the Director General of the BBC, Greg Dyke stated it to be so. The 2004 Mubarek enquiry raised the idea explicitly that something akin to institutional religious prejudice existed, by highlighting anti-Muslim praxis at the Feltham young offenders institution where Zahid Mubarek was killed by an avowedly violent racist cell mate.

Part of the backlash against the idea of 'institutional racism' was expressed by Munira Mirza et. al. in their report for right wing think tank Policy Exchange (2007) 'Living apart together: British Muslims and the paradox of multiculturalism'. Whilst attacking the idea of a Muslim polity encouraged to develop by successive governmental policies focused on multicultural norms, the report specifically seeks to undermine the Macpherson Enquiry's recommendations, claiming that "Despite its high-minded aim, the preoccupation with monitoring racism seems to coincide with increased racial tensions between groups."

Not only does this set out an anti-Macpherson stall, it claims that Macpherson, or rather the implementation of Macpherson's recommendations (in particular those around the identification of a hate crime or attack based on a victim's perception of it as racist) leads to racial tension.

Whilst Policy Exchange is a right leaning think tank, the New Labour government by the mid-2000s had already distanced itself from Macpherson's recommendations. The discourse of a post-racial society was one that New Labour fostered using, ironically, cases like that of Stephen Lawrence. The family-based campaign around the Lawrence case represented a shift in advocacy on 'race' issues, with campaigners acknowledging that campaigns for structural change were no longer actionable in the current climate, leaving campaigns for individual justice the only effective campaigning option (Merali, 2014).

The New Labour government also sought from its outset to change the equalities culture in the UK. This has been critiqued in depth by Sayyid et al (2013). Suffice it to say here that the proposal to create a single equalities body, the Equalities and Human Rights

Commission (EHRC) (which required the abolishment of all other
equalities bodies including the Commission for Racial Equality),
has been instrumental in shifting the cultural understanding of
how racism works, as well as enshrining in praxis the idea of a
post-racial society:

> "The danger then is that this simplification of equality
> laws and the joining up of the distinct equality strands
> enables Britain to construct itself as a progressive, 'post-
> racial' liberal society, thus racism becomes invisible and is
> instead understood as a human rights issue. That is the
> bringing together of all groups and dispensing with single
> issue bodies such as the CRE, sustains and strengthens the
> notion that 'we are all the same' and as such reinforces the
> discourse of colour blindness, universalism and unification
> which masks the persistence of structural inequalities that
> remain embedded within contemporary Britain. For
> example within the strategic plan it is quoted that, "racism
> appears to be less prevalent among younger generations,
> though it is far from absent. [EHRC, 2012 cited in Sayyid et
> al 2013]"

The authors go on to cite exactly how much worse the
situation vis a vis experiences of racism are. As with this work,
Sayyid et al argue that there is significant worsening of many
experiences of racism, and claims like those made by EHRC are at
best disingenuous.

The Con-Dem coalition, and at the time of writing the new
Conservative government, covering the years since 2010 (a few
months after the previous study of Ameli et al was concluded)
have taken the idea of the post-racial further, on the one hand
creating a working group on anti-Muslm hate crime, but on the
other fostering the ideas of a homogenous and politically active
Muslim polity that can be viewed as an existential threat not just
in terms of violence and killing but also through the destruction of
institutions and values. These latter themes will be discussed in
detail later looking at the recent anti-terror laws and strategies and
the role and impact of the so-called Trojan Horse affair.

It is worth noting at this stage that a facet of the post-racial
belies the myth that the post-racial is based on. The post-racial
society arises, in part, out of the idea that previous policies that

developed institutions of integration have fulfilled their role. As Lea (2003) points out with reference to the experience of black communities following the 1980s riots, but also Asian and white working class groups:

> "We have moved a long way from Scarman. He did not doubt, even though he produced his report when a Conservative government was already established and determined to begin the process of rolling back the state, the social nature of citizenship. It meant inclusion in the economy, inclusion in welfare rights and inclusion in legal and civil rights. The focus was on the relationship between the community and the state, how to break down discrimination and extend equal rights to ethnic minorities. The multicultural settlement was a particular way of doing this which served the interests of pacification by establishing separate institutions which would facilitate the development of a middle class in the black community which would have a pacifying 'leadership' effect rather than see black workers as a militant section of the working class. Nevertheless many black and Asian people moved into influential positions in local government."

Lea's critique of the pacifying effects of multicultural praxis, by socialising communities' leaderships to the state rather than confronting, transforming or demanding transformation of the state, is seen as evidence that structural racism (in so far as it was ever acknowledged officially to exist) is now over. Repeated speeches and articles by Tony Blair and David Cameron, as well as other political figures and commentators, play on the idea of the UK as a tolerant country of equal opportunity, the only barriers to which are (a) a recalcitrant Muslim community unwilling to integrate; (b) the existence within state structures and institutions of Muslim community figures who are symbols of the failure of multicultural praxis. Thus the frequent 'outing' of Islamists by the media of the 2000s (e.g. the 'exposé' of Azad Ali, a senior civil servant at the Treasury as a so-called Islamist that led to his removal from his post), has now changed in tone. Even participation by appointment by a minister (if that minister is Muslim) is seen as entryism, not legitimate political participation (Gilligan, 22 February, 2015).

Azad Ali and the Case of the Disappearing Civil Society

Azad Ali was a civil servant at the Treasury, as well as holding various civil society posts as a Muslim spokesperson and activist. Amongst these he was a member and latterly chair of the Muslim Safety Forum (a body that at one stage was in consultation with the Metropolitan Police over anti-terror policing), as well as spokesperson for the Islamic Forum of Europe, based in London.

A number of targeted media attacks in 2009 and 2010, labelled Ali an Islamist extremist and led to his resignation firstly from MSF and subsequently from his job at the Treasury.

Ali had held a post at the Treasury for many years, and indeed had been cleared to join the Metropolitan Police's Communities Together Strategic Group, which involved the sensitive task of 'engagement and consultation with the Met's key strategic partners, stakeholders and networks, as well as London's diverse communities, within the context of counter terrorism and security' (Metropolitan Police, undated). The charge that he was unfit for purpose suggests that either those seeking to 'expose' him felt that the government and Metropolitan Police Services had poor intelligence and security OR that Muslim activists do not have a role to play at this level of society.

A number of the attacks on Ali were spearheaded by Andrew Gilligan, a neo-conservative leaning journalist who has held roles under the London Mayoral administration of Boris Johnson, as well as working on stories like the Trojan Horse affair (see Chapter 3). His 2015 attack on Muslims sitting on the 'cross-Government working group on anti-Muslim hatred' and their appointment by erstwhile minister Baroness Sayeeda Warsi (also a Muslim), re-coined the term 'entryism'.

The charge of entryism, according to Faisal Bodi, has been:

"...devised [as] a new term for Muslims exercising their right to compete for and hold political positions. It's called entryism. Apparently it's the process whereby extremists consciously seek to gain positions of influence to better enable them to promote their own values. Wait a minute, doesn't that look like the right wing of the Tory Party?"

Even a socialised, pacified and uncritical (Muslim) middle class is now evidence of both a post-racial society, but also a failed multicultural praxis that must be rolled back. The anomaly is that to do so, the post-racial society must be undone. This is then in some ways an oblique call for the shoring up rather than breaking down of structural racism. Recent polling in the run-up to the selection of party candidates to stand as Mayor London has found that 1 in 3 Londoners (a city where 65% of the population are not white British) is uncomfortable with the idea of a Muslim mayor (Yougov / LBC cited in 5Pillars.com, 13 August 2015). This is despite the fact that the two key Muslim mayoral candidate candidates (Sadiq Khan of the Labour Party and Syed Kamall of the Conservative party) have held high ranking political positions. Khan was an erstwhile government Minister and a member of the Shadow Cabinet, as well as Chair of the human rights organisation Liberty. Kamall is an MEP and also leader of the Conservatives at the European Parliament.

NGOs / Civil Society and Victorian Models of Social Responsibility

As referred to above, campaign methodologies regarding racism have gradually shifted from demands of the state and the law to family campaigns (Merali, 2014). This mirrors the rise of the obfuscating idea of the post-racial society. The explosion of frustration that the so-called 2011 riots showed in the wake of the killing of Mark Duggan, augurs a sense of (a) understanding amongst the grassroots working class of the structural nature of the problem they face, and (b) the futility of existing campaigning in the face of such problems.

Bridges (2012) highlights the discourse surrounding causality but also outcomes regarding the riots of the summer of 2011.

Departing from previous precedents in setting up a judicial led inquiry, the government of the day set up a cross-party panel whose findings cited criminality and poor character amongst rioters as a causal factor, again ignoring the possibilities of there being pre-existing structural and institutional problems:

> "Its final report After the Riots, resonates with the Victorian values and underlying notions of the 'deserving' and 'underserving' poor... This focuses on what are seen as personal defects and social development problems of rioters - their lack of 'resilience', inability to 'defer gratification', ill discipline, absent fathers and lack of 'proper role models' - rather than attempting to address the sources of their grievances or structural factors in society."

This shift in discourse from the days of Scarman et. al., is described by Lea (2003) with reference to the white riots of the 1990s and riots of Asian youths in the northern towns in the summer of 2001, thus:

> "The subtle change between 1981 and 2001 is that in 1981 the issue was the relationship between the ethnic minority communities and the state: were the ethnic minorities being treated as citizens? When we come to read Ouseley, Cantle and Denham the issue is different: how have the socially excluded communities—poor whites and Asians—got into this mess, and what can be done—in particular what can they do—to restore their 'community cohesion'?"

The shift in focus had particular specificity with regard to the Muslim experience vis a vis the multicultural settlement. Whilst the idea of a lack of culture amongst rioters in the early 1980s and in 2011 are consistent, the idea of Asian grievances can be read as the idea of Muslim grievance and, as Kundnani (2001, cited in Lea, 2003) sees it, as having 'too much culture' i.e. an aggravating a sense of identity fostered by multicultural practice.

With or without 'culture' communities thus tarnished, are seen as the cause of their own and mainstream society's problems, requiring state intervention as well as self-reform. The appellation of Victorian is apposite not only to this form of political organising around social issues. As the latest coalition and Conservative governments have shown, the rollback of the state from the Thatcher era has resulted in the reintroduction of welfare provision via non-governmental organisations. This has taken on particular momentum in terms of food banks and other forms of welfare provision since the economic crash of 2008, whilst state welfare provision has been dramatically and ideologically cut away.

Additionally the rise (and at the time of writing, dramatic fall) of charities such as Kids Company (Guardian, 5 August 2015) has shown that the outsourcing of services, but also solutions to the charitable sector, has been large scale and broadly along the lines of a Victorian model of social responsibility that rests beyond the state (though on occasion as the recipient of some form of financial and / or political largesse of the state)

KIDS COMPANY and the Rise and Fall of Favoured Partners

Kids Company, a charity set up in 1996, provided practical, emotional and educational support to deprived and vulnerable inner-city children and young people, in London, Liverpool and Bristol.

Up to 36,000 vulnerable children and young people received support and Kids Company employed more than 600 people.' (BBC, 7 August 2015).

During its 19-year history it sported many high profile supporters, including the leader of the Tory Party and subsequently Prime Minister, David Cameron, who in his famous 'hug a hoodie' speech described Kids Company as a 'visionary social enterprise' (Cameron, 2006 in Guardian 10, July, 2006). The charity was in receipt of both state funding (at a time when state grants to the voluntary sector were being curtailed) and large donations from the public including high profile figures e.g. Richard Branson, Sting and Trudi Styler etc. Its chair of the board of trustees for 18 years (and at the time of closure) was BBC Creative Director Alan Yentob.

The charity was forced to close in 2015 after a rapid public decline in confidence, which the charity claims, was based on media demonisation of the charity coupled with the support of establishment figures. Notably, the publicising of the recommendation of a senior civil servant not to advance a £3 million grant to the charity (which was initially rejected), followed by conditions attached to the grant namely the resignation of the CEO Camila Batmanghelidj, followed swiftly by allegations about non-reporting of criminal acts, saw the downward spiral that led to the closure.

The charity claims that the reports (which have at the time of writing not been substantiated) led to the withdrawal of other donors, causing a funding crisis, forcing the closure.

Given the public praise heaped upon Kids Company and its founder, and its high profile supporters and members, it is clear that even this level of patronage either does not prevent (in the detractors' analysis) either wide-scale mismanagement or worse, or (in their supporters' analysis) a capricious witch-hunt and lack of regard for the vital importance of services outsourced to the charity sector.

For her part Batmanghelidj claims that the company was targeted because she knew of details of the Westminster child abuse allegations (see below) and this was a way to tarnish her. Whether true or not, it is clear that the government, with this charity alone, outsourced services hitherto thought to be the responsibility of the state, and in allowing Kids Company to fold, has now left adrift those in need of such services (although the government has stated it has taken emergency action to support the most vulnerable).

The whole process has seen the outsourcing not just of services, but also of responsibility. If the charity sector cannot provide these services, there will it appears in the long run, be no services.

Part of the rhetoric of the post-racial society in this context is the rhetoric of human rights which reduces the experience of and redress from racism to the individual, but also encourages a model of 'good citizen' intervention in seeking such redress not just from racism, but also poverty, child abuse, lack of educational opportunity etc. A company like Kids Company can (could) operate with a multi-million pound budget in providing services for disadvantaged children, whilst its CEO could give evidence to parliamentary committees explaining some of the crises within black communities, particularly with young black men, as stemming from the failure of black women to love and nurture them (Bathmaleghji, 2006 quoted in House of Commons Home Affairs Committee, 2007). She stated in evidence to a Home Affairs Committee on Black Youth and the Criminal Justice System:

> "I also think that actually the mothers are hugely responsible, because they have created a culture where they can get rid of the adolescent boy; they can get rid of the male partner; they can survive on their own. Often people think it is the males who are the culprits, the irresponsible people who actually come along and make these girls pregnant and walk off, and they underestimate the level of rejection and cruelty from the females towards the males. I actually think the males are vulnerable. It starts the minute the adolescent boy looks slightly like a male and behaves like a male and often the mother wants that young male banished from the house and a hate relationship often develops. I really think we underestimate the vulnerabilities of young black men."

Again, the focus is turned away from systemic bias within the criminal justice system and towards the (demonised) culture of the community in question. The ambiguity over human rights, as something that is deserved rather than universal also has Muslim specificity.

A combination of negative reporting of human rights cases in particular with reference to anti-Muslim racism, prisoners and child abusers, became a trope in criticism of human rights laws in the 2000s. The then Lord Chancellor Lord Falconer made a speech in February 2007 reiterating that human rights are common sense, averring to the idea of 'common sense' as a subjective marker of right and wrong amongst the majority community. Ameli et al (2004b) highlight that this type of common sense undermines 'human rights' rather than fosters them.

Thus Muslim and / or Black rights are conditional - they must be earned. Human rights are not then universal, and Muslim and/ or Black grievances can only be seen as non-sensical rather than common-sensical, and must be dealt with by an entirely different regime.

This regime uses state intervention in a punitive sense. With regard to communities marked as Black, this takes the form of inter alia overpolicing and in the case of Muslim communities, the anti-terrorism regime of laws and policies that includes surveillance and social engineering. Interventions through law are not then about justice or transformation but regulation and ultimately rule.

As will be discussed later, the authors argue that anti-terrorism laws have created not just an unnecessary body of law that targets primarily Muslims, they have been used to expel the Muslim subject, as Razack argues (2008) from the law and society. Once expelled, the Muslim subject can be tortured and denied in ways that citizenship does not allow. This is literally done through laws e.g that strip nationals of their citizenship, but is also done by the creation of differential laws themselves (Ameli and Merali, 2014). Welfare reforms based on the need for austerity as argued by successive governments have borrowed from this rhetoric, so whilst anti-Muslim discourse, law and policy has specificity its impact is much wider.

The expulsion of unwanted and / or dissenting subjects by and from the law can be in part attributed to the new model of social responsibility. By shifting responsibility from government shoulders, government institutions relieve themselves of moral responsibility for societal ills and can thus concentrate power to govern or to in fact rule without the need to subject laws to moral requirements.

Thus to overcome poverty the poor must learn to buy within their means, and learn the skills of austerity cooking. Charities can help with teaching these skills and in worse case scenarios supply food. The government is not obliged to supplement incomes or provide support to new arrivals, asylum seekers etc.. Muslims must amend their expectations, curtail their sense of grievance and show blind loyalty to the 'tolerant' state that has nurtured them and their ingratitude. In this case the state has no need to look at grievance but must surveil and socially engineer these outcomes.

Working within this paradigm however is also precarious, as the downfall of Kids Company has shown. The rolled back state is also a more authoritarian and capricious one.

Anti-democratisation as the outcome of subalternisation

Hate Environment (Ameli, 2012) in the context of the UK, is born out of the operation of Hate Practice (PREVENT and Contest) and Hate Representation (Political and Media Discourse). From the Hate Environment comes the impetus for street level hate, which the authors will elaborate on later as something not simply located 'on the street' but something which exists at school, in the workplace and in other public spaces. The authors will argue that it also impacts internally within communities, and as such an 'Islamophobic' lens of understanding Muslim identity is being used by community organisations and leaders within Muslim communities.

The anti-terrorism laws, notably the Counter-Terrorism and Security Act 2015, have been instrumental in creating not only a hate environment but solidifying in law a state of reasonable fear on the part of Muslims that they are under pervasive surveillance. The analogy of the Stasi state pertains, whereby under the CTS Act public servants be they teachers, lecturers, nursery school staff, doctors etc. are under a duty to report anyone they believe to be an extremist. The issue is further compounded by the fact that no concrete definition of what 'extremism' might be is proffered, leaving such referrals open to the subjective vagaries of those referring. Already the authors were made aware of the case of a 15 year old school student referred to the police for handing out leaflets calling for the boycott of Israeli goods, and for asking a dinner time supervisor if the food being served came from Israel. His story, later taken up by Al-Jazeera (Hooper, 23 July 2015) also includes details of his treatment once visited by the police who asked him if he supported ISIS. His response - that he was a Shia Muslim - did not register with the police officer as a denial. Thus all Muslims are tarred with the same brush, in this case as potential ISIS (herein after referred to as Daesh) supporters, regardless of whether they are Muslims who are the actual target of Daesh and Daesh ideology. Legitimate anti-racism campaigning in the form of boycotting Israeli apartheid, when undertaken by a Muslim, is deemed to be extremist.

The authors refer to their previous works to outline the slow drip of demonisation that has created a subaltern space and identity for Muslims in the UK.

That subaltern space is a space of fear for Muslims, who are in turn feared and / or despised by the majority in greater numbers. A shocking 55% of people polled accepted the claim that:

> "There is a fundamental clash between Islam and the values of British society' (YouGov, March, 2015). A further dissection of the results in terms of political affiliations shows little improvement:
>
> "Among Tory supporters, this gap increases to 68 per cent who say "clash" versus 17 per cent who think "compatible". Ukip supporters look almost unanimous on the issue (89 per cent "clash" versus 4 per cent "compatible") while roughly half of Labour supporters take the negative view (48 per cent "clash" versus 27 per cent "compatible") and Lib Dems are divided (38 per cent "clash" versus 39 per cent "compatible)." (Faulkner Rogers, 30 March 2015)

Political commentary posits Muslims as country haters, disloyal, haters of soldiers, and Muslim leadership capitulates to this discourse, as Kundnani (2014) explains:

> "Everyone who rejects the game of fake patriotism falls under suspicion, as opposition to extremism becomes the only legitimate discourse... the spectacle of the Muslim extremist renders invisible the violence of the ... empire. Opposition to such violence from within the imperium has fallen silent, as the universal duty of countering extremism precludes any wider discussion..."

This fake patriotism is not new, and is a familiar racist trope levelled previously against Jews in particular but also Catholics and Christian non-conformists as (racialised) religious groups and ethnic groups marked for unacceptable (extreme) cultural practice.

Such a widening of the trope of disloyalty can also be seen implied in the attacks on former Labour leader Ed Miliband's father, the late academic Ralph Miliband. Articles saying he hated Britain - a place that he came to as a Jewish refugee fleeing persecution - claimed that he hated the UK based on his teenage diaries. Whilst not explicitly associating this 'hatred' to Miliband's Jewish heritage, the emphasis on his arrival in the UK as a Jew fleeing the Nazis raises the same flag of disloyalty used against Jews at that time and also against Muslims today.

Anti-Semitism, which has for a long time been taboo, if not eradicated from British society, has now found space in public discourse with the failure to address, and political and media ratcheting up of Islamophobia.

Whilst the primary targets of the witch-hunt post the so-called Trojan Horse affair (to be discussed in Chapter 3) were Muslim governors, teachers in / and schools with a Muslim majority, it is notable that Jewish schools have become caught up in the anti-Muslim discourse, finding themselves also marked out as extremist and thus failing new governmental and OFTSED criteria. According to Adams, (14 October 2014):

> "The experience of the Jewish schools mirrors that of a conservative Muslim primary school in Luton this year, where angry parents confronted inspectors over their questioning of children regarding gay marriage.
>
> "The use of snap inspections came in the wake of the Trojan Horse affair, alleging Islamic involvement in state schools in Birmingham, along with a government requirement for inspectors to judge attitudes to discrimination and exposure to British values."

Additionally, after years of far-right mobilisation against Muslim communities and sites, with groups like the EDL organising protests in Muslim areas and outside mosques, or Britain First invading mosques, the last year saw the organisation of a protest against the 'Jewification of Britain' organised in Stamford Hill in London. The police rearranged that protest to take place outside Downing Street and away from the Jewish community that has been targeted (itself in stark contrast to policing of anti-Muslim protests, see Majeed (2010) for further details).

This real and alarming rise in anti-Semitism is not attached to the concern it deserves, but rather the issue of anti-Semitism is also used as a brush with which to tar Muslims, with anti-Zionist activism by Muslims and Jews alike targeted as evidence of anti-Semitism. During Operation Cast Lead, anti-Semitic graffiti and incidents were reported by the Community Security Trust - a charity set up to provide security to the British Jewish community. A further document attributed to the CST and allegedly sent to the Crown Prosecution Service (CPS) listed such incidents as well as names of organisations it deemed were anti-Semitic. The list included a number of vocal pro-Palestinian Muslim groups, as well as Jewish organisations involved in pro-Palestinian advocacy and calling for the boycott of Israeli goods (IHRC, 2009c) [1].

Thus spaces for dissent whether regarding domestic or foreign policy, are closed down, and democratic participation by Muslims as groups or individuals is not only curtailed but surveilled, stigmatised and criminalised. A parallel process which borrows from Islamophobic tropes but is not located solely against Muslims is that of anti-refugee and migrant discourse. At the time of writing a so-called 'migrant crisis' has been reported as facing the UK, whereby some thousands of refugees and possibly economic migrants, are encamped in Calais (though various evictions have taken place), waiting to cross over illegally into the UK. Maya Goodwin (30 July 2015) summarises the discourse thus:

> "Migrants and asylum seekers have been dehumanised to the point that their lives are of no importance. The papers report that "migrants storm the Eurotunnel", as if they're part of a medieval army making a power grab. In April in the UK's highest selling paper a columnist described them as "cockroaches" and "feral

---

[1] At the date of writing the CST have not responded to a request from IHRC to confirm or deny the authorship of the document attributed to them or various questions arising out of it. See IHRC, 2009c

humans". And today Cameron has argued that a "swarm" of people want to come to Britain, despite the fact that most migrants and asylum seekers don't try to enter this country. This is scaremongering, plain and simple. As has been pointed out whenever papers talk about "the Migrant Crisis", they rarely refer to the crisis of being a migrant or refugee (the majority of people in Calais are the latter). In this context it's easy to forget that these people are human beings, most of whom are fleeing war, poverty and trauma that Britain has played some part in creating.

"This dehumanisation fits in well with the Government's xenophobic policies, which are pursued in the name of balancing the books. Last year in the face of evidence that advised them to do otherwise, the Government decided they would no longer support any search and rescue operations for migrants and refugees drowning in the Mediterranean. By mid-April over 1,500 people had died. Then, just last week, they decided to cut the amount of money asylum seekers are entitled to, estimates suggest they will receive around 50% less than British benefit claimants. This tells us that the British-born poor are worth little, but foreign-born poor are worth even less."

All of this masks yet again, that asylum seekers and migrants without full documentation or with expired documents are subjected to detention in centres akin to prisons, where adults and children reside side by side, or moved around the UK to towns miles away from areas of location under dispersal policies often with little access to services, and have for years been subjected to harsh regimens including the provision of vouchers to buy supplies from shops. In particular the documented cases of pregnant refugees in the UK has raised alarming questions about the treatment of those seeking shelter and safety on these shores (Refugee Council, 2013).

Militarisation and subhumanisation, militarisation and securitisation

A key pillar of government supported critique over the years of the Muslim community is their concern with the plight of Muslims in other parts of the world. This critique requires Muslim to show loyalty to the British state by disavowing any concern for foreign affairs. This political conditionality was discussed by Shadjareh and Merali (2002). Ironically, the call for conditionality has been expressed by race relations advocates and conditionalises Muslims' political participation not only vis a vis the State's foreign policy but in sharp contrast to and in a subaltern position to other racialised groups in the UK. Discussing, the Runnymede Trust's 1997 report 'Islamophobia: A Challenge for us All' Shadajreh and Merali state:

> "The idea that Muslims hold unacceptable views is a thematic of demonisation that recurs repeatedly over the years. Whilst Salman Rushdie's right to free speech was deemed absolute, Muslims' right to hold not just so - called 'extreme views' but political values has been continuously undermined, often by the lobby that references itself as opposing Islamophobia... we would contend that the terms of Muslim participation in wider society have an inbuilt political conditionality to them which we do not see attached to other communities. The Runnymede Trust's recommendations on 'Bridge Building' in a subsection entitled 'Making common cause' calls on communities to make 'solidarity at times of tension.' Whilst suggesting that the communities affected by this are principally the Muslim and Jewish communities, and by implication this would mean both should do so, it goes on only to cite examples of Muslims doing so and receiving appreciative letters of response from Jewish figures. This is a dangerous precedent to suggest.

"Apart from generalising as to the nature of the Arab / Israeli conflict and the understandings of both communities to it, it advocates that British Muslims must disassociate themselves from what the British Jewish community feels to be the cause of tension. Would they suggest the opposite? We doubt it. Likewise we have not seen such recommendations made to other communities e.g. the Hindu community with regard to the rise of Hindu nationalism in India and its effects on minorities there and the situation here. The report therefore has already taken on board a slant or bias in favour of the views of one community over another in a general and not particular manner...

"This is dangerous in that it allows crass generalisation to be exploited by those with strong political views to the disadvantage of those who oppose those views. Last year, Richard Stone, now chair of the British Commission on Islamophobia stated in an article in The Independent that Muslims and Jews can make common cause easily, if only Muslims would isolate the young anti-Zionists that exist within their community. Whilst Muslims should and often vociferously do condemn anti-Semitism, why should they be asked to accept Zionism? It is like the white chairman of an anti-racist group stating in the 1980s that black and white communities could easily make common cause if only the blacks isolate the anti-Apartheid elements of their community. Apart from the glaring political conditionality, it also polarises perceptions of community relations. Maybe whites and Jews also oppose apartheid and Zionism."

It is clear that it is not just Muslims for whom 'here and there' are connected. However the demand for conditionality and disavowal applies to Muslims alone. There is also however further development in this discourse.

Whereas at the time Shadjareh and Merali (2002) wrote, the UK was not involved in full scale wars, it is now involved in or has participated in or supported several military interventions, wars and in some cases uprisings. Collyer et. al. (2011) highlight the type of impact on communities in the UK of involvement in Afghanistan / Pakistan: on refugee flows, on Muslims generally and Pakistani communities already living in the UK and on military families but also the wider majority communities:

> "The conflict has produced large flows of asylum seekers and refugees from Afghanistan, including large numbers of unaccompanied children. It has also drawn in members of settled Pakistani communities in the UK, who had a sense of insecurity about travelling to Pakistan and felt profiled as a suspect community in the UK. The conflict has drawn in the armed forces community too, particularly through the charity 'Help for Heroes', in challenging public perceptions of soldiers and raising money for the families of soldiers injured or killed. In addition, the conflict has impacted on the local communities in which Afghans, Pakistanis and members of the armed forces live in the UK."

Quaker Witness & Peace have gone further and highlighted (Walton, 2014) the clear militarisation of British Society which it lays at the door of a drive by the armed forces for recruitment and explicitly as part of a deliberate agenda by successive recent governments (which includes the impetus to normalise authoritarian responses to events and to promote the arms industry):

> "A huge cross-party government programme dedicated to ensuring that the military are popular in society has implications other than the popularity of the armed forces and ease of military recruitment."

According to Scott (8 July 2015): '[T]he Chancellor pledged £50 million to create cadet forces in 500 state schools. Most would be in "less affluent areas".'

Currently there are about 275 cadet units across the UK. Of these, only a third (fewer than 100) are in state schools.

According to the Ministry of Defence (MoD), as of April 1 last year there were about 131,000 cadets in the UK, divided between the Combined Cadet Force (42,950), a scheme run through schools, and the Army Cadet Force (41,000)."

Worley lists the impact of deliberate militarisation as: stifling criticism of war; glossing over negative aspects of the military; the wrong motivations for youth work; the danger of becoming an overly militarised society and failure to support members of the armed forces properly. The impact on society then and the concomitant need for the dehumanisation of Muslims in order to pursue this agenda is clear. As Worley points out however, the British public has been largely unaware of the creeping militarisation. With the presence of the armed forces on ceremonial and royal occasions always the norm the newer presence of military on the streets, e.g. the huge presence at the London Olympics of troops, the mooring of a warship for the event and the placing of missiles atop nearby roofs, and subsequently the deployment of soldiers at other events e.g. Wimbledon has largely gone unnoticed. There has been in Worley's opinion, a lack of media critique of this process which impacts in the failure of the development of concerns and critique at large resulting in an uncritical environment.

This process has happened in the wake of huge public criticism and concern over British wars in Afghanistan and Iraq, and the role of the media in uncritically advancing the ideas promoted by the government, in particular the Ministry of Defence, in lionising the armed forces, whilst not addressing deliberate and institutional dehumanisation of inter alia Muslims, leading to polarisation amongst communities. This polarisation has resulted in inter alia, the type of poll results referred to above where over half of all those polled see Islam as clashing with British values. It is also a contributory factor to the mobilisation of far-right street organisations like the English Defence League (EDL) who often tie their activism to armed forces events.

Grosfoguel (2012) argues that this type of dehumanisation corresponds to the Fanonian idea of zones of being and non-being. Again this links the idea of here and there, with 'here' being a zone of being in a colonial world context, where there exist structures, stability and law, but from whence violence is perpetrated 'there' ie in the zone of non-being, ie the colonised and latterly the developing / post-colonial world. People from the latter who now reside in or are born in the former also form something like a zone of non-being, experiencing the same subalternisation reserved for those in the actual zone of non-being, and suffering their own forms of structural violence. Grosfoguel connects Fanonian theory to Desousa Santos' idea of the line of the human, whereby universal rights are obviated by law and in public perception.

Thus the type of 'Victorian' arguments of the 'deserving' and 'undeserving' poor and ethnic communities, and the political conditionality placed on Muslims in terms of responding to Islamophobia (already discussed), form part of the delineation of what or whom is considered to be human and thus protected by universal codes of rights.

Griffin (2012) - a dissenting veteran - has highlighted how dehumanisation has worked to aid military policy and how it is linked to social mores:

> "The reality is killing people from the safety of an attack helicopter or drone control room. As if you are playing a computer game, with no regard for the lives of people who have been dehumanised.
>
> "Haji, Raghead, Sand Nigger, Chogie, Argie, Paddy, Gook, Chink, Jap, Kraut, Hun. All terms used by our armed forces. The product of a society which still believes in its superiority over other peoples and cultures.
>
> "We pretend that we wage war for higher, noble causes. We claim that our armed forces fight for Freedom, Democracy or Human Rights.
>
> "This is not the case. We wage war according to Policy. It is a choice determined by Government. This policy is influenced by those who gain the most from war. Politicians, Generals, The Arms Industry and The Media."

Griffin's identifcaition of the discourse of human rights, democracy and freedom and the role of media, politicians and the military in promoting them, mirrors various other critiques. Ameli and Merali (2014) state:

> "…these ideas, however idealised, are now also under threat from a rapacious public, political and media narrative that seeks to ensure supremacist ideas of 'white' / 'Christian' /' secular' / 'liberal' values and culture are understood to be the values of the state as a nation. The spectre of Razack's (2008) 'civilized European' pervades law and discourse, the normative citizen who is 'seldom explicitly named' but forms part of the 'underpinning of a clash of civilization' ideology."

In so doing, i.e. undermining the idealised ideas of freedom, human rights and democracy, the British state has created a climate wherein Muslims' existence is surveilled and criminalised. In particular the PREVENT strand of the CONTEST strategy (to be discussed further in Chapters 2 and 3) has created the hate environment wherein such state violations can occur. Even before the CTS Act 2015 came into force, the ubiquity of PREVENT measures operating on a non-statutory basis for almost a decade have been exposed as profiling and impacting Muslims and ethnic minorities whilst avoiding actual or potential issues around white extremism. Newman (31 March 2015) reports on how schools in areas with high EDL and BNP mobilisation were in fact explicitly profiling only ethnic minroity / Muslim students:

> "Schools in an area with a history of far-right activism have been singling out black and ethnic minority pupils in monitoring for signs of radicalisation – while suggesting white children are not at risk due to their skin colour.
>
> "The three schools, in Barnsley, South Yorkshire, have published adapted versions of the same "Radicalisation and Extremism Risk Assessment" document on their websites.
>
> "The document relates to the government's PREVENT counter-extremism strategy, which requires schools to protect children from being drawn into all strands of radicalised ideas, including from the far-right.
>
> "Each of the schools' assessments say that white pupils are at low risk of radicalisation on account of their skin colour and because many families have links to the Armed Forces.
>
> "This is despite a relatively recent history of far-right activity in Barnsley, where the English Defence League and the British National Party have traditionally enjoyed strong support."

Now under a statutory duty in the CTS 2015, PREVENT must be implemented by doctors, nurses, teachers, lecturers, nursery staff and other public sector workers. Given the anecdotal evidence compiled thus far, in particular in The PREVENT Diaries (ed. Mohamed, 2015), it is clear that Muslims will continue to be the prime if not sole target.

Grassroots backlash

A crisis of perception as described by Worley (2013) over militarisation is not restricted to this issue alone. There is heightened perception and misperception of Muslim related issues as a result of hate representation by media and politicians and concurrent lack of critical perception of institutions and the state.

Whilst there have been repeated stories about Pakistani and Muslim men grooming children after a series of cases involving all or mainly Muslim and / or Pakistani men, it has been observed that no similar stories highlighting the ethnicity or religion of perpetrators have been noted. Harker (22 July 2012) reflecting on the conviction of white male perpetrators of child abuse said:

> "There was no commentary anywhere on how these crimes shine a light on British culture, or how middle-aged white men have to confront the deep flaws in their religious and ethnic identity. Yet that's exactly what played out following the conviction in May of the "Asian sex gang" in Rochdale, which made the front page of every national newspaper. Though analysis of the case focused on how big a factor was race, religion and culture, the unreported story is of how politicians and the media have created a new racial scapegoat. In fact, if anyone wants to study how racism begins, and creeps into the consciousness of an entire nation, they need look no further."

Three years later and the narrative has continued unabated. Harker's premonition in the same article: "I am also certain that, if the tables were turned and the victims were Asian or Muslim, we would have been subjected to equally skewed "expert" commentary asking: what is wrong with how Muslims raise girls?" has come to some reality by analogy with regard to the issue of so-called jihadi brides, young women leaving the UK to marry Daesh fighters. The current government and media narrative is demanding scrutiny of Muslim parenting in regard to this and other issues.

Harker further laments:

> "While our media continue to exclude minority voices in general, such lazy racial generalisations are likely to continue. Even the story of a single Asian man acting alone in a sex case made the headlines. As in Derby this month, countless similar cases involving white men go unreported.
>
> "We have been here before, of course: in the 1950s, West Indian men were labelled pimps, luring innocent young white girls into prostitution. By the 1970s and 80s they were vilified as muggers and looters. And two years ago, Channel 4 ran stories, again based on a tiny set of data, claiming there was an endemic culture of gang rape in black communities. The victims weren't white, though, so media interest soon faded. It seems that these stories need to strike terror in the heart of white people for them to really take off."

Whether by striking terror into the hearts of white people or not, there is now some critical reflection on the British establishment after the revelations of widespread child abuse in the wake of the inquiry into the late celebrity Jimmy Savile, and at the time of writing, allegations into widespread child abuse by senior political figures including former Prime Minister Edward Heath and ministers and peers including the late Leon Brittain and Lord Greville Janner.

Nevertheless it appears that the same generalisations, as mentioned by Harker above, are still not applied when dealing with the establishment. Cases surrounding Savile relating to the TV celebrity culture of the 1970s and 1980s in particular and allegations about a paedophile ring in Westminster have not elicited the same discussions about the possibilities of cultures of abuse within white, middle aged, middle class and upper class cultures. As Neale and Lindisfarne (March 2015) argue about the Oxford gang abuse case the:

"[G]reat majority of the men recently prosecuted for organised abuse of children and young people are non-white. These are a tiny minority of non-white men in the country.

"Meanwhile, the great majority of guilty men who have not been prosecuted, but protected at the highest level, are white. None of this abuse has anything to do with Islam. One fact shows this very clearly. The gang members abused no Muslim girls. This is because they knew the girls' families would have reacted with effective fury. It was also because the abusers own extended families, and their communities, would have found out and disapproved deeply.

"Moreover, the motives for the abuse were criminal – to make money illegally. Look at the example of the United States. There organised prostitution has long been controlled by the Italian Mafia, the Irish mafia, and the Jewish mafia, and the Russian mafia. Immigrants are poor, many routes are blocked to them, and some always turn to crime. It is not an accident that Tony Soprano is shown owning a titty bar, and that his life is full of goombas. It reflects how the sex trade works in the US, and how some of it now works in Britain.

"Finally, the trade in young people in care was until recently the work of white people. For example, Simon Danczuk, in his biography of Cyril Smith, points out that Smith was involved in a ring of white abusers in Rochdale for many years that prostituted boys to people who visited from many other towns. As Danczuk has pointed out, the men of immigrant background recently convicted of gang abuse in Rochdale are only continuing a long local tradition.

"However, it is not enough just to say defensively that non-white people and Muslims are not the problem. In the current situation, we do have to say that. But it is also necessary to go on the offensive, to stop abuse by gangs of poor men and rich men alike."

Nevertheless there is media reportage and discussion and the taboo of critiquing the establishment is somewhat broken.

However, this critique is not coming from Muslim community leadership, who, as in Kundnani's (2014) description, have thrown in their lot with the official narrative of defeating (Muslim) extremism. As Dodd (14 May 2013) pointed out even child abuse experts countered the narrative that there was an overrepresentation of perpetrators from Asian / Muslim communities, yet the Muslim Council of Britain organised a conference on the issue. Whilst clearly opposing the idea that there was a Muslim - child grooming connection, the MCB's responses simply reinforced what it sought to distance Muslims from (MCB, 2014).

Depsite the silencing of Muslim leadership, there is grassroots and some civil society backlash against establishment policies. There have been notable student protests in the last five years, as well as Occupy London protests and more recent anti-austerity protests. At the time of writing Polish workers in the UK have announced a one-day strike in protest at the demonisation of migrants. Despite continued demonsiation of Muslim political participation and leadership on issues, the annual Muslim-led protest for Palestine, Al-Quds Day, continues with several thousand protestors of different backgrounds attending each year.

Even the CTS 2015, despite the climate of fear and the possibility of criminal sanction, has found opposition amongst teachers' and lecturers' unions.

The University and Colleges Union (UCU) has opposed the CTS Act 2015 (UCU, Sunday 24 May 2015) calling for 'a boycott of the implementation of the PREVENT Agenda in colleges and universities', whilst committing to oppose all forms of Islamophobia and racism.

The National Union of Teachers (NUT) has said the rules are stifling debate in schools, with its leader Christine Blower warning against a heavy-handed approach to counter-extremism (Richardson, 6 April 2015).

The National Union of Students (NUS) have passed a motion against it (SACC, 2 April 2015) and called for it to be boycotted in the new academic year (NUS Connect 13 August 2015).

The possibilities of mobilisation and grassroots backlash per se, are also manifesting at the time of writing in the bid of veteran left wing MP Jeremy Corbyn to become the new Labour leader. A mobilisation around his candidacy has seen over 400,000 people join the party, it is thought in large part, in order to vote for him. Corbyn's foreign policy, which takes an anti-war stance and a pro-Palestinian stance, sets him out from establishment figures and puts him in line with the ertswhile critical discourses of inter alia Muslim communities.

Whilst some of these developments are heartening, there remains the reality of polarisation in perceptions of Muslims that inform far-right street mobilisation that has surged in the last five years, as well as fuelled spikes in backlash attacks against Muslims e.g in the wake of the killing of Lee Rigby. This rise and its possible causes will be discussed in Chapters 3 and 5. The role of the political commentariat as well as policies that are ostensibly unrelated to Muslims e.g. the creation of the EHRC (Sayyid et. al, 2013) in legitimising a status quo of inequality, will be further analysed along with the results of the survey that accompanies this volume. Not only do state policies and commentary cement existing inequalities, but the authors argue that they produce further stratification and demonisation.

So, to the British Stasi State of 2015

The new 'Stasi state' impacts everyone, as the revelations about the profiling of Occupy London as a terrorist organisation in a police training manual testifies (Quinn, 19 July 2015). The idea of a problem of the Muslim / the minority (of which Daesh is just the latest) becomes the enabler of the project that Worley (2013) identifies as a move towards authoritarianism in the manner of the US and Israeli state models.

The State meanwhile is attempting to airbrush racism out of the picture, partially by shifting the burden of responsibility for dealing with racism to the racialised individual/community and their supposed deficiencies. It is further promoting discourse that feeds the subhumanisation of Muslims and other minorities, outsourcing services whilst rolling back the state, but intervening punitively in communities to promote its own authoritarian agenda, including increasing militarisation.

Left and right mainsteam political parties have little or nothing to separate them on Muslim and minority issues. Muslims in particular are discussed as a problem outside of political discourse - as an existential threat. Their expulsion from the state (as defined by the praxis of law) (Razack, 2008) mirrors the anxiety of Arendt, which she:

> "...describes as the transformation of the state from the instrument of law to the instrument of nation, i.e. where a citizen is only defined by her / his adherence to national identity, itself enshrined in legal codes, precedent, policy and normalised in the social, public, political and media discourses." (Ameli and Merali, 2014)

This dilemma of the Nation State as / and Eurocentric ideas of political organisation and praxis - are brought into sharp focus by the issues and the existence of Muslims both 'domestically' and 'abroad'.

Chapter 2

Talking the Talk – Anti-Muslim Racism in Media and Political Discourse

The Domination Hate Model of Intercultural Relations (Ameli, 2012) expounds the Hate Environment within which minority groups experience being hated as an effect of structural prejudice. As such it is the accumulation of various factors including hate representation by the media and politicians, as well as law and policy. It is only once these effects kick in that the phenomenon we understand today to be 'hate crime' comes into effect, that is the attacks committed by people on the street, at work or at school, from staring, spitting, name calling to murder, as well as discrimination and exclusion.

From the mundane and largely unacknowledged day to day profiling of minorities by law enforcement agencies, to the more spectacular cases, profiling did not start after 9/11 nor is it a Muslim-specific issue. Rather, as the authors have argued elsewhere, and in these pages, such policy is mutually constituted through demonised representation, law and policy, and creates a hate environment for out-groups / hated societies. (Ameli and Merali, 2014:54)

This chapter looks at the rise of anti-Muslim representation in the media and political discourses. It will look specifically at certain sections of the commentariat, the editorial choices for front pages and headlines, and their relation to neo-conservative think tanks and government. It also looks at the type of discourse propounded by politicians of different parties in discussing Muslims and Islam. However this critique can be made of media content that is seen as art, entertainment or news reportage.

These discourses, the authors argue, create the climate whereby Muslims are feared and loathed, as Ciftci's (2012) analysis of various Pew Research polls highlights:

> "…that fear of Muslims and perceived threat accounts for much of the variation in the realm of attitudes. Western citizens view Muslims as fanatical, violent, and supportive of terrorism because they perceive them to be threatening of their physical well-being and cultural values."

Both of these discourses are instrumental in creating the Hate Environment within which, in the case of the UK, policy and now the statutory duties of PREVENT operate. PREVENT was formulated by the New Labour government to tackle 'extremism'. It is the second strand of the four-pronged CONTEST, counter-terror strategy (IHRC, 2015).

The original 'Counter-Terrorism Strategy of the United Kingdom' was released in 2003 and elaborated upon in 2006 when the strategy was split into four distinct strands; 'Prevent, Pursue, Protect and Prepare'. Of the four strands, the thinking behind the 'Pursue' strategy has been extensively responsible for the introduction of draconian anti-terror laws, racial profiling and the arbitrary arrest and detention of an overwhelming number of Muslims who have usually by the end of their ordeals found to be innocent. The inability to recognise and understand the detrimental effects of the arbitrary application of such legislation upon Muslims in Britain is reflected in the 'Prevent' strand of CONTEST which, whilst seeking to 'actively promote shared values (including democracy and the rule of law)', fails to see that the prevention of violent extremism is wholly dependent upon not only an understanding of the reasons behind it, but a subsequent rectification of flawed policies that result in it. (IHRC, 2009a)

The Home Office has funded PREVENT for many years, supposedly to prevent violent forms of extremism. The basic rationale is that people advocating 'non-violent extremism' create an environment in which terrorists can operate and so encourage 'violent extremism'. Thus entire Muslim communities (and communities from specific ethnic backgrounds) are being monitored for 'extremist' ideas or ideas that oppose the government's policies– officially defined as hostility to 'British values'. This phrase conflates universal human values with the British state, whose foreign policy regularly contradicts these supposed values. In practice, the PREVENT programme has interpreted 'extremism' to encompass Muslim criticism of some UK government policies.

This practice has spread fear within Muslim communities, as well as among voluntary organisations and public-sector employees who are expected to implement the programme. Under the last coalition government the programme was given a statutory basis by the Counter-Terrorism and Security Act 2015. This imposes monitoring and reporting duties on all public-sector institutions, and in doing so institutionalises the promotion and normalisation of Islamophobia.

Kundnani, speaking at the Preventing Violent Extremism? Conference organised by IHRC and CAMPACC in June 2015 (IHRC, 23 July 2015) highlighted the connection between the idea of policing the presumed inherent violence of the Muslim community and the state's march to militarisation already discussed in Chapter One. Firstly, it manipulates concepts like radicalisation, extremism, terrorism etc so that certain types of violence can be 'associated with certain communities, while more pervasive state violence needs to be seen as normal'.

Since the introduction of the PREVENT strategy in 2005, IHRC has consistently engaged in formulating counter-narratives to it. Surveillance specifically focussed on Muslim communities is counter-productive; by conceiving of Muslims as guilty (or suspected) of terrorism by association, the programme institutionalises racism and discrimination against Muslim communities. It alienates entire communities, while allowing the government to ignore the communities' own efforts against violent extremism. (IHRC, 23 July, 2015)

Hate Representation - The Media as Oracle

Multicultural misery

In January 2010, the acclaimed and popular screenwriter Lynda La Plante was quoted bemoaning the BBC's commissioning practices. La Plante, whose many TV dramas like Prime Suspect have had primetime slots over many decades on mainstream British channels stated that the BBC would rather read a script by a "little Muslim boy," than one she had written implying that there was in fact preferential treatment for Muslims. She continued, "If my name were Usafi Iqbadal and I was 19, then they'd probably bring me in and talk,.." (Midgeley, 2 January 2010). In using the name Usafi Iqbadal (neither of which have an actual provenance in Muslim heritage languages) she reverts to age old racist practice. Whilst the story was covered, there was little revulsion.

The Telegraph (Midgeley, 2 January 2010) reported the story in terms of a discussion about the values of the BBC and a more general critique of its commissioning practices. The implication was that new commissioning editors have exceeded the corporation's remit (as highlighted by the critique of another author P.D. James) with regard to the quality of the their programmes (she spoke of dog themed entertainment shows and made no reference to ethnicity or religion) and programmes which are by implication mindful of trends rather than focusing on British classics and classical programming e.g. shows like Pride and Prejudice (a critique cited from Andrew Davies, another well-known scriptwriter). La Plante's criticisms are then attached to unrelated critiques and legitimised. By doing so, in this article, they also attach a sense of cheapness to the idea of Muslim creativity (akin to shows on dog training) and undermining of British classics (like the very famous adaptations of Andrew Davies), as well as mooting the idea of misplaced favouritism for Muslims which discriminates against a beloved elderly screenwriter i.e. La Plante.

This article and incident speaks to an idea of failure of multiculturalism resting not in the failure of Muslims to integrate, but that Muslims are undeserving of integration into (in this case) the cultural fabric of the nation.

The authors, in their 2014 work on Canada, look at the role of discursive racism in the creation of the Hate Environment. As Ameli (2011) argues, hate representation, i.e. the media / political / academic / elite discourses impact on the ordinary understanding of people within a state both from the majority and the minority. While the minority then become victims to the social attitudes of the majority expressed in acts of hatred, hostility, discrimination and violence, the majority, including perpetrators of such acts are also a type of victim (Ameli et. al, 2013) incited by those they trust to undertake otherwise unimaginable acts of hostility. According to Van Djik (2000):

"...social practices also have a cognitive dimension, namely the beliefs people have, such as knowledge, attitudes, ideologies, norms and values. In the system of racism, thus, racist stereotypes, prejudices and ideologies explain why and how people engage in discriminatory practices in the first place, for instance because they think that the Others are inferior (less intelligent, less competent, less modern, and so on), have fewer rights, or that We have priority for a house or a job. These beliefs or social representations many members of the dominant (white) in-group have about immigrants and minorities are largely derived from discourse.

"That is, discourse as a social practice of racism is at the same time the main source for people's racist beliefs. Discourse may thus be studied as the crucial interface between the social and cognitive dimensions of racism. Indeed, we learn racism (or anti-racism) largely through text or talk. Because they control the access to, and control over, most public discourse, the political, educational, scholarly and media elites have a specific role and responsibility in these forms of discursive racism (van Dijk 1993, 1996). By their control over the crucially important power resource of public discourse, the various elites at the same time are dominant within their own in-group (of which they are able to influence the prevalent ethnic opinions), as well as over minority groups, whose everyday lives they are able to control by their discourse, policies and decisions in positions of power."

The impact of the idea of Muslim favouritism by the media can be seen to be having an impact on the public at large. In 2011, Channel 4's decision to broadcast the Islamic dawn call to prayer in May, received the most complaints from viewers. Given the small audiences at that time of the night and the likelihood that Muslims (awake for prayer at that time) might be a significant demographic, the decision to do this by Channel 4 was not as surprising as some of the critique suggested. Yet, complaints from members of the public (not necessarily those who had watched the broadcast) were the most for that year with 1,658 objections registered. Ralph Lee, the head of factual programmes at Channel 4 stated that "The level of Islamophobia we encountered with the 4Ramadan season was unexpected, though much of it came from communities that were either very polarised or very undiverse." He also stated that he had received hundreds of emails directly after giving an interview to the Radio Times (The Guardian, 8 May 2014).

Multicultural depravity - Sex and Sexuality

Even before 9-11, the reportage of Muslims has been identified 'as exoticism, fanaticism, and delinquency' (Brown, 2007). Poole (2011) analysed hundreds of articles from British newspapers over three years before 9-11 and identified the following themes: Muslims' involvement in deviant activities that threaten national security; Muslims as a threat to British values provoking integrative concerns; the idea of inherent cultural difference between Muslims and the majority; and Muslims increasingly making their presence felt in the public sphere. These themes are illustrated further by examining the dominant topics of coverage: politics; criminality; relationships; education and fundamentalism.

Poole (2011) further highlights (citing Moore, Mason and Lewis (2008)), that such coverage has come to the forefront again as the threat of terrorist attacks declined after 7/7. It can be argued that this cycle repeats as and when attacks happen. However, Poole further argues that despite the shifts in the type of stories, the core message remains the same since before 9-11 with the idea that 'we' the British have been too tolerant of them, the Muslims, who have sought to impose their way of life on us. She highlights the link between this type of coverage, the legacy of New Labour's integrationist / assimilationist project and David Cameron's Munich speech blaming multiculturalism for Islamic extremism (due to minority separatism). Cameron's speech, as Poole notes, is seen as more symbolic in that it set out a test for "extremism" (see below) on the day the English Defence League staged an anti-Islamic march in Luton, UK.

An overview of certain headlines in popular media, both tabloid and broadsheet, in the last year give a sense of the pervasiveness of anti-Muslim terms. Pitt (Islamophobia Watch, various years) lists various terms, a sample of which are set out below. Others contain terms and ideas that are patently ludicrous to anyone with knowledge but which pass unchallenged. Pitt (29 July 2014) highlights two articles about the Commonwealth Games, one of which appeared in the Telegraph, containing the line: 'Some overseas Muslim groups have reportedly previously called for a jihad on dogs.' (Fong, 28 July 2014)

Imams Promote Grooming Rings, Muslim leader claims
by Hayley Dixon, The Telegraph, 16 May 2013

Welcome to East London: Muslim gang slashes tyres of immigration-raid van before officers showered with eggs from high-rise
by Michael Powell, Mail on Sunday, 26 July 2015

Woman beheaded: 'Muslim convert' known as Fat Nick suspected of slaughtering grandmother pictured for first time
by Ben Morgan, Matt Watts, Anna Dubuis and Justin Davenport
The Evening Standard, 5 September 2014

Nick Salvadore, suspect for beheading of Palmira Silva, is would-be cage-fighter and Muslim convert
by Patrick Sawer, Gordon Rayner, Keith Perry, Tom Whitehead and Tom Brooks-Pollock
5 February 2014

Face of a killer: Father who shot his seven-year-old daughter dead when her mother rejected Islam then killed himself is pictured for the first time
by Paul Bentley and James Tozer and Tania Steere for the Daily Mail
12 September 2014

The changing face of Britain: A child in Birmingham is now more likely to be a Muslim than Christian
by Mark Howarth for The Daily Mail
14 September 2014

British man, 58, kidnapped, tortured and held to ransom by 'Muslim gang' when he went to Ukraine to find a bride
by Will Stewart for Mailonline
24 September 2014

The conclusions drawn from this type of description are that the descriptive term Muslim inherently contains meanings of violence, perverse and extreme violence, sexual depravity, misogyny, and disloyalty. All of these feed into the idea of inferiority to a Western i.e. white British majority, but also of inherent lack of values, a deficiency that can never be overcome.

Privot (2014) argues that gender equality is one such idea, used to define a sense of identity of the 'European' against the 'Muslim':

> "The issue of gender equality is a good example... violence against women (1 in 3 European women faces violence in her life), lack of representation in top jobs and politics and the gender pay gap in countries like France (20% in 2012), should all be unheard of in a continent so proud of upholding the principle of gender equality as one of its core values.

> "Such dissonances between reality and principles demonstrate that many political discourses about gender equality as a defining principle of European democracies are actually only cultivated to serve as a powerful means of exclusion by mobilising negatively a powerful ideal."

According to Progler (2008 cited in Ameli and Merali, 2014), the specificity of Muslim stereotyping provided in the Age of Enlightenment through the repackaging of tropes from the times of the Crusades (see also Ameli et. al, 2012 on how this also impacts discourse in France), illustrates many contradictory, yet important affirmatory images of Western superiority. The authors argue that these images continue to be relevant at the present time, with Progler citing the following as examples:

1. The concept of despotism which provided a foil to internal European excesses, be they of the Republican or monarchical variety
2. The imposture of the Islamic Prophet, used by the likes of Voltaire to discredit all religions
3. The seraglio, which negated sexuality

In 2015, these tropes can be found regurgitated in various ways. This can be seen in the idea of sexuality negated. Muslim male perversion – child groomers, predators against vulnerable white women etc. – has been the staple of much media and political representation. Likewise an idea of Muslim female perversion has developed (further) around 'veils', 'burqas' and 'headscarves'. This also inheres in headlines and stories relating to the undermining of British values by the so-called Trojan Horse affair, whereby the idea of single-sex schooling or gender segregation again infer perverse sexuality. Issues around the normative teaching of homosexuality are also invoked repeatedly, highlighting again an idea of Muslim moral failure.

The stigmatisation of the face-veil is not new in the last five years but has gathered pace and found more succour from legislation in France and Belgium, thus providing space for the commentariat to make repeated accusations of the veil being a sign of separation (first propounded by a politician, the then Home Secretary Jack Straw in 2006) or a sign of misogynistic value and male control, or both. Bans on face veils in the UK (e.g. at some schools), however have often been made on the grounds of security (i.e. not being able to identify the wearer). Stories relating to a bombing suspect fleeing in a burka have stoked this, but Williamson and Khiabany (2010) provide other examples:

"A… story in the *Mail*, 8 February 2007, under the headline 'School veils allow new Dunblane', similarly collapsed the issue of security into that of 'threats to our way of life'. This reported the comments of a judge to the effect that allowing veil wearing in schools could allow a recurrence of the primary school massacre which took place in Scotland in March 1996. According to the article:

"'Allowing Muslim girls to wear full-face veils to school could make Dunblane-style massacres more common, a judge suggested. Judge Stephen Silber was hearing a case brought by a 12 year old Muslim girl against her headmistress's ban on her veil. The judge suggested veils would make it hard to identify intruders in schools, making murderous attacks more likely'."

Whilst this idea has fuelled a securitisation idea around face-veiling, the past year has seen this idea of threat extended to the idea that face-veiling is a form of or engine to radicalisation. Janice Turner (5 July 2014) states in The Times:

> Moreover, the anger that the veil provokes unsurprisingly makes them suspicious of non-Muslims, less likely to mix in white-British areas. And while some, often at the insistence of worried parents, cast off the veil to feel safer, others are only galvanised by hostility. "If I were to be stabbed or have stones thrown at me for the sake of my religion," says Faridah, "I would feel proud because Allah is testing me. This person is just the means."
>
> The veil is not only radicalising women but their brothers and sons. When they see female relatives stared at for covering their faces, it only confirms the messages from the mosques that Muslims are a separate and beleaguered people, justifying a righteous anger whose logical conclusion is jihad.
>
> The veil is so much more than a garment or even a symbol of faith like the cross, yarmulke, turban or headscarf, whose British wearers live largely free from abuse. It is a Trojan horse for an extreme form of Wahhabi

Islam that provokes western Muslims to rage against their non-Muslim compatriots rather than to co-exist in peace with them. The veil is both a means to banish women from public life and a tool for provoking social unrest.

The face-veil and the act of face-veiling are in fact seen as violent threats to British society. This piece comes in response to Dr. Irene Zempi's research into the experience of being face-veiled in the UK (Zempi and Chakraborti, 2014). Not only did Zempi and Chakraborti interview women who wore the niqab, Zempi dressed in a burka for four weeks and presented her findings, which included being victimised and oppressed by non-Muslims. Zempi and Chakraborti outline in some detail the horrors of victimisation, highlighting that part of this is the exclusion of the Muslim women who wear it from social spaces, thus fulfilling a concomitant function to the expulsion created by law that Razack discusses (2008):

"In this regard, there are distinct emotional harms associated with this victimisation. Throughout interviews and focus group discussions participants highlighted that they had low confidence and low self-esteem because of experiencing Islamophobia in public. They also pointed out that they were made to feel 'worthless', 'unwanted' and that they 'didn't belong'. For converts in particular, experiences of Islamophobic victimisation often left them feeling confused and hurt, compounding their sense of isolation. Seen in this light, Islamophobic victimisation disrupts notions of belonging whilst maintaining the boundaries between 'us' and 'them'. This highlights the immediate effect of Islamophobic victimisation which is to undermine victims' sense of security and belonging whilst the longer-term or cumulative impact is to create fear about living in a particular locality and to inspire a wish to move away (Bowling, 2009). In this way geographical spaces are created in which 'others' are made to feel unwelcome and vulnerable to attack, and from which they may eventually be excluded (Bowling, 2009). (Zempi and Chakraborti, 2014)

Part of that exclusion comes from the exclusion of Muslim voices from the spaces of discourse. Ameli et al (2004b) highlight how conversations around the face veil are considered to be part of a 'common sense' discussion that finds expression in newspaper columns whereby everyone can be an expert (even TV sports presenters) except Muslims. In the last few years, this narrative space has been extended to include Muslims who accept the extremes of the narrative.

Turner's piece cited above comes alongside a call from Taj Hargey, Director of the Muslim Educational Centre of Oxford:

> "The increasing fashion for young Muslim women in Britain to wear the burka (in contrast to their mothers, who do not) is one of most sinister developments of our times.

> "Supporters of this garment like to pretend that it is a welcome symbol of our society's multicultural diversity and philosophical tolerance. But such warped thinking is woefully misguided. In reality, the burka is an archaic tribal piece of cloth that is eagerly used by fundamentalist zealots to promote a toxic brand of extremist non-Koranic theology.

> "Everyone in Britain, including Muslims, should oppose the insidious spread of this vile piece of clothing, which imprisons women, threatens social harmony, fuels distrust, has grave health implications and is a potent security risk."

Sinister, toxic, insidious, and vile, the face veil 'imprisons women, threatens social harmony, fuels distrust, has grave health implications and is a potent security risk.' This acceptance by a leading Muslim figure emphasises Kundnani's point that Muslim leadership has acquiesced to government narratives when opposing extremism, and the government line is the only discourse available.

The issue of face-veiling however is not the full extent of demonisation of Muslim female identity. It is a marker of it. Social and cultural mores regarding Muslims, seen through the prism of sexuality are, as with other tropes, prone to shifting symbols and narratives. During the course of colonisation in Africa and Asia, where Islam was prevalent, the idea of Muslims as having a licentious sexual culture (in comparison to a modest, chaste Christian culture) abounded, hence the seraglio and the harem. However, come the last one hundred years this has reversed, as the narrative for post-colonial domination has turned to 'freedom' and individual liberty. The harem - previously a sign of sexual licence, is now seen as an arena of sexual subjugation. The only constant is the idea that whatever Muslims and Islam are, culturally they can only be seen through a homogenised and limited narrative lens.

To this end, however Muslims are (veiled, unveiled, rich or poor, left wing or right wing), ultimately they are still Muslim and thus a danger (morally, culturally, physically).

This theme can sit in plain sight or be suggested through imagery that invites the viewer to see it as a representation of something 'other'. A case in point is the idea of Muslim womanhood, sexuality and threat in the blockbuster film The Dark Knight Rises (2012). Though Hollywood produced, this third film in a trilogy of films about Batman was written and directed by Christopher Nolan, who like many of the main cast, is British. Whilst the nuances of interpretation may only have direct significance with those familiar with the graphic novels and comic strip, the level of success of the film (it is ranked in the top 20 highest-grossing films of all time (not adjusted for inflation)) gives it wide reach and the general implications of the portrayal of the character Miranda Tate / Taliya al-Ghul emphasises the fixation both on Muslim female sexuality, existential threat to society, disloyalty and untrustworthiness, and undeserving citizenship.

The Arab villain Ras al-Ghul and his equally villainous daughter Taliya, are in the original comic strip story, though whether explicitly Muslim is a subject for discussion (Taliya, though is a Muslim name which means a woman who recites the Qur'an often). Both characters represented Al-Qaeda type organisations, methods and ideologies (Muslim Reverie, 2013).

Taliya al-Ghul is first presented as a wealthy businesswoman and philanthropist. She is presented as noble and caring, aspiring to creating sustainable clean energy for the world. She becomes the paramour of Bruce Wayne (the protagonist's true identity) and appears to be his saviour on a personal level, and part of the good citizens of Gotham fighting the resurgent Al-Qaeda-like League of Shadows (once led by Ras al-Ghul). What transpires at the dénouement of the story however is the revelation that she is in fact Batman's nemesis and the arch villain of the movie intent on detonating a nuclear device that will kill every inhabitant of the city including herself. A revelation which comes with the line, "While I am not ordinary, I am a citizen." Hereinafter we are told her story through the lens of an orientalised world of Middle Eastern / Central Asia warlords, the imprisonment of her mother by her grandfather for secretly marrying Ras al-Ghul, a vision of her escaping the dungeon into which she was born and donning a head veil, the revelation that her actual love is the man who saved her as a child (invoking again ideas of child grooming and Muslim male sexuality) and above all her fanatical belief in the need for mass murder in order to 'restore balance to the world'.

Taliya al-Ghul represents the closet Muslim woman, who even when socialised to all the norms and privileges of Western society is always hell-bent on destroying it, seeing it as decadent. Even her sexuality is poisonous in that she does not heal the hero's broken state (it is implied he has not been in a relationship since the death of a previous lover many years before), but seduces him in order to weaken him and ultimately kill him and millions of others. Whether puritanically face-veiled, secluded and chaste or glamorous, integrated and promiscuous, the Muslim woman is a threat. And in the current age, that threat is one of totalitarianism and mass death dressed in the language of rights and justice.

Whilst this characterisation exists in fiction, it finds its mirror in real world practices that exclude Muslim women, veiled or not. In particular the university space, where activism and identity formation are thought to be par for the course, Brown and Saeed's study (2014) identifies the university as part of the government's strategy of managing radical identities of Muslims. Based on interviews, Brown and Saeed show that Muslim female students' activism, university experience and identities are constrained. Ultimately this keeps them 'out' of the nation, i.e. it prevents integration (despite the demand for it):

> "The term 'radical' instead folds them into a securitized student life. If this archetypal elite liberal subset of 'acceptable Muslims' - 'good', 'moderate', integrated, educated, female Muslims - cannot be free from suspicion and be critical citizens, then there is little space for other less privileged Muslims to escape the radical ghetto (Turner 2007; Tyrer 2010)."

Politicians, extremists and despots

Hoskote (2007 in ed. Merali, 2008) describes the portrayal of the 'House of Islam' post-9-11 in the global media as a 'politics of image which presents the House of Islam as a repository of horror, showing it chiefly through images of violence, terror, desolation, the unreason of the mob, the intolerance of pulpiteers – the model of reportage from zones of crisis and conflict.'

The idea of despotism and mass death - finding cartoonish reality in Daesh (much as it did a decade ago in the Taliban, see Merali, 2002) - also finds itself reinvented in the theme of British values and Muslims' (inherent) inability to accord with them. The links between media and political discourse are many but some are concrete. In 2002 Boris Johnson, then editor of The Spectator, claimed Muslim extremists feared women (Merali, 2002), now as Mayor of London, his remarks claim that statements made by Muslims, including those expressing concern over Islamophobic language, are somehow promoting an 'extremist' violent agenda.

MCB - ISIS

"I often hear voices from the Muslim intelligentsia who are very quick to accuse people of Islamophobia.

"But they are not explaining how it can be that this one religion seems to be leading people astray in so many cases. They are not being persuasive in the right way with these people." (Stone, 2 March 2015)

This is not a new intervention by Johnson (and also clearly with the same target i.e. the MCB in mind). Writing after the London bombing of 7 July 2005, in The Spectator, of which at the time he was editor, he states:

"The Islamicists last week horribly and irrefutably asserted the supreme importance of [their] faith, overriding all worldly considerations, and it will take a huge effort of courage and skill to win round the many thousands of British Muslims who are in a similar state of alienation, and to make them see that their faith must be compatible with British values and with loyalty to Britain. That means disposing of the first taboo, and accepting that the problem is Islam. Islam is the problem.

"To any non-Muslim reader of the Koran, Islamophobia - fear of Islam - seems a natural reaction, and, indeed, exactly what that text is intended to provoke. Judged purely on its scripture - to say nothing of what is preached in the mosques - it is the most viciously sectarian of all religions in its heartlessness towards unbelievers....

"It is time that we started to insist that the Muslim Council of Great Britain, and all the preachers in all the mosques, extremist or moderate, began to acculturate themselves more closely to what we think of as British values. "(Hill, 8 September 2009)

At the time of writing Johnson is widely considered to be the likely next leader of the Conservative Party. In 2013, he called for parents who taught their children 'extremist views' to be treated as child abusers and their children taken into care (Johnson, 2 March 2014):

> "The law should obviously treat radicalisation as a form of child abuse. It is the strong view of many of those involved in counter-terrorism that there should be a clearer legal position, so that those children who are being turned into potential killers or suicide bombers can be removed into care – for their own safety and for the safety of the public.

> "That must surely be right. We need to be less phobic of intrusion into the ways of minority groups and less nervous of passing judgment on other cultures. We can have a great, glorious, polychromatic society, but we must be firm to the point of ruthlessness in opposing behaviour that undermines our values. Paedophilia, FGM, Islamic radicalisation – to some extent, at some stage, we have tiptoed round them all for fear of offending this or that minority. It is children who have suffered."

'Our values' in this piece by Johnson, are set against Islamic ones (earlier in the piece he refers to British values again). By associating paedophilia and FGM with Islamic radicalisation he further catalyses the imagery of the Muslim as sexual predator.

Johnson's use of 'British values' back in the 2000s, predates that of David Cameron (indeed in 2007, David Cameron spent a week with a Muslim family where he claimed he learned a lot about British values (Cameron, 13 May 2007) but followed close on the heels of Tony Blair. The former Labour Prime Minister set out a stall for governmental intervention and social engineering in the Muslim community through PREVENT, with his so-called 'Rules of the Game' speech (Blair, 5 August 2005). Successive statements set out ever increasing restrictive ideas on what constitutes normative Islam, and acceptable speech from Muslims. Pro-Palestinian activism and beliefs, support for any type of political Islam, in particular the idea of the Caliphate, considering homosexuality a sin, supporting armed resistance, were some of the issues flagged up by Blair and his colleagues (IHRC et. al., 2009). These ideas have been repeatedly promulgated, creating an environment whereby laws and policies that target solely Muslims can be found.

Since Jack Straw's direct targeting of Muslim niqab wearers in 2006, various ministers have made interventions in minority issues that would have once been thought of as taboo in a multicultural society. Though later forced to retract his statement, defence secretary Michael Fallon claimed British towns were being "swamped" by immigrants and that the towns' residents were "under siege". Despite being forced to withdraw his remarks by Number 10, he received significant public support on social media including from other MPs (The Guardian, 27 October 2014). Additionally the impact on the public psyche of such comments coming from the Defence Minister has largely passed without mention.

In June 2014, Phillip Hollobone, a conservative MP, proposed legislation to regulate the use of "certain facial coverings" in public. He described the burka as "against the British way of life". "We are never going to get along with anyone with having a fully integrated society if a substantial minority insist on concealing their identity from everyone else." He had previously stated in 2010 that "Wearing the burkha is the religious equivalent of going around with a paper bag over your head". He made that remark in a public debate on immigration and was referred to the police by Northamptonshire Race Equality Council. At that time the Crown Prosecution Service decided not to prosecute him for inciting religious hatred.

Although many similar cases can be cited, there is enough from senior governmental figures to keep us occupied. David Cameron's speech in Munich in 2011, attacking 'Islamist extremism', proposed among other things a litmus test for engaging with Muslim organisations:

So let's properly judge these organisations:
Do they believe in universal human rights – including for women and people of other faiths?

Do they believe in equality of all before the law?
Do they believe in democracy and the right of people to elect their own government?
Do they encourage integration or separatism?
These are the sorts of questions we need to ask.
Fail these tests and the presumption should be not to engage with organisations.
No public money. No sharing of platforms with Ministers at home.
At the same time, we must stop these groups from reaching people in publicly funded institutions – like universities and prisons."

This litmus test has been applied and reapplied and used to exclude many organisations from positions in public spaces in which they they had hitherto been present, and to keep many others out. Andrew Gilligan, a journalist and close associate of London Mayor Boris Johnson (who appointed him an advisor) and other Tory figures, has written many articles accusing various organisations and individuals of failing this test (see e.g. Gilligan, 22 February 2015). Repetition of these ideas, needless to say, impacts on the readership and audiences of such commentators.

In July 2015, Cameron revisited this theme in another speech in which he accused Muslims of quietly condoning Daesh. Bodi (2015) summarises the trajectory of the governmental disourse of Muslim extremism thus:

What makes the 'new' strategy any different from CONTEST, the euphemistic acronym for Britain's counter-terrorism strategy in place since 2003? Judge for yourself:

This is Gordon Brown, writing in the Guardian in 2009 about his government's plans to revamp the strategy.

"Al-Qaida terrorists remain intent on inflicting mass casualties.... They are motivated by a violent extremist ideology based on a false reading of religion......The approach we are taking ....addresses the longer term causes - understanding what leads people to become radicalised, so we can stop the process."

And this is PM David Cameron speaking in 2011:

"We have got to get to the root of the problem... That is the existence of an ideology, Islamist extremism... Islamist extremism is a political ideology supported by a minority. At the furthest end are those who back terrorism to promote their ultimate goal: an entire Islamist realm, governed by an interpretation of Sharia. Move along the spectrum, and you find people who may reject violence, but who accept various parts of the extremist worldview, including real hostility towards Western democracy and liberal values..."

Fast forward four years and plus ça change. This is what the PM announced last week:

Islamist extremism, is an ideology. It is an extreme doctrine... And like any extreme doctrine, it is subversive. At its furthest end it seeks to destroy nation-states to invent its own barbaric realm. And it often backs violence to achieve this aim...: But you don't have to support violence to subscribe to certain intolerant ideas which create a climate in which extremists can flourish. Ideas which are hostile to basic liberal values such as democracy, freedom and sexual equality."

So there we have it. The conveyor belt theory of terrorism where Islam is the first step of a journey along which extremist ideology is a staging post and acts of terrorism the possible destination.

This definition of 'extremism' is a catch-all for making everything about Muslims suspicious. Even the lack of anything to suspect is something to suspect in a culture that finds Muslim existence itself anathema. How this environment impacts on Muslims day to day will be discussed further in Chapter 5. The following chapter will look more closely at how PREVENT has worked to create this environment, and will focus on education, in particular the so-called Trojan Horse affair, as well as how hate crimes and hate policy have operated in the last five years.

Chapter 3

"PREVENT" as the Socialisation of Hate

Statistics from Ameli et. al (2011) show that the numbers of Muslims experiencing physical attacks ran at 13.9% of the sample. This and other statistics will be analysed in comparison to the findings of 2014 in Chapters 5 and 6. To set the scene of the last five years the following further key experiences from 2010 were reported by the sample as follows:

Key findings 2010	
	Percent
Numbers of Muslims experiencing verbal abuse	44.5%
Numbers of Muslims witnessing or hearing Islamophobia	57.1%
Numbers of Muslims experiencing discrimination at work	28.1%
Numbers of Muslims seeing negative stereotypes in the media	66.9%
Numbers of Muslims experiencing discrimination in an educational setting	37.2%

Table 1: Key findings 2010

The experience of hatred is multifaceted, yet the experience that is acknowledged is the one called hate crime, which is now legislated for. The statistics above confirm that Muslims are living with a high level of violence enacted against them as individuals, through attacks, insults and discrimination, as well as symbolically via representation of Muslims in the media and in political discourse.

This chapter will overview some of the incidents reported in the last few years of attacks of an individual and symbolic nature, with the aim of highlighting the way that violence is enabled through prevailing media and political commentary. As Ameli et. al. (2011) argues, even when minorities become victims of social attitudes with the majority of hate crimes expressed in acts of hatred, hostility, discrimination and violence, the majority population, including perpetrators of such acts are also a type of victim (Ameli et. al, 2013) in that they are incited to commit acts of violent hatred by the environment created by media, political elites, academia and other institutions. In Ameli et. al. (2011)

research was cited making clear that the majority of perpetrators of hate attacks were not members of organised groups but individuals with no history of criminality, who often after the event would express remorse and surprise at their actions. This may still be the case, but the following overview suggests that there is a significant trend in far-right street mobilisation evidenced in the operation of groups like the English Defence League, Britain First and to a lesser extent the British National Party, as well as supporters who may simply share their goals but have no formal affiliation.

This 'street-level' view of hatred will be contextualised through a short discussion of the PREVENT policy implemented by successive governments that the authors argue constitutes a significant policy factor in the intervening periods. Whilst pre-dating the first survey, PREVENT has been revamped and pushed (sometimes in the face of strong opposition and sometimes almost by stealth via conceptual laxness) into institutional frameworks, including and especially education, but also in the discourse of media and politics. Following the end of the survey the PREVENT duty has now been enacted as part of the Counter Terrorism and Security Act 2015.

The discursive praxis of PREVENT, according to the authors, may be one of if not the most significant factor in the rise of 'street-level' hatred against those perceived to be Muslim, as well as normalising differential treatment of communities of colour and culture using the rhetoric of community cohesion and British values (as a challenge to and heralding the end of state sanctioned multi-culturalism).

The authors argue that a more detailed and systematic study, including mass data collection be undertaken to assess how the conceptual underpinnings of the discourse of PREVENT as represented in media, policy and political discourse inhere in ideas of supremacism and right (including the right to individual and collective violence) against the 'other' (for a possible methodology see de Bolla (2013).

Such an enterprise falls outside of the remit of this book. The following discursive terms contained in the PREVENT policy however, are meaningful in terms of the following overview: gender (rights), democracy, security, British (values), human rights, loyalty.

Thematics of individual attacks

Hate crime as a legal concept is an act actionable under the criminal law. However the following overview takes examples of cases of hate crime and discrimination and looks at the motivating factors behind the incidents. This collapsing of the legal differentiation between criminal and civil provides a prism through which the operation of a hate environment can be understood. Hate crime does not operate in a vacuum nor is it the only manifestation of hatred. It is simply one that carries penalties (if proven) under criminal law, as opposed to sanction under civil law (discrimination).

When looking at the incidents, it is worth referring to media and political discourse referenced in Chapter 2. Again motivation comes from a point of belief or instigation based on an authoritative voice.

Child grooming

October 2014

Asian taxi drivers in Rotherham claim they are facing racist abuse from passengers on a daily basis. Cabbies in the town say they have been the target of bigots since the Jay Report into child sexual abuse by largely Pakistani men was published in August. (Pitt, 22 October 2014)

Security

Veil-wearing Muslim students Yasmin and Atoofa were refused entry on a London bus.

The bus driver claimed they were seen as a "threat" to passengers. They were ordered off the bus even though they had valid tickets.

Yasmin began recording the confrontation and the bus driver hid his face. She said "It's ok for you to cover your face on my recording but it is not ok for my friend to cover her face out of choice." (BBC News Online, 23 July, 2010)

Taher Gulamhussein was detained unlawfully under terror laws after trying to make a complaint on a train. (5pillars.com, 14 July 2014)

Loyalty

December 2014

False accusations levelled at Muslim workers at a petrol station, claiming they refused to serve a customer who was wearing a Help for Heroes top.

Police confirmed this is a false allegation.

The mother of the boy in question posted online that the workers are 'Taliban supporters' (Pitt, 22 December, 2014)

Veils

April 2010

William Baikie racially assaulted 26-year-old Anwar Alqahtani by forcibly removing her niqaab in Glasgow. (BBC, 26 July 2010)

April 2013

North Cheam. Four teenage girls attacked and mocked a Muslim woman for wearing a headscarf.

They knocked and kicked the 26-year-old to the ground, afterwards trying to remove the hijab. The attackers have not yet been found. (Sutton Guardian, 21 April 2011)

May 2013

Tracy Davis, 46, was fined over £300 for racially abusing and punching a 55-year-old woman in Woolwich for wearing the niqab (The Voice, 4 October 2013)

July, 2014

Muslim women who wear a full veil say there are no-go areas in Leicester which they feel frightened to visit – even in a car. They claim they are subjected to abuse every day and that it is getting increasingly difficult to avoid such incidents in the city centre. (Pitt, 8 July, 2014)

July 2014

A Muslim girl was spat at and racially abused in Bristol City Centre and no one came to help.

A teenage girl was walking home from school through Bristol City Centre when a man hurled insults at her then proceeded to spit at her. No one assisted the girl.

The young girl's counsellor said: "She was picked on because she was wearing a headscarf. As if somehow wearing a headscarf ought to single someone out as a foreigner. This has led to many of her friends who also wear headscarves to be worried about being alone in public."(Onions, July 17, 2014)

September, 2014

A teacher has been suspended after she allegedly made a comment about a Muslim student's headscarf. It is claimed a girl at the school was fidgeting with her headscarf and the teacher involved was heard to say: "If she was in my class I would chuck the scarf in the bin." (Pitt, 13 Septmeber 2014)

September 2014

London's Camden School for Girls has stopped a 16-year-old student from attending because she wears the niqab despite being a student there for the past five years. (Owen, Tuesday 23 September 2014)

October 2014

Emiliano Sanchez, 59, confronted Shirin Akter and asked "why are you wearing this? This is not the Quran and it is not allowed in this country." He then pulled off her niqaab and said "Did you see that Paki? I told her to take that thing off her head."

He was let off very lightly as he was ordered to carry out 250 hours of unpaid work in the community. (Taylor, 1 November 2014)

An investment banker was caught on camera launching a racist rant at a woman on an Inter City train in front of shocked passengers, claiming that Muslim men are raping British women. (Pitt, 14 October, 2014)

Nurun Ahmed, who wears the hijab, was fired from the BBC show, The Apprentice. In response to her departure Katie Hopkins tweeted: "Nurun has left the building. Thank crap for that. The token headscarf wearer is no more." (Pitt, 23 October 2014)

November 2014

A 19-year-old Muslim student was subjected to a racial attack in Piccadilly Gardens. Her headscarf was torn from her head.

Maryam, a first-year photojournalism undergraduate at Staffordshire University, was confronted by a group of white girls after expressing her disgust at the way they were treating a beggar.

Yet she was subjected to a torrent of racial and physical abuse by the gang, which left her in tears. The gang shouted: "Go back to your country you f*cking terrorist p*ki, I will bomb your face off." Then they slapped her face, before pulling her headscarf off and kicking her on the left side on the hips. (Wilson, 5 November 2014)

December 2014

A Muslim woman who was spat at during a racist rant in Cabot Circus has spoken of her shock at the people who turned a blind eye. As reported by the Bristol Post when it happened in July, Hughes spat on her hand and hijab headdress while launching into an Islamophobic rant. (Emanuel, 11 December 2014)

An Islamophobic thug who threw a can of alcohol over a Muslim woman and her child as they walked along the street has been sent to jail. In December 2014, Leeds Crown Court heard the details of a July case where the victim was a young white woman who had converted to Islam and married a Muslim man. Her attacker was jailed for throwing alcohol over her and her child as well as hurling foul-mouthed racist abuse and threatening the woman with a butcher's knife. He targeted the 21-year-old as she walked past his home on Berkeley View, Harehills.

Nick Addlington, prosecuting, said the attacker approached

the woman and said: "Why are you with a p***? Why are you wearing those clothes? You are not a Muslim!" He then followed her down the street and called her a "Muslim bitch" before throwing the can of alcohol over her and her child.

The woman asked him why he was behaving like that and he replied: "Because I hate Muslims." He then produced a silver butcher's knife and began waving it around as children stood close by. He then said: "Watch what I am going to do when your husband comes out."

Police were contacted and went to the house. Mr Addlington, prosecuting, said there was a "total lack of co-operation" from anyone at the party despite what had happened. (Yorkshire Evening Post, 6 December 2014)

Far-right ideas and symbols

May 2010

A 38 year-old, was given a 10-year CRASBO in 2011 for his involvement in an incident the previous year. The CRASBO prevents him from attending any public meeting organised by the EDL. He entered a guilty plea at Doncaster Crown Court for racially aggravated order (section 5 Public Order Act) following an incident on a train when he racially abused a family while travelling from a demonstration, for which he was arrested by British Transport Police. (Lincolnshire Police, 10/03/2011)

July, 2010

A 26-year-old father and a 17-year-old were charged with racially aggravated behaviour against a group of Muslim men and an off-duty officer in Lincoln.

30 to 40 Muslim men were discussing the building of a mosque when David Odling and the unnamed 17-year-old, barged in and began spewing anti-Muslim sentiments. Both were also members of the EDL. They then assaulted off-duty police officer Rizwaan Chothia when he asked them to leave. (Gainsborough Standard, 16 May 2011)

September 2010

In Burnley a 77 year-old-widow had her car torched and a swastika sprayed on her shop.

The food store owner said she would not be forced out of her home or shop and is not scared by what happened. "I can forget about the spray now it has vanished. I'm not scared by it.... I don't understand why it has happened. It is a close neighbourhood here and everyone that comes in is friendly and I've had no trouble with anyone. But if they come back then maybe it is just my time. I am not scared of death" (Jackson, 20 September 2010)

June 2014

Two Pakistani men racially attacked after attending an anti-racist rally in Belfast. Muhammad Khattak and Haroon Khan were assaulted and had their home set upon by thugs. (Porter, 02/06/2014)

June 14 2014

Turkish man assaulted in broad daylight in racist attack.

Musa Gulusen, 45, has been working in Belfast for the past 20 years. He says he "is subjected to racist abuse almost every day but it goes in one ear and out the other."

However during June he was assaulted by two men who were passing by his stall. They punched him to the ground, ripped his shirt and broke his wrist before stealing £120 from his pocket.

It is said the attack occurred following the controversy over Pastor James McConell's comments about Islam. (Williamson, 14/06/2014)

The foregoing highlights a number of tropes.

Poole (2011) argues that obsessions with culture, deviant behaviours and inferior behaviours are manifested in media coverage before 9-11. She argues further that once security concerns lessened in the aftermath similar tropes have come to the fore in reporting again.

As the general discourse of securitisation has set in, incidents in spaces like public transport are given a context. The argument of a post-racial society is that the discourse of security simply provides a cover for individual racists to spout their pre-existing prejudices. Even if true, a prevailing discourse of securitisation still supplies a legitimisation of discrimination and / or attacks (verbal or physical). The domination hate model argues that the prevailing discourse influences everyone and conditions modes of representation and perception.

In this case it is the idea that Muslims, their dress or their sense of grievance (in Gulamhussein's case in a matter unrelated to security) that makes them a potential threat.

Taint by association is another theme that recurs with people of different backgrounds being attacked for their (perceived) association. In addition to the type of cases cited above, even those with little or no affiliation can fall foul of the taint of association or the taint of sympathy. Parris (21 March 2015) outlines the number, level and also background of those posting aggressive comments in response to a columnist from The Times newspaper's piece on negative attitudes to Muslims. The columnist, Janice Turner, quoted in Chapter 2 for a negative piece on the niqab, is not known for any type of sympathy towards Islam or Muslims, yet received some 500 comments, of which in Parris' opinion 90% were "hostile and many of them biliously so." Parris recounts a similar experience when writing on the same topic and describes reading the comments as "feeling you've been spending time somewhere pretty unpleasant." Significantly Parris notes that in Turner's case, her piece was in the subscriber only online version of The Times. This is not the space for working-class right wing street organisers or an open space such as Twitter or Facebook or other social media platforms where the phenomenon of 'trolling' including racist trolling has become a feature. Awan (2013) argues that such comments 'consist of an 'extremist' and incendiary undertone', which he further argues stokes 'up more hatred particularly in the case of online Islamophobia.'

The obsession with face veils and head coverings for women and their link to both security and threat in the public imagination as well as citizenship and belonging become evident in the case of physical attacks, but also exclusions from educational spaces. Such cases have been reported year on year, in particular after Jack Straw's rather public interventions on the subject. These individual attacks fulfil (as do all hate attacks) a dual purpose of not just hurting the individual but sending a message to the group (Ameli et al. 2011). Fearfulness, as described above, is created in the group targeted by the message, described by Ameli et al (2012) as the hated society. Zempi and Chakraborti (2014) describe the state of fearfulness they found amongst wearers of the niqab:

> "...both the fear of being attacked and incidents of Islamophobic victimisation can have significant and ongoing consequences for veiled Muslim women, their families and wider Muslim communities. Everyday experiences of both explicit and implicit manifestations of Islamophobia produce, *inter alia*, feelings of inferiority, loss of confidence and self-esteem, depression, flashbacks, guilt and self-blame. Moreover, incidents of Islamophobic victimisation are likely to increase feelings of insecurity, vulnerability and fear amongst veiled Muslim women. Consequently, the threat of Islamophobic victimisation limits both the movements and the social interactions of actual and potential victims, thereby resulting in social isolation."

Ameli and Merali (2006a) highlight how women who cover their hair are also made intensely vulnerable by the increasingly negative rhetoric. In the 10 years between the two studies, it can be argued that the sense of vulnerability has turned into outright fearfulness, and that the consequent impact on mental health and well-being, health and social mobility need to be properly addressed.

According to Sian (2013):

> "...government policies and institutions initiated the change from what David Gillborn (2008) refers to as 'naïve' to 'cynical' multiculturalism, and called for the return of assimilationist logics which dominated the political and social imaginary in the 1970s (Gillborn 2008; Law and Swann 2011, 35). As a result of such global, national and local events also including the 2001 riots and 7/7, discourses surrounding education

have been saturated by a rhetoric of assimilation, community cohesion, integration and security (Law and Swann 2011, 36)."

On the one hand there is confidence in individuals of whatever ilk to commit attacks or perpetrate discrimination and indeed to revert to racist modes of behaviour associated with decades gone. Part of this behaviour is mobilisation against anti-racist activism. State mobilisation against those challenging societal ills, including racism, gives succour to pre-existing right-wing groups, legitimising such thinking and providing a recruiting tool.

Whilst those provoked to attack are a minority, the hate environment also breaks bonds of compassion and empathy. As described above, when attacks take place, there can often be a veil of silence amongst those also present with no one offering to help. Ameli et al have remarked on this previously (2004b) as a worrying precursor to a serious breakdown of social bonds that can precede mass action against an out-group. The idea of the post-racial society assumes a teleology that results in this 'ideal' social reality. This ideal is an end-point from which there can be no return. With this default assumption of 'no going back' warning signs can be missed e.g. detentions without charge based on profiling turning into mass detentions and internment of communities.

Before addressing incidents of a symbolic nature (including certain attacks on individuals) it is worth noting that these incidents show that the idea that there can be shared citizenship between perpetrator and victims is in itself anathema to perpetrators. Part of the 'message' is that the victim does not belong in this space or can only be tolerated on certain conditions that are so pressing they require in some cases a criminal act from the perpetrator to enforce them. With individuals who commit such acts instigated to be enforcers, it is hard to assign this motivation to random individual hatred.

Symbolic crimes / attacks

A number of individual attacks outlined below, take place near to someone or their property while they are at, or on their way to and from a Muslim place of worship or Muslim space. Whilst targeted at an individual their proximity to a place of worship is clearly deliberate, and the victims' affiliation to practices associated with being a Muslim is a target.

October 2014
A racist teenager was jailed for throwing a pot noodle at two Asian boys walking home from a mosque in Darwen. (Lancashire Telegraph, 14 October 2014)

December 2014
A Middlesbrough football fan who ripped up pages of the Qur'an during a match has been banned from every football ground in England and Wales for three years. (Pitt, 16 December 2014)

December 2014
A man branded a "vile, reprehensible bigot" by police after he sent offensive photographs and social media posts to an Islamic community centre near Truro has been spared jail despite saying he will continue to share his views on Facebook. (Pitt, 17 December 2014)

Organisation against Muslim places of worship and schools, is based again on the idea of denied citizenship. Attacks on other religious symbols, including the Qur'an fall into a similar category. If the binaries of unfettered speech, civil society mobilisation, as well as discrimination and hate crimes are collapsed, we can again find shared motivations.

June 2014
Douglas Murray links up with Christian fundamentalist homophobe to smear Newham 'mega-mosque' supporters.

Murray is associate director at the right wing neo-conservative Henry Jackson Society which has acquired a reputation for writing bigoted anti-Muslim articles. In this instance he authored a piece which repeated baseless accusations that the local Muslim community in Newham, east London, was intimidating a witness from speaking out against plans to build a mosque. (Piit, 17 June, 2014)

July 2014

A former footballer has been fined £1,000 for a post on a social network inciting racial violence. The man, from Tayside, aged 19, posted on Facebook asking people to start terrorist attacks after the murder of soldier Lee Rigby. (BBC News online, 17 July 2014)

July 2014

A UKIP councillor has been accused of "scaring people with made-up information" after he branded an Islamic procession in Ilford "a call to war". (Pitt, 29 July 2014)

September 2014

Plans to build a mosque on a Basildon industrial estate were attacked by a local UKIP councillor who claimed "Basildon needs jobs, not a mosque."

The planning application was put forward on 23 July for Buckwins Square, on the Burnt Mills Estate, to be used for a place of public worship by Basildon Islamic Centre leader Sarfraz Sarwar, 66, of Gordons, Pitsea.

But the decision caused uproar among local councillors as the industrial unit, which was previously a call centre, would be "putting businesses into the background for a religious organisation".

Brother Sarwar, who has also faced attacks on his Pitsea home, said: "It is not a mosque. You know there will never be a mosque in Basildon, because of all the opposition. All this will be is an education centre. It is an Islamic centre for British and cultural studies. The problem is everything to do with Muslims ends up being a propaganda war." (Echo, 1 September 2014)

December 2014

A man who was being spoken to by police shouted abuse at people who were watching from across the road. Blackburn magistrates heard that Phillip Anthony Townley told onlookers he would burn down their mosque. (Pitt, 16 December 2014)

December 2014

Britain First were encouraging people to avoid Muslim majority areas around the UK on their Facebook page. (Yorkshire Standard, 16 December 2014)

December 2014

A 19-year-old from Leeds, West Yorkshire, who was arrested in connection with an offensive video he posted on a social media website has been released on bail.

A video, which was shown to the *Yorkshire Standard*, showed a man ripping apart an English translation of the Qur'an with his teeth and putting it in the toilet before burning it. (Yorkshire Standard, 30 December 2014)

Thus fixation with negating 'Muslim' cultural space, and even eradicating it physically, begs the question as to why certain acts are dealt with or not by the law and the category of law they fall into.

Mobilisation against mosques and schools, as well as Muslim communities is now a feature of life for communities in various parts of the UK. The killing of Lee Rigby, the child grooming scandal reported in racialised terms (discussed in Chapter 2), are both cited as actual or perceived motivations for protests or attacks against mosques, community spaces, schools etc. These descriptions come again from perpetrators but also victims. The operation of a hate environment involves the internalisation of discourses by all sectors of society, so as a hating society forms and bases its motivation on e.g. the racialised reporting of the child grooming case, so too does the hated society see its problems through the lens of attacks mistakenly laid at their door because of the 'bad reputation' given by rotten apples within the community. This latter gives succour to policy makers, and is a feature of the climate of fear Kundnani (2014) identifies. Thus comments by Taj Hargey (Hargey, 16 May 2013) claiming that Islamic preachers have encouraged a culture of grooming young white girls, plays to a state and street fascists' narrative that excuses structural subalternisation but also justifies attacks on those who do not take part or are actually victims of, street mobilisations.

February 2014

Four English Defence League (EDL) members have been convicted of a religiously aggravated offence following a Thatcham town centre protest.

The prosecution was brought after up to 20 people, some draped in St George Cross flags and one wearing a rubber pig mask, descended on The Broadway on the night on Friday, February 28. Their target was Hosans kebab van.

Chants of "Muslim groomers off our streets – go back to your own country," and "no surrender to the Taliban" filled the room at Reading Magistrates' Court on Tuesday as footage from police officers' body cameras was screened. Naomi Edwards, prosecuting, said: "Protesting is fine and proper but this went beyond what's acceptable." (Pitt, 8 September 2014)

June 2014

Second far-right protest against planned Bolton mosque (Pitt, 30 June 2014)

Protestors took to the steps of Bolton Town Hall to rally against plans to build a new mosque in Astley Bridge.

More than 100 campaigners, who insisted they were not representatives of any political party, demonstrated in Victoria Square today.

Plans have been submitted to Bolton Council for a mosque in Blackburn Road with space for more than 1,000 prayer mats by the Taiyabah Islamic Centre. (Culley, 17 June 2014)

On July 18 (Pitt, 18 July 2014) it emerged that the BNP, NF and Infidels were jointly and variously organising campaigns against the mosque.Two men were convicted of making Facebook threats to "torch" and "blow up" the proposed new mosque.

Leon Richmond, aged 18, wrote on the page that he would not be bothered if the mosque was built as he would "blow it up" himself.

23-year-old Darren Hubble posted: "Bolton people say no, Wigan says not a chance, I'll torch the place if I get half the chance".

July 2014
Police are hunting for two racist thugs who smashed windows and screamed abuse at people in the mosque in Warrington town centre. (Pitt, 8 July 2014)

August 2014
On Friday, members from Britain First turned up outside the North West Kent Muslim Association mosque in Crayford. This is the same mosque they barged into last month, harassing the imam and threatening to remove the "sexist" signs outside the building that indicated separate entrances for women and men. They handed out copies of Britain First's 'Islam and Women' pamphlet to worshippers and passers-by. ("Most folk know that Islam exists", the pamphlet begins, "but have no clue as to its true horror.") (Pitt, 3 August 2014)

August 2014
Peaceful vigil for Palestine becomes noisy protest in Middlesbrough as EDL members arrived to 'disrupt' it. (Evening Gazette, 7 August 2014)

August 2014
About 200 protesters marching in Portsmouth against Israel's campaign in Gaza were confronted by around 15 far right counter-demonstrators. The anti-war protesters were stopped at the roundabout between Guildhall Square and Commercial Road by police as more officers rushed to the scene. (Portsmouth News, 9 August 2014)

August 2014
The BNP organised a rally against a mosque in New Addington, near Croydon. They accused the statement's signatories of "putting ethnic minority groups before the indigenous Brits" and setting aside their political differences to "conspire on an issue they all very much agree on – the Islamisation of Britain". (Pitt, 21 August 2014)

August 2014

30 members of the right wing South East Alliance demonstrated close to offices they say are used as a recruiting centre by the Muslim Brotherhood in Cricklewood, north west London. Police kept the two groups apart but there were some scuffles and arrests.

SAE, which has held similar protests in the area, deny they have links to the English Defence League claiming they are 'a non-political community based street movement'.

However, their Facebook page is filled with anti-Muslim posts. (Pitt, 22 August 2014)

September 2014

Police investigate as semi-naked man in homemade 'burka' does ice bucket challenge video while waving sausages and bacon outside Bolton mosque.

A clip of the man doing this was later posted on the Stop Astbridge Mosque (see above) Facebook page but was later removed. (Bolton News, 10 September 2014)

September 2014

A Cardiff mosque has been forced to close after being smashed up by intruders. Police are investigating after the Rabbaniah Islamic Cultural Centre suffered thousands of pounds of damage after what news reports described as 'burglars' pulled down the ceiling and ripped charity boxes from the walls. (ITV, 18 September 2014)

September 2014

Burglars have targeted a town centre mosque in an apparent hate attack. Raiders broke into Chapel Walk Mosque in Rotherham in the early hours of Tuesday morning. They ransacked offices, stole money from a collection box and damaged microphone equipment. They also threw copies of the Qur'an on the floor, leading one faith leader to blame right wing elements. (Doyle, 18 September 2014)

September 2014

The English Defence League came to London, "to demand the government take firm action urgently about the many Islamic threats to this country, its people, its culture, its heritage and its future", as they put it. (Pitt, 20 September 2014)

September 2014
  A minibus, which was used to ferry elderly worshippers, was torched outside the Manchester Islamic Centre. (Manchester Evening News, 23 September 2014)

October 2014
  Hundreds of Britain First supporters marched through the centre of Rotherham on two occasions after the publication of the Jay report into child grooming. (Parry, 5 October, 2014 and Pitt, 5 October, 2014)

October 2014
  Protesters angry at a planned Muslim school marched through Portsmouth on 11 October.
  Around 20 people including members of the English Defence League (EDL) gathered at Lake Road, where the Madani Academy is to be based. (Pitt, 11 October 2014)

November 2014
  Members of far-right party the National Front tried to disrupt a peaceful march of more than 500 Muslims from across Wales in Newport today. The marchers were commemorating the anniversary of the death of the Prophet Mohammad's grandson, Imam Hussain, who was martyred more than 1,300 years ago. (Pitt, 16 November 2014)

November 2014
  A march by a far right group was banned after police said it would have incited violence. (Roberston, 2014)

November 2014
  EDL protest in Luton draws around 400 (Luton on Sunday, 22 November 2014)

December 2014

Britain First were reported to be continuing to disseminate videos of their Birmingham branch protesting a 'Muslim only' cinema despite the story being proven to be false several months earlier.

Vue Cinema in the Star City entertainment complex was accused of turning away customers based on religion back in July.

Leon Jennings claimed he and his friends were denied entry because they "did not look like they celebrated Eid", a story which was picked up in the Mirror and Daily Mail.

The centre's manager however, denied the allegations stating the men had been turned away simply because it was too busy.

Local police soon confirmed they had received no complaints into the alleged incident either.

This didn't stop Britain First leader, Paul Golding, from storming down there with some heavies to confront the manager.

In the video, re-posted again on their Facebook page, the group were allowed into the building with absolutely no incident.

Despite repeatedly denying the incident ever happened, the manager was forced to listen to Golding issue a threat if it ever happens again.

After sufficiently intimidating the man the burly group then set about handing out their leaflets to both Muslims and non-Muslims alike who are all quite happily enjoying their day in the centre.

A Vue spokesperson said: "Everyone is welcome at Vue. During peak times, holidays and celebrations Star City does get very busy and we unfortunately have to turn some customers away if our screens are up to capacity.

"This has no bearing on the religious and cultural backgrounds of our customers and everyone is welcome at Vue at Star City."

(Huffington Post, 17 December 2014)

December 2014 onwards

A series of demonstrations by far right groups against a proposed mosque in Dudley have gradually increased in size and created mayhem for locals. First the EDL, then Britain First followed by All Football Fans Against Islamisation have held protests and rallies. (Express and Star, 21 May 2015) The cost of policing the marches has at the time of writing come to £414,700 (Express and Star, 21 September 2015)

• A mosque was damaged during a nearby arson attack on a caravan. (Macpherson, 17 December 2014)

• Luton Islamic Centre organised a conference refuting the teachings of ISIS. However the EDL spread misconceptions about the conference online arguing the conference was promoting ISIS teachings. (Pitt, 30 December 2014)

• The EDL ushered in the New Year with a call for a boycott of Muslim-owned taxi companies and Muslim-owned restaurants. (Pitt, 31 December 2014)

• Small numbers of English Defence League supporters appeared at a demonstration against Luton Islamic Centre but were largely outnumbered by the police. (Luton on Sunday, 31 December 2014)

*****

There are many issues raised by the treatment of cases relating to violations of Muslim spaces, as well as the reporting of such. Lenient sentences (particularly in comparison to crimes of causing gross offence that various Muslims have been prosecuted for), and reasons for such leniency (e.g. the perpetrator was drunk), emphasise once more that there is a double standard and indeed a separate legal regime for Muslims. In news reporting intruders and vandals in mosques have been described as burglars, thus marking the crime in a different manner and undermining its significance.

The violation of Muslim spaces, in particular mosques and schools, again speaks to the idea of being able to 'touch' (See

Chapter 2) - in this case Muslim space, in the name of desegregation.   In actuality it serves to reinforce expulsion because it also denies the legitimacy of identity and violates the psychological sanctity of the community targeted.

Public disconnect and 'threat'

According to Choudhury and Fenwick (2013):

> "There is a damaging disconnect between the state and communities in their conceptions of 'threat'. From the perspective of the state and officials who work in counter-terrorism, the threat from international terrorism is the most significant and real threat that Britain faces today. Given the nature of the actual and planned attacks from Al Qa'ida-inspired terrorism in Britain and elsewhere, the existence of networks and groups involving around 2,000 individuals that are involved in planning or supporting attacks in this country or abroad pose a real and grave challenge to national security. From the perspective of a Muslim population of over 2.5 million, however, those individuals are a tiny and virtually invisible minority. In the face of state claims about the threat posed by Al Qa'ida, focus group participants consistently identified a range of other issues, from drugs and gangs to unemployment and racism, that to them posed an equal or more immediate and real threat to their families and local communities. The research suggests that a state-centric approach to threat that is unable to acknowledge or respond to community conceptions of threat will struggle to attract community acknowledgement and cooperation. For example, it should be recognised that the English Defence League (EDL) are, for many Muslims in this research, a visible and real manifestation of violent extremism and one that many are more likely to encounter than an Al Qa'ida extremist. The research suggests that the policing of EDL marches, if handled correctly, could provide an opportunity for partnership and cooperation between local Muslim communities, the police, local authorities and other communities."

The thematics of the symbolic attacks and incidents again show the breaking of bonds of empathy and shared citizenship. The continued attacks on the idea of multiculturalism from political discourse in particular, makes multiple non-majority spaces vulnerable. The replacement discourse of social cohesion, which places responsibilities on minorities to integrate and desist from separation, only serves to emphasise that community-specific places like mosques are a mark of separation.

As Khan describes:

> "discourses surrounding community cohesion set the stage for the acceptance of Islamophobic measures in public and political spheres promoted by PVE [Preventing Violent Extremism] and associated counter terrorism initiatives. As a consequence negative, reductive and stereotypical constructs have been played out to represent Muslims as 'something of a congealed mass, both impenetrable and inassimilable' (Khan 2010, 86). Such depictions both reinforce and escalate fears about the Muslim 'other' whereby all Muslims come to embody a 'danger,' even young Muslim children in primary schools" (Sian, 2013: 7-8).

The idea of separateness is also tied in to the material and thinking of groups such as Britain First who have staged a number of mosque invasions in the last year. These typically involve entering mosques wearing shoes, distributing bibles, calling on worshippers to integrate into society and condemning women only spaces as 'sexist' and un-British. There has not been a systematic condemnation or legal penalty for these incidents.

The visibility of Muslim symbols like mosques, is also often interpreted as a sign of takeover. The long-running idea that Muslims in the public space are problematic as expressed before 9-11 (Poole, 2011), has turned into arguments of entryism and takeover of public life. This found extreme reflection in the so-called Trojan Horse affair that started in early 2014.

The Trojan Horse, renamed Trojan Hoax by some analysts and commentators, for reasons that will follow, focused on six schools in Birmingham which were all Muslim majority schools.

Background to Trojan Horse / Hoax

Richard Adams, writing in The Guardian (8 June 2014) summarises the affairs and its shifting goalposts as follows:

If anyone is looking for the ingredients for a British version of The Wire, the Trojan horse affair has them all: race, politics, education, media and law, wrapped up in one toxic, Birmingham-sized bundle.

But unlike in HBO's acclaimed crime drama, there is no evidence that anyone caught up in the Trojan horse row in Birmingham has acted illegally. In fact, there's not much evidence of anything.

That is the most bizarre element of an affair that has thrown 21 Birmingham schools into the heart of a cabinet row over how to tackle extremism.

It began with a letter sent to Birmingham city council in November last year [2013]. The letter, quickly dubbed the "Trojan horse", purported to be a plan of attack sent from a Birmingham circle of Islamist plotters to counterparts in Bradford, advising them how to carry out a similar takeover of Bradford schools, by hijacking boards of governors in state schools in mainly Muslim areas and forcing out opposition.

The letter was detailed and refers to events in Birmingham going back years. But it is widely thought to be a fake or hoax, because it is also strewn with errors. The letter then bounced around inside Birmingham city's administration, a hot potato that got passed on to the West Midlands police and back again. Eventually someone forwarded it to the Home Office, which forwarded it to the Department for Education. And there it rested, until February, when it became public through leaks to the media... The affair has led to four separate inquiries: three ordered by the education secretary, Michael Gove, including the Ofsted inspections of 21 schools that will be published on

Monday. There are also investigations by the Education Funding Agency,.. and then a separate inquiry into extremism led by the former Met police anti-terrorism chief Peter Clarke. The fourth inspection is a city-wide inquiry being conducted by Birmingham city council, which is waiting on the Ofsted reports.

In the past few days an extraordinary public spat between Gove and Theresa May has seen the education secretary forced to apologise and one of May's special advisers forced to resign. The row has even seen one national newspaper report that Gove's future in cabinet was even under threat.

Labour's position has been little more coherent: the shadow education secretary, Tristram Hunt, has used the letter to paint Gove as "soft" on extremism, which some in Birmingham have called disgraceful. But then again, both parties appear to have been briefed by Khalid Mahmood, the Labour MP for Birmingham Perry Barr, who argues the letter reveals a truth about an Islamist takeover that has eluded others.

Just what that takeover entails is central to understanding what the Trojan horse row is all about, and the fall-out between May and Gove. It comes down to a definition of extremism.

The claims that have bounced around include allegations of segregated classes, compulsory prayers and incendiary preachers at school assemblies – but most have crumbled under examination. So the focus for investigation has slipped from extremism to "an awareness of the risks associated with extremism" in the elided phrase now used by Ofsted inspectors to condemn the schools most heavily involved, such as Park View academy.

In the process, the DfE's definition of extremism has shifted from actual bomb-throwers to religious conservatives. That is a definition that is dangerously wide – and one that the Home Office objects to, hence the May-Gove rift. After the Ofsted chief inspector, Sir Michael Wilshaw, agreed to Gove's redefinition of extremism so enthusiastically, he now has to put its cards on the table... Ofsted's reputation is also under fire. Several of the schools were previously praised for their academic results and record for improving community relations.

Despite a House of Commons Education Committee also investigating the matter and being deeply critical of the whole affair, there have been no repercussions for any of those in power, whether ministers or local authorities who pursued the extraordinary investigations. Instead there has been major damage perpetrated on the schools involved. Other schools in areas such as Tower Hamlets became the victims of what was dubbed Trojan Horse 2, as well as actual Muslim schools. Additionally, the idea of dual educational space (Ameli et al., 2005), religious rights and basic recognition of students' identities, the rights already conferred on students by Department of Education guidelines, have all been undermined. Legitimate aspirations, such as those of Muslim educationalists, including teachers and governors, have been portrayed as sinister.

Sir Tim Brighouse (7 June 2014), a former chief education officer of Birmingham and schools commissioner for London, lambasts the denial of agency (and again shared citizenship):

> "…the arrival of academies and free schools has created an open season for lay people and professionals keen to pursue their own eccentric ideas about schooling: and when trust or governor vacancies occur, some perpetuate the very English tradition of inviting friends to join them. When the community is white it doesn't cause much comment. In mono-ethnic east Birmingham, however, it is seen as a Muslim plot to expose pupils to an undefined "extremism"."

An Insted Report (2014) states:

> "The notion of a plot has been given credence by widespread and longstanding Islamophobia in British society and culture. The recurring themes and tropes in moral panics about Islam, clearly present in most of the media coverage of the Trojan Horse affair, are that all Muslims are the same, all are wholly different from non-Muslims in their values and aspirations, and all are a threat to non-Muslims both physically and culturally, for they are more likely than non-Muslims to condone or to engage in violence.

"The affair in Birmingham is being used by certain organisations, groups and think tanks, some of them linked to the EDL and the BNP, to further their interests and agendas. Such organisations are funded in part by sources in the United States and are components in what is sometimes known as the global Islamophobia industry. Also the security services and counter terrorism units in Western countries are involved in this industry. The industry overall is concerned primarily with global oil supplies and Middle East politics, not with (for example) schools in a West Midlands city in England."

The above mirrors Ameli et al's findings in 2005 and the idea amongst parents seeking faith education that a Muslim school environment helps create confident citizens. Yet the idea of Muslim educational space, both in terms of faith schools and as space within mainstream schooling has not only continued to be pilloried, it has also become a trope reproduced by law and policy makers as well as in political and hostile media discourse. Repeated discussions around the idea of (self) segregation are usually unfounded, (see Billings and Holden, 2008 outlined below). Merali (2013), writing before Trojan Hoax, observes the continued obsession with the Muslim educational space nearly a decade after the research by Ameli et al (2005) was undertaken:

"… we find ourselves subsumed by a pernicious debate about Muslim schools (again), where government and opposition politicians jump over each other in attempts to placate an Islamophobic mob mentality over red herrings such as gender equality and discrimination, and the demonising of the wearing of hijab as inimical to this. Whilst paying the same taxes as everyone else, it appears Muslims have no right to demand the type of schooling they want, and thus having to put up with whatever is on offer, often low on academic standards and institutionalised against diversity, or pay for private Muslim schools."

As a result of the furore around Trojan Hoax, many governors and teachers now face lifetime bans from involvement in education (Kerbaj and Griffiths, 5 April 2015 and Taylor, 7 September 2015) despite there being no evidence of any wrong-doing or indeed any discernible type of 'extremism' bar one isolated incident (House of Commons Education Committee, 2015):

> "The one example given by Ian Kershaw is clearly unacceptable and action should have been taken by the school to prevent it, but a single instance does not warrant headline claims that students in Birmingham— or elsewhere in England—are being exposed to extremism by their teachers. The Birmingham City Council Trojan Horse Review Group was firm that it did not "support the lazy conflation–frequently characterised in the national media in recent months–of what Ofsted have termed issues around 'a narrow faith based ideology' and questions of radicalisation, extremism or terrorism". We agree.

> "... We also note that we have seen no evidence to support claims of an organised plot to take over English schools. We discussed this in some detail with witnesses. (HC Education Committee, 2015:7-8)"

Despite harshly criticising the Trojan Horse investigations, the House of Commons Education Committee repeats supremacist notions of universalism. The British values which are now to be promoted in all schools are universal and an important part of what children should learn.

Grosfoguel (2013) highlights how values e.g. human rights, gender equality, democracy, are represented as already existing European norms (norms which are used in clash theories like Huntington's (Foreign Affairs, 1993) which are inherently European and mark our Eurocentric societies as superior to all others. This runs counter not just to decolonial theories but even minority rights regimes developed after the Second World War through international covenants and treatises. Whilst the right to educate your child in your faith is a right given to all parents, rights protecting various aspects of minority cultures form the basis of minority rights and were developed specifically as a result of the Holocaust and the lead up to it. Adams, quoting the assistant deputy head at one of the affected schools (Lee Donaghy) identifies how that runs counter (Adams, 14 May 2014) to the idea of raising achievement through cultural values, and actually marginalises minorities.

> "Part of us getting excellent results has been about reflecting the wishes and needs of the community in the school. We would not have got those results without doing those things that mean that parents trust us and that kids are comfortable here."

Just as Progler (2008) identified recurring post-Enlightenment tropes in the depiction of Muslims in Anglophonic culture, Khan (2014) sees specific tropes come to the fore in the Trojan Hoax affair, which the authors here see reflected in the general narrative used in the run up to the enactment and implementation of the CTS Act, i.e. the slave and the witch.

> "... The slave or the subordinate - the dangerous street mugger who threatens the law and order of society, a figure reflecting fear of rebellion and insurrection. This is the fear of the ghetto and the street. A fear of a Muslim physicality expressed through the language of self-segregation or segregated communities, espoused by Ted Cantle and Herman Ouseley a decade ago in a language now embedded in public policy. A body of people depicted as a congealed unmovable mass, unable to integrate or penetrate into wider society; allegedly a space whose counter values have been fostered by a multicultural egalitarianism that has compromised the cohesiveness and safety of Britain.
>
> "This is the Muslim imaginary space referred to by former New Labour Minister, Hazel Blears, as non-governed spaces, where notions of *jihad* are born, take shape and take action. It is a fear that creates 'no go' areas in people's minds, a fear of Muslim ghettoes that challenge the aspirational 'Middle England' and you can

hear it echoed in both the rhetoric of the EDL and that of mainstream UK politicians. It is the fear expressed in the charge of 'Muslimification' of state schools as self-segregated institutions producing self-segregating young people and communities. A charge that interprets acts of demography as acts of ideology.

"… the Witch: a fear of the disguised, the hidden, and the stranger seeking vengeance or retribution. This fear exists in the breakdown of trust within a community or nation leading to it becoming divided against itself, neighbour suspecting neighbour, colleague suspecting colleague. One can see this here in state measures that place a duty on teachers, employers, colleagues, neighbours and families to look for signs of radicalisation in their colleagues, students or children. This form of Islamophobia conveys the fear of a hidden agenda, of an intelligence planning and designing, a trope that the 'Trojan Horse Plot' has cultivated brilliantly."

A persistent trope manifested in the Trojan Hoax affair, but long-running, expressed even in the thinking of former race relations pundits is 'sleepwalking into segregation' (Phillips cited in the Guardian, 19 September 2005). Trojan Hoax, within the current environment, highlights the idea of segregation as an incubator of ideas that undermine British values as discussed above. However research is counter-intuitive and rather shows the locus of extremist White ideologies in enclaves of the 'host', as in the Burnley report (Billings and Holden, 2008). The report studied inter alia three schools (one mainly white, one mixed, one mainly Muslim) in the Burnley area with a view to looking at the negative impacts of enclavisation and how this may have contributed to the riots in Burnley in 2001. The authors however found that:

"The all-White school is unable by itself to overcome the entrenched White extremism that is mediated through the family, the peer group and the enclave. This strongly suggests that in towns with sizeable ethnic minorities, unless White young people are exposed during their school careers to fellow pupils of different ethnic and religious backgrounds, attitudes of White superiority and hostility towards those of other cultures are unlikely to be ameliorated and smouldering resentments will continue into adult life. Enclavisation, however, assists the development of liberal and integrative attitudes among young Asian/Muslim people by providing an oasis of liberality in a strong and cohesive sub-community." (Billings and Holden, 2008: 4)

At that time the report, originally commissioned in part by the government, was sidelined. Yet, a letter, widely thought to be a hoax from the time of its exposure, triggered what has been repeatedly observed (see e.g. Adams, 2014) as a crusade and witchhunt.

Writing before Trojan Hoax erupted, Sian critiques the existing Preventing Violent Extremism (PVE) measures being implemented in schools:

> "The rehashing of such accounts including the 'culture clash,' religious hatred, alienation and so on (Alexander 2000, xiii), are never deployed to explain white activity, as such they remain locked into assumptions replete with elements from the immigrant imaginary (Sian 2011, 118), that is a series of discursive representations based around the ontological and temporal distinction between host and immigrant (Hesse and Sayyid 2006)... As David Tyrer (2003) points out the specific marking of Muslims reinforces and '...fixes the representation of Muslims as criminalised, and thus valorises the logics of racist pathology' (184)." (Sian, 2013:6)

Professor Gus John sums up the fiasco and where it has ultimately led:

> "Michael Gove, under the pretext of responding to anonymous claims in an unsigned letter, appears to be seeking to establish grounds for extending the *'Prevent Terrorism'* agenda to schools with a certain percentage of Muslim students. British-born school students, teachers

and governors belonging to this particular faith group are therefore likely to be subject to surveillance in much the same way as they are in further and higher education.

"Mr Gove presumably makes no connection between this saga, the xenophobic support for UKIP that we witnessed in the latest elections and the British Social Attitudes survey results regarding the percentage of people in the population who describe themselves as *'racist'*." (2014)

Preventing Terrorism or Promoting Demonisation and Violence?

Sian (2013) identifies how managing of the term Islamophobia (pre-dating the current security focus on Muslims) fuels the ability of state organs to enact hate policies with a purpose as ideological as anything the Trojan Hoax governors were wrongly accused of:

"I follow this argument and also suggest that PVE is stitched together by the logic of Islamophobia. Here I think it would be useful to draw upon S. Sayyid's conceptualization of Islamophobia (2010) which departs from framing Islamophobia as simply a set of distinct attitudes reducible to individuals holding 'closed' views as presented in the Runnymede Trust report, "Islamophobia: A Challenge For Us All"... Rather, for Sayyid, Islamophobia can be defined as 'the disciplining of Muslims by reference to an antagonistic western horizon' (Sayyid 2010a, 15), that is, the heart of Islamophobia comes not in the form of unfounded hostility, but instead, through the 'maintenance of the violent hierarchy between the idea of the west and Islam' (Sayyid 2010a, 15). I find Sayyid's definition a more helpful way to proceed as it shifts the focus from daily incidents of name calling and harassment to a wider critique of structural operations of power which govern and regulate Muslim bodies. This governing or 'disciplining' of Muslim bodies can clearly be seen at work in the PVE initiative."

This meta-narrative of discipline links the foregoing to the current praxis of PVE, commonly referred to as Prevent.

Surveillance, suspicion, self-censorship and behaviour modification, threat from wider society, are all facets of Muslim experience that will be disaggregated through the statistics generated by the 2014 UK-wide survey. As the prevailing discourse disciplines Muslims not to speak out against injustices either at home or abroad, any attempt not to conform to this containment or to have any sort of agency is seen as evidence of deviance.

The hate environment created by negative political and media discourse, mutually constituted with laws that discriminate including the CTS Act 2015, work together to create a hate environment within which the negative experiences of hated societies are produced and as this research shows, in the UK context, have worsened over the five-year period.

The role that anti-terror laws per se have played in creating this environment has led a coalition of organisations to call for the scrapping of all anti-terrorism laws enacted since 1997 (Guardian, 5 February 2015). The call comes amid the understanding that successive consultations with the state have simply given credence to ever more draconian laws with successive governments using the consultation process to claim legitimacy for them.

Some have described the impact of PREVENT as having "a chilling effect on open debate, free speech and political dissent. It will create an environment in which political change can no longer be discussed openly, and will withdraw to unsupervised spaces. Therefore, PREVENT will make us less safe." (various authors, Letter in The Independent, 10 July 2015) Its reality is far more disturbing and perverse than just a chilling effect on free speech and dissent. It is the creation of a police state in all but name. A state in which the state is actively shaping the beliefs of communities using coercion and demonisation.

PREVENT imposes a duty (The National Archives, 2015) on public bodies (schools, universities, NHS, social services etc) to identify individuals at risk of being drawn into extremism or terrorism. Those identified at risk are then referred to a panel whose job it is to come up with a "de-radicalisation" plan, referred to in the legislation as a 'support plan'. The focus of PREVENT is overwhelmingly on the Muslim community with a token mention of right wing extremism, which seems by and large to be ignored by those implementing PREVENT (Newman, 2015).

The Channel programme is the process by which the government tries to 'de-radicalise' people at risk of being drawn into extremism. It is part of PREVENT, and was introduced by the government in 2006. The panel is made up of local police, social services, PREVENT officers, and their job is to create a de-radicalisation plan for those identified at risk of being drawn into extremism or terrorism. Little is known of how the programme operates as most of those who have been put through the programme have refused to speak (Mohamed ed., 2015).

While the Channel programme conjures up images of Orwell's thought police, the PREVENT programme goes further in seeking to control people's ideas and beliefs. As one commentator put it: PREVENT has created a category of thoughtcrime for Muslims by which certain ideas and beliefs such as the right to armed resistance, wear religious attire or conscionably oppose homosexuality is referrable to the PREVENT police (Bodi, 2015). Recently David Cameron spoke about how some in the Muslim community were quietly condoning extremist ideology and that it was not sufficient to be law abiding citizens: "For too long, we have been a passively tolerant society, saying to our citizens 'as long as you obey the law, we will leave you alone'." Under PREVENT, Muslims are now required to reject normative Islamic values that have become unfashionable with the government, and actively uphold British values, a term that is vague and which many consider to be racist (IHRC, 21 July 2015). Cameron's speech was reported perversely as "UK Muslims Helping Jihadis" by the Daily Mail. (Groves, 19 June 2015)

PREVENT has moved us towards an Orwellian nightmare where police call on parents to report their children (Dodd, Laville and Pidd, 24 April 2014), where teachers (Richardson, 6 April 2015), doctors, social workers and other public workers are asked to spy on those they are supposed to serve, where teenagers are labelled extremist for handing out leaflets printed by a legitimate charity (Hooper, 2015), where being a law-abiding citizen is not enough to guarantee a life free from harassment from the state (Beech, 13 May 2015). It is a police state in which people's ideas will be actively moulded, where communities will be required to disavow ideas and practices stemming from their religious beliefs and actively display ideals dictated by the state.

Chapter 4

Domination Hate Model of Intercultural Relations and the Expansion of the Hate Environment

The authors and various colleagues have undertaken several studies using Ameli's Domination Hate Model of Intercultural Relations. This model has been developed to reflect on the absence of a proper critical theoretical framework to study minority groups' mistreatment in westernised countries. This model has several elements and each element is inseparably connected to other elements. In general, this model puts hate crime in a wider context and explains which forces are in operation when a member of a minority group is subjected to a hate crime. Thus, the victim of a violent assault is simply experiencing hatred somewhere along a spectrum of experiences that is the culmination of the interaction of various structural forces enabled by institutional discourse and praxis. Likewise the perpetrators of hate attacks and discrimination, as well as other forms of prejudiced behaviour are not social outliers but in fact victim citizens who have been mobilised by structural forces and are themselves a type of victim of those structural biases.

Hate Environment

The very term "hate crime" is associated with organised hate groups like the Ku Klux Klan, skinheads, or neo-Nazis. Yet, in our view, the majority of hate crimes are committed by individuals and not organised hate groups. Many studies have shown that although hate crime offenders can commit their crimes in groups, they are not usually affiliated with any organised gangs. These groups of offenders tend to be young, white males with no prior criminal record. Moreover, in many cases the offender may even be a neighbour or live in close proximity to the victim (Martz, 2009: 341). Studies such as that of Law et al. highlight areas in the UK where hate crimes are repeatedly perpetrated against residents in social housing complexes by neighbours (Law et. al., 2013). Law et. al. record that in Leeds, levels of racist hostility two decades ago were recorded as sporadic, whereas at the time of writing they had reached 4,000 – 5,000 per year across the geographical area. In their study of racist motivators amongst white estate residents, Law et. al describe both the immediate environment, the motivators expressed by respondents and the causes of those motivators:

> "One centrally important contextual factor was community self-policing: power and mobilisation of local family and community networks to enforce hostility, drive families out and maintain an atmosphere of fear and intimidation. There was an instrumental promotion of racial hostility where it was seen to be useful to achieve family, community or criminal goals. Several tensions in the area were linked to very specific social and geographic boundaries of trust and safety, and racism on this estate was linked to fear of the 'other' and fierce allegiance to those who are close to oneself."

The fear of the 'other' is here directly expressed as violence. Law et. al's report describes the 'routine 'everyday' nature of this hostility and violence' as a troubling list of experiences that resulted in many families being moved away from the estate, with at least one family moved with a police escort because a large group of estate residents had gathered outside their home. The nature of the incidents reported by victims included: "..verbal abuse, graffiti, eggs thrown at houses, cars burnt out, physical assaults on children and adults, and petrol bombing."

Residents on the estate generally were able to deny or were seen to be in denial about their motivations as racist due to the entanglement of issues e.g. sense of abandonment by authorities and social exclusion with the fictionalised notion of the privilege of the other, and the need to look after 'one's own': 'Therefore for many households in these areas racist hostility met a test of practical adequacy and sense-making and fitted with core norms and values."

Thus 'value' making, the internalisation of tropes about the 'other' and the idea of a mono-cultural community, although arising out of 'fear' amongst majority groups, result in the marking out of the hated society. The hated society is formed out of such 'fear'. Whilst that 'fear' is expressed as a means of empowerment for the majority community grouping, the hated society experiences this process as violence – both physical and psychological.

The hate environment described above at a micro-level does not arise in a vacuum. However, the idea of the post-racial society has already curtailed existing cultures of tackling racisms, as Law et. al. (2013) note:

> "…the climate across Leeds in 2011-2012, in relation to racist hostility and violence, was still one of denial, or 'racism fatigue', with a move to deny explicitly racist elements of incidents and move away from a language of 'race' through responses such as 'it's all just ASB (anti-social behaviour), and the incorrect 'branding' of racism as a 'cohesion issue'."

The shift in discourse itself further enables a hate environment wherein flawed if not deliberately racist policies can be enacted. With the focus off racism, discourses of 'human rights' inevitably refer to the idea of the individual as the primary unit of society and law and obviates the need to understand, protect and legislate for the protection of identities. Instead the idea of a hegemonic identity becomes the law, and law and policy is developed to protect that identity from threat. Thus the idea of community cohesion shifts focus from racism and structural prejudices to the idea of failed citizenship amongst minorities that creates disharmony – in some cases it can be argued that the claim equates to blaming the victim.

Ameli et al. (2011) also include cases that show how a hate environment can even turn law-abiding citizens into hate crime perpetrators. Whilst there has been a fuelling of this by the rhetoric of anti-Islamic nativism by far-right groups (Pupcenoks and McCabe, 2013), this is set within a context of 'mobilization against Islam and Muslims… in Western Europe. Some observers argu[ing] that [perceptions of "Islamization" have melded with immigration concerns and spurred anti-Islamic reactions that are part of a quest for European identity.[2]' Pupcenoks and McCabe (2013) argue that this rhetoric has transformed mainstream political party positioning, taking the rhetoric to its logical conclusion as:

---

[2] Betz and Meret (2009) cited in Pupcenoks and McCabe (2013)

"More than the religion of Islam, or even Muslims as individuals or communities, the *very idea* of having Muslims in Europe has come to represent the "threat of death" for native Europeans, in both a cultural *and* physical sense."

Such alarming conclusions can be internalised and embedded within the minds of those in majority communities. Studies have shown that the majority of so-called hate crimes are not perpetrated by organised groups but by individuals, often with exemplary records, and who having committed such acts, feel that their behaviour has been out of character. Such acts are characterised by the perpetrator feeling incited to do something uncharacteristic. This suggests that (hate) ideology operating within structures is more of a motivator than the attachment by individuals to a hate ideology directly. Thus while the rise of the far-right across Westernised settings including the UK is notable and alarming it does not necessarily explain the rise in recorded hate attacks, or in the case of this study experiences of hate per se. Law et. al. (2013) describe the decline in support for the British National Party between 2007 and the time of their research but cautions that the policies of successful criminal prosecutions, and the tackling of ideologies together with:

"an overemphasis on crime prevention, extremist ideologies and the role of particular individuals can risk neglect of wider, underlying and durable experiences of racism. These strategies illustrate Lentin and Titley's… suggestion that race is buried or made invisible, because 'racism is understood as an irrational attribute or behaviour', and irrational sentiment exhibited by extremist individuals and, therefore, 'it has diminished purchase in a social vision that places the rational and autonomous actors centre stage."

The authors argue here that the focus on the idea of the individual as the symbol of a monolithic British identity is repeatedly contrasted by political and media discourse with the idea of the hated society / ies e.g. Muslims (terrorists, oppressed women, Trojan Horses for alien value), blacks and black youth (promiscuous, violent, rioters), Roma and Travellers (criminals, lazy, ignorant), immigrants and refugees (swarms, hordes) which act as groups (not individuals) to threaten the individual but also are an existential threat to the society of the individual.

Whilst these types of enabling narratives result in local acts that, with a proper enforcement of existing legal regimes can be addressed (Ahmed, 2011), there is no enforceable mechanism of accountability for the fostering of the 'fear of the other' or the perpetuation and in some cases creation of stereotypes by powerful elites that can instigate hate, and which ultimately create cultures of hatred that can be triggered into micro or even macro events (see section on 'Confrontation' below). This poses a dilemma for the judicial system of any country. It is very hard to hold people accountable, in this case powerful elites, who have not directly committed a hate crime. What they have created is a "hate environment", which is something not less than committing an individual, direct, actionable act of hate itself.

The situation of Muslims as subjects of discriminatory and violent praxis by society and state is almost masked. Instead, ideas of Muslim deviancy persist e.g. that of self-segregation. As Law et. al. (2013) and Billings and Holden (2008) describe there are issues around white self-segregation that result in Muslim segregation or enclavisation. Samad (2013) looking at Bradford argues that there is no evidence of Muslim self-segregation (contrary to the post-2001 riots' narrative by media and political elites), with Muslims particularly in sub-ward areas and particularly from established communities mixing in housing locations but also in social interactions. Yet the discourse of social cohesion that developed from those riots through 7-7, and eventually the 2011 riots, focuses on the idea of forced assimilation in practical terms as well as cultural terms. Samad (2013) argues that rather than deal with core issues of deprivation, marginalisation and discrimination that resulted in the 2001 northern riots, successive governments have instead invested in raising a moral panic about Muslims, turning the debate into a victim-blaming exercise (p.287).

Likewise Hussain and Baguely (2012) citing Maxwell (2006) argue that British South Asian Muslims have been demonised as 'rejecting Britishness, living in segregated ghettoes and subscribing to anti-establishment views.' Their studies, like many others, showed precisely the opposite. They argue however that demonisation (surfacing after the 2001 riots in excessive political narrative) has been 'elaborated and embellished as part of the government's counter-terrorism policy...' effectively resulting in differential treatment of Muslims in their social interactions, in the case of their study in getting 'funny looks' from their white non-Muslim counterparts and being perceived as different (Bauman's familiar yet unknowable stranger).

Hate Policy

If the hate environment is a powerful predictor of hate crime occurrence, then how is this environment created or indeed who is the creator and director of this hate environment? Is it possible to think that this powerful social phenomenon develops spontaneously? Clearly not. The hate environment, fed by such discourses as described above (hate representation), are effected by hate policy, which can be defined as a method of creating and managing hate in a collective manner. Most of the hate policy in apparently less violent societies is formulated through decisions on legal as well as executive procedures.

Successful hate policies have resulted in a condition in which many victims may be forced to hide their victimhood because they perceive a lack of support from the general public and among law enforcement officials. Besides, the very revealing of their victimhood might make them more susceptible to further attacks. Research has documented a significant degree of mistrust of the police among some hate crime victims (Rayburn et al, 2003). Of course this is something more than a matter of pessimism. For example in the US, crimes against immigrant groups are not considered to be "hate crimes", and immigrants are not a protected category in hate crime law (see Stacy et al, 2011: 279).

Hate Representation

Researchers generally define a criminal act as a hate crime if it was motivated by the perpetrator's hatred for the victim's gender, race, ethnicity, religion, national origin, or disability (Rayburn et al, 2003).

Hate crime is quickly becoming a routine category in popular and scholarly discourse about crime (Jacobs and Potter, 1998). In 1985, 11 hate crime articles appeared in newspapers nationwide. In 1990, there were 511 stories about hate crimes, and three years later, more than 1,000. The term "hate crime" first appeared in a popular magazine in the October 9, 1989 issue of U.S. News and World Report, in an article entitled, "The Politics of Hate." The author, John Leo, questioned the wisdom of a proposed District of Columbia law that enhanced the sentence for criminal conduct motivated by prejudice (Jacobs and Potter, 1998: 4).

Hate representation helps the hate policy to be executed in an expansive manner at the service of hate ideology. Hate representation plays a vital role in the chain from ideological hate to hate practice. It creates a steady flow of negative ideas about minority groups. The very fact that some elements in this current of information are true will make it very effective in creating a hate environment.

The Model

Ameli has elaborated on these concepts in his publications and added hate related concepts to develop his model. Hate is generated at different levels of mental structures of the individual, primary and secondary group, the media, political apparatuses and ideology. Therefore, all of these elements contribute to the process. Synergy between all elements makes the creation and implementation of hate policy much easier e.g. a pre-existing culture of media and literary representation of 'Muslims' as inherently terroristic or 'black' youth as inherently violent, allows for the formulation of anti-terror laws or stop and search policies that target these communities, without much if any protest from wider society.

Hate representation by the media and also individuals fuels the entire system of hate. In a hate environment, society divides into a mainstream hating society versus the minority hated society. Rather than taking hate crime as a personal crime, DHMIR invites us to place the issue in the broader context of hate policy, hate representation and hate environment. DHMIR takes both perpetrator and victim, as the victims.

Most of the models in this area suffer from over-emphasising one level at the expense of other levels of intercultural perception and practice. DHMIR tries to fill the gap between the abstract and the practised. It endeavours to reveal how shocking daily behaviours against minorities are a natural and common output of well-designed hate environments. Killing people on the grounds of their difference seems to be unjustified and only bigots do this. However, DHMIR reveals that many of the apparently innocuous speeches by politicians can in fact affect public behaviour in hateful ways.

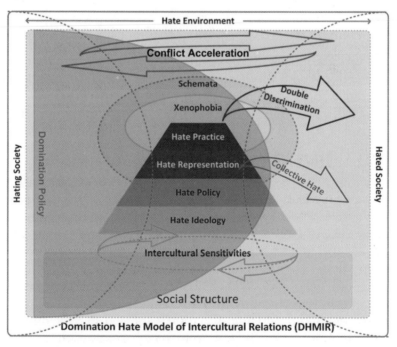

Figure 1: Domination Hate Model of Intercultural Relations (DHMIR)

Review of Previous IHRC Research on anti-Muslim Discrimination and Hate Crime against Muslims in North America and Europe

Saied Reza Ameli, Arzu Merali and their colleagues have worked with this model since at least the late 1990s. This approach however is ontologically different from existing approaches as it is a critical model and locates intercultural relations within wider concepts of power, discourse, ideology and representation. There are many members of minority groups in the West who become victims of hate crimes just by virtue of being - or being deemed to be - part of a certain minority community. There have been many reported instances of such cases involving Muslims in the West. According to a 2012 Amnesty International report, Muslims in Europe are frequently subjected to discrimination, abuse and even legal prohibition. In an environment where discrimination is expressed in a very subtle and complex way, only a sophisticated and compatible model can address the issues that arise.

DHMIR deals with this in a number of ways. In a broad study by Ameli et al. (2004), about 40% of Muslims believed there was no support from British authorities for British Muslims, with an almost equal number believing there was some support, albeit not very significant. The primary reason for respondents who felt little or no support from British policy makers towards British Muslims was the lack of legal protection for Muslims from discrimination similar to legislation protecting other religious communities. They also revealed that Muslim experience of discrimination is diverse ranging from hostile behaviour to abuse, harassment, assault and alienation. They also showed that overall about 80 percent of respondents reported that they had experienced discrimination because they were Muslim. This study showed that the extent of discrimination is much higher in comparison with previous surveys: the IHRC survey in 1999 showed that discrimination was already high with 35 percent of respondents reporting discrimination. By 2000 this had risen to 45 percent.

Ameli et al. (2005) studied experiences of discrimination and school preference in the UK and revealed that 71.8% of those who experienced discrimination 'almost daily' favoured Muslim schooling. In the largest category, experiencing discrimination 'only on some occasions', preference is almost equally spread between the 'best school' and 'Muslim School'. The highest preference for mainstream education, 17.2%, is in the category of those who do not experience discrimination at all. The findings of the report negate the view that Islamic faith schools are counterproductive in fostering a sense of citizenship and promoting segregation. It shows that underachievement can be combated by faith schools, because they foster a culture of inclusion. Furthermore, the report highlights several problems with mainstream schools and the national curriculum, which, inter alia, cause underachievement and a sense of isolation and segregation. Out of 1125 British Muslims surveyed, 47.5% indicated they would prefer to send their children to a Muslim school rather than a state school. The majority of remaining respondents stated they would choose the best school (regardless of whether it is mainstream or Muslim), while only 8.5% chose the option of a mainstream school.

Ameli et al. (2006b) emphasised that if minorities are deemed a threat by law, this is reflected in legislation which in turn confirms social stereotypes, ultimately validating racism, Islamophobia, anti-Muslim backlashes and hate crimes. Conducting a survey of 1125 Muslims in Britain, Ameli and his colleagues found that more than 91% of the respondents said they respected the law in varying degrees. Nevertheless, most of the respondents contended that British laws are unfair. From these reactions emerges a sense of intelligent and passionate engagement with the issues of law, equity and fairness for all. Shockingly, what is also obvious is the lack of trust in the legislature to address the numerous concerns raised. These concerns raise the spectre of systemic separation inside the legal framework and the harsh and selective usage of law from stops and searches to detentions without trial – all seen to disproportionately target Muslims.

Ameli and Merali (2006a) conducted a survey of Muslim

veiled women in Britain and showed that before 9/11, 60.8% of women who wore some form of hijab experienced being talked down to or treated as if stupid. This figure rose to 68.5% after 9/11. This report particularly aimed to voice the views of both men and women who recognise or affiliate to the concept of hijab and to present recommendations to the government by analysing responses from a nationwide survey of 1200 Muslims, the qualitative answers of 56 Muslims and 365 quantitative questionnaires.

Ameli et al. (2011) also summarises the hate crimes situation against Muslims in the UK. Their study includes cases that show how a hate environment can turn good citizens into hate crime perpetrators. They based their study on analysis of data collected from 336 questionnaires, among them 135 conducted online and the remaining 201 in print format. The majority of the survey's respondents reside in the UK. The questionnaire considered demographic data about Muslims, questions relating to forms of implicit and explicit discrimination, ranging from discriminatory remarks and jokes to threats and physical violence, and an open ended section for views to be more freely expressed.

The respondents were asked to consider 29 categories of negative encounters they may have experienced. For every category, the respondents were offered six choices from which to rate the frequency of their experience, extending from once a year through to more than once a week, including the choice to express that they had never experienced such an episode.. Numerous negative encounters predominated inside the overview aggregate, and made up 40% or greater of the study bunch.

Additionally, other cases of discrimination and abuse were reported by significant minorities in the survey group, including, as examples, 38.6% reporting having experienced not being taken seriously, 37.2% having experienced unfriendly behaviour in their place of work or study, and 37.1% experiencing being left out of conversations. Some of these statistics are noteworthy despite their relatively low prevalence due to the severe nature of the offence, such as 13.9% of respondents reporting having been subjected to violent physical assault.

Ameli, Merali and Shahghasemi (2012) conducted a study of Muslims in France using DHMIR. Data gathered from 244 print questionnaires revealed that the highest percentage of those experiencing hate reported doing so in the area of media representation. The media's negative representation of Muslim people affects non-Muslim attitudes towards Muslims. Hate policy was also reflected in the participants' experiences of Islamophobia, Islamophobic expressions by politicians, exclusion of Muslims from political decision-making or examining particular policies on them, and finally, policies which target Muslims in France. Moreover, politicians resort to Islamophobia to design their election campaign strategies. War between Israel and Palestine, Sarkozy's right-wing agenda and the events of 9/11 were also cases which were frequently mentioned as pretexts and reasons for making hate policy.

In relation to the frequency of personal hate crime experience, 27.6 percent of respondents reported experiencing it at least once a month. After this, twice a year and once a year were reported by 24.7 percent and 24.5 percent respectively. 12.4 percent said they had experienced it once a week with 10.8 percent saying more than once a week. The respondents in this study were also asked to answer some open-ended questions. Muslim respondents described in detail how they were physically attacked or verbally abused or professionally discriminated against. Ameli and his colleagues categorised these answers in order to provide an overall summary of how Muslim respondents felt they were victimised.

Ameli et al. (2013) show that 30% of Muslims in their study have experienced a hate-motivated physical attack. This outcome is one of many statistics gathered from a sample of 1200 participants undertaken in 2012 by IHRC in California. About 88% reported negative experiences in everyday life, the media, political discourse and policy. They analysed their findings within discrete categories – demonised media and political discourse fall within the category of ideological hatred; being mistreated, demeaned, patronised, insulted on the basis of one's faith are included in the category of being a member of a hated society; and finally the category of Discrimination and Double Discrimination, which includes discrimination at work or school, as well as discrimination or repercussions when reporting discrimination to supervisors or agencies.

Five Steps for Expansion of Hate Environment

As described above a hate environment is important in linking other elements of hate and eventually facilitating structuralisation of hate crimes. DHMIR perceives that the hate environment is not a homogenous and rigid body of concepts and sentiments. In order to know its differences and intensities, we have divided it into five incremental steps: 1) Otherisation, 2) Xenophobia, 3) Collective Hate, 4) Confrontation and 5) Chaos and Global Harassment. These five steps constitute the process by which hate is gradually expanded to take the hate environment from a local to a global environment.

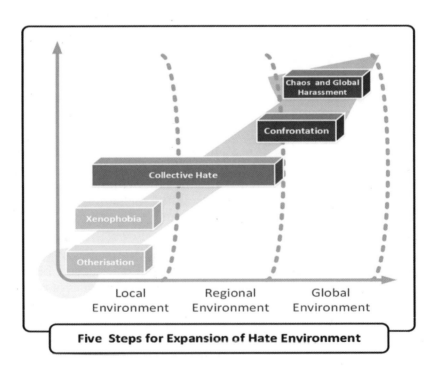

Figure 2: The Five Steps of Expansion of Hate Environment

Otherisation

Over the last couple of decades and particularly after 9/11, many Muslim scholars and critical academics have written about the otherisation of Muslims in the West (see for example Afshar, 2008; Jamal & Naber, 2008; Afshar, 2013; Eliassi, 2013; Zahedi, 2011; Ameli, 2006; Schreiber, 2014).

Simplistic characterisations of the "us" and the wider society have led to false representations of the Self and the Other. Therefore, otherisation is naturally a reductive process that attributes an imagined superior identity to the Self and a supposed inferior identity to the Other. In all of us there is a tendency to portray ourselves as having an identity that is desirable and developed while assuming the identity of people who are racially, ethnically, or linguistically different as undesirable and inferior (Kumaravadivelu, 2008). Over the decades scholars have considered the ways that this process of otherisation has misrepresented and caricatured the Oriental Other in terms of sex, gender, race, ethnicity and religion (Afshar, 2008). Most often a significant power differential is involved in the process of otherisation, particularly cultural otherisation. Although the process of cultural otherisation has always been with us, it became much more pronounced during the colonial history of the twentieth century (Kumaravadivelu, 2008). Psychiatrist Frantz Fanon and philosopher Albert Memmi who had both personally experienced the French colonisation of North Africa, have critically theorised the relationship between the coloniser and the colonised, and in the process have elaborated on the process of cultural otherisation. In two of his well-known works -Black Skin, White Masks, and The Wretched of the Earth- Fanon showed how the coloniser deliberately creates a sense of inferiority in the soul of the colonised by destroying and burying local cultural originality (Kumaravadivelu, 2008). Therefore, we can see how otherisation can be systematically exploited and implemented through a project which can be programmed for several decades and even centuries.

Xenophobia

Use of the term Xenophobia has become rampant in recent years but ironically, it has its roots in the Western view of a place which is now known as a Muslim region in the so-called Middle East. More than 24 centuries ago the historian *Xenophon* emphasised the contrast between the people of Greece and the barbaric world. For Xenophon, barbaric regions were vast, diverse, wild, and exotic while Greece was united, educated and modern. This Greek nationalism was shared by many other writers. The term *"xenophobia"* has its roots in Xenophon's arrogant viewpoint (Harle, 2000: 42).

In the past few decades and particularly after 9/11, Muslims have experienced bitter xenophobia in the West. In an extensive study, Hjerm (1998) studied the theoretically proposed positive sides of different forms of civic national attachment. His data came from the International Social Survey Programme (ISSP) 1995, which is a programme for cross-country comparative attitude studies. His results showed that both civic national identity and national pride go together with xenophobia, whereas the reverse holds for ethnic national identity and national pride in four Western countries, Australia, Germany, Britain and Sweden, despite their different conceptualisations of the nation-state. El Hamel (2002) used the controversy over the hijab to question and challenge the conventional reading of the integration of the Muslim Maghrebin people into secular French society. He explored the concept of integration and the way this integration functioned as a source of privilege as well as a source of discrimination. He employed the debate over the hijab to further investigate the interplay of religion, immigration and citizenship in France and concluded that the debate over the hijab culminated in a negative policy towards Muslims because prohibiting it is against personal rights and freedom of religion. Although France is a signatory to the European Convention on Human Rights, which guarantees religious freedom, the ban has showed the intolerance of France towards Muslims and ignited disrespect of the religion and Islamic culture.

In the UK context Alam and Husband (2013) note:

"… the pervasive presence of culturally determinist thinking in the contemporary zeitgeist as part of the framing of epistemological context in which government and popular exclusionary discourses that marginalize Muslims have their impact. We must also note the equally politically important fact that the success of culturalist Islamophobic discourses, in entering into the routine explanatory repertoire of a wide range of citizens, reciprocally reinforces the perceived legitimacy of such thinking."

Collective Hate

In general, there are a variety of influences that contribute to hate. They include culture and what it communicates to people, social conditions such as hard life conditions and the processes they create, group relations such as conflict (especially intractable conflict), and the personal experience of individuals and the orientation it creates for human beings in general, to the self, and to members of particular groups (Staub, 2005). When hate is systematically spread in the body of a society, we will confront uncontrollable and even unbelievable outcomes. From 1882 to 1921, the United States alone was the scene of more than 3,405 cases of lynchings. A majority of the victims were black men, women and children. The scale of lynching was so high that it was sometimes called "unofficial execution." Although there was great effort to ban lynching, the government effectively resisted passing anti-lynching laws (Williams, 2001: 3-4). This kind of systematic fuelling of hate by the government and powerful elites thus has a very long history. That is exactly what happens when xenophobic sentiments rise in the aftermath of terrorist attacks or narrow representation. Stigmatising minorities may have no immediate effect on them, but, in the long run, it can have catastrophic consequences. Some scholars try to account for the role of hate crime in co-constructing the relative identities and subject positions of both the victim and the offender, individually and collectively. Hate crime, then, involves acts of violence and intimidation, usually directed towards already stigmatised and marginalised groups (Perry, 2001). It therefore aggravates the problem and paves the way for more intense

versions of intercultural communication.
This is propounded by and perpetuates:

> "Hierarchies of oppression that feed into and off each
> other, and the nurturing of anti-Muslim prejudice in
> recent years, have also been a vehicle for the rehearsal of
> seemingly legitimate hierarchies of dominance, and their
> attendant ideological justifications that can be readily
> adapted to stigmatize and exclude other minority groups.
> Bitter anti-asylum-seeker sentiments and policies, rising
> anti-semitism and the casual and brutal dismissal of the
> life chances of an urban 'underclass' of 'welfare
> scroungers', all feeds at the same ideological trough in
> which essentialist deployment of culture is a staple."
> (Alam and Husband, 2013)

Confrontation

The fourth level of development of hate is confrontation. At
this stage, a conflict is inevitable. In confrontation, the previous
–perhaps constructive- approach is abandoned and the weak are
literally targeted as the guilty. This stage is very dangerous
because it is the gateway for chaos. The governments of the
destination countries are unfortunately in control of the situation
but they choose to evade responsibility. In times of social
turbulence, the American government has always perceived
Arab and Muslim citizens and residents as outsiders.

There are many other instances of confrontation as a result of
underestimation of the threat at previous stages. On June 7, 1998,
in Jasper, Texas three white supremacists chained James Byrd, an
African American man, to the back of their pick-up truck by his
ankles and dragged him to his death (Martz, 2009). This event
was often framed as an exception and located within a post-racial
society, an idea of the US that was given additional succour after
the election of President Obama in 2008 (Sayyid, 2010 in Sian,
2012). As the Black Lives Matters movement has demonstrated
in the last two years, the phenomenon of police killings of black
people is in fact a modern day equivalent to the process of

lynching, which had passed without comment for a long time.

According to Muslim Advocates (2011), the threat of being harassed, assaulted or even killed because of one's faith, race or ethnicity has become an increasing concern for Muslim, Arab, Middle Eastern, Sikh, and South Asian Americans. During the period from January 2010 to August 2011 alone, there were numerous cases of alleged hate motivated physical violence or threats of physical violence to individuals across the country (Muslim Advocates, 2011: 26). The shocking case of three young Muslims killed by a neighbour in Chapel Hill, North Carolina, and a number of similar shootings and killings after this event and in the wake of the release of the film American Sniper, raised the spectre of a very ideological shift towards extreme acts of violence against those perceived to be Muslim (American-Arab Anti-Discrimination Committee quote in Woolf, 24 January 2015). Khalek (22 January 2015) documented the responses of hatred in the 'twittersphere' highlighting the violent rhetoric and incitement to violence therein.

In 2001, the US Department of Justice recorded a 1,600 percent increase in anti-Muslim hate crimes from the previous year, and this number rose 10 percent between 2005 and 2006. The Council on American-Islamic Relations processed 2,647 civil rights complaints in 2006, a 25 percent increase on the previous year and a 600 percent increase since 2000. The largest category involved complaints against US government agencies (37 percent) (Read, 2008).

Confrontation is a dire state and has grave consequences. However history has shown us that we may see far more devastating consequences.

Chaos and Global Harassment

After all the previous steps have occurred, global confrontation ensues. It is at first glance an easy game, but once entered into, there is no escape. Powerful groups in the Western world use nations in this step to advance their own interests. From the terrorist attacks of September 11, 2001 until the end of 2010, the US Congress has appropriated more than a trillion dollars for military operations in Afghanistan, Iraq, and elsewhere around the world. The House and Senate considered an additional request for $33 billion in supplemental funding for the remainder of FY2010, and the Administration also requested $159 billion to cover costs of overseas operations in FY2011 (Dagget, 2010). Factoring in the value of the dollar and other connected issues, at the end of 2014 the cost of wars in Iraq and Afghanistan was estimated at about $4.4 trillion and rising (Cost of War, 2014). The costs of war are not only monetary. The total number of casualties as a result of Western campaigns in Iraq and Afghanistan is estimated to be between at least 250,000-340,000 (Costs of War, 2015). But, there is still more to come. A further development of this step is seen in what the so-called ISIS (Daesh) is doing in Iraq and Syria.

The results of the above-mentioned stages may be summarised in the diagram above. The development of hate has been classified into five steps, each step more intense in hate than its previous one.

Resolution

If one wants to solve the problem, he or she should look for conflict resolution by using reverse engineering to come back to collective peace—peace in local and global environment - so this strategy should start by prevention of any types of 1) xenophobic ideology, 2)xenophobic representation, and 3) xenophobic behaviour. In the second step otherisation policy should be replaced by promotion of understanding of differences and diversity of culture, values and practices. Prohibition of any collective hate requires, according to Staub (2005), some processes that help prevent hate. They include love and affection that children (and adults) experience and the constructive fulfilment of basic human needs; humanising the other and the experience of positive connections to people who belong to different groups, which help develop inclusive caring; self-awareness both as an individual and as a group member, which among other benefits, enables people to see the impact of their actions on others; healing from past victimisation, and reconciliation between groups and individuals who have harmed each other.

Chapter 5

From the Multicultural to the Hierarchical: Experiences of Everyday Hate for Muslims in the UK

This is the second such study in the Domination Hate Model of Intercultural Relations Project in the UK. The first was part of the pilot study for the project with a survey undertaken at the end of 2009 and early 2010. The results were published as *Getting the Message: The Recurrence of Hate Crimes in the UK* by Ameli et. al (2011). Comparisons with that study will be made where there is significant change.

One of the original aims of this project was to create a method of data collection that could be repeated regularly to assess levels of hatred and hostility. After reporting on 4 different countries over the course of 5 years, this work is the first repeat survey of any country. The following results show clearly that there is a worsening environment when it comes to anti-Muslim sentiment and experience in the UK.

Demographic overview

A total of 1782 respondents answered the quantitative questionnaire. The questionnaire was available online and in hard copy (handed face to face). A total of 1,148 completed the questionnaire in hard copy (64.4% of the sample), with the rest completing it online.

Type of Questionnaire (Quantitative)		
	Frequency	Percent
Printed version	1,148	64.4
Online version	634	35.6
Total	**1,782**	**100**

Table 2: Type of questionnaire frequency

Country of birth and citizenship; ethnicity

Those responding to the quantitative survey were overwhelmingly citizens and residents of the UK at 75.4% and 88.4% respectively. Of the sample, 52.9% were born in the UK.

Country of Citizenship		
	Frequency	Percent
United Kingdom	1,344	75.4
Pakistan	72	4
Bangladesh	22	1.2
India	19	1.1
Netherlands	15	0.8
France	12	0.7
Saudi Arabia	9	0.5
Germany	8	0.4
Nigeria	8	0.4
Tanzania	7	0.4
Canada	6	0.3
Malaysia	6	0.3
USA	6	0.3
Italy	5	0.3
Sri Lanka	5	0.3
Brunei	4	0.2
Sudan	4	0.2
Turkey	4	0.2
Indonesia	3	0.2
Iran	3	0.2
Scotland	3	0.2
Other countries	94	5.3
Total	1,659	93.1
Unknown	123	6.9
Total	1,782	100

Table 3: Country of Citizenship Frequency

Ethnic origin frequency

Ethnic origin		
	Frequency	Percent
Pakistani	454	25.5
Bengali	187	10.5
Asian	123	6.9
Indian	111	6.2
Arab	57	3.2
British Pakistani	48	2.7
Muslim	31	1.7
British	25	1.4
Somali	24	1.3
Iraqi	24	1.3
White British	16	0.9
Iranian	16	0.9
British Indian	15	0.8
Afghan	14	0.8
Kashmiri	12	0.7
Black	11	0.6
British Asian	11	0.6
British Bangladeshi	10	0.6
Yemeni	10	0.6
White	10	0.6
Other ethnicity	325	18.2
Unknown	248	13.9
Total	**1,782**	**100**

Table 4: Ethnic origin frequency

The majority of respondents cited Pakistan or British Pakistani as their heritage followed by Bengali / British Bangladeshi. The results conform generally to the MCB analysis of the UK census 2011 (Ali, 2015) which found that 'the Muslim population is ethnically diverse – 68% Asian (1.83 million of 2.71 million) and 32% non-Asian. One in 12 is of White ethnicity (8% of the Muslim population).' There is possible underrepresentation of 'white' Muslims in this survey.

Level of Education

Level of Education		
	Frequency	Percent
BA	205	11.5
A Level	203	11.4
Degree	178	10
MA	145	8.1
GCSE	93	5.2
University	82	4.6
College	64	3.6
PhD	31	1.7
Msc	30	1.7
Graduate	28	1.6
Postgraduate	28	1.6
High school	25	1.4
Diploma	23	1.3
BTEC	21	1.2
Undergraduate	15	0.8
HND	13	0.7
University degree	11	0.6
MBA	10	0.6
Other Levels	234	13.1
Unknown	343	19.2
Total	1,782	100

Table 5: Highest level of education frequency

Gender and age

Just over 31% of the sample has some sort of undergraduate degree. With a total of 43% having some sort of degree or postgraduate qualification. This is higher than the general population of Muslims, in which the figures are 24% and 27% respectively (Ali, 2015).

Gender		
	Frequency	Percent
Male	912	54
Female	777	46
Total	**1,689**	**100**

Table 6: Gender frequency

Just over half the respondents were male (54%) and 46% female.

38% of respondents were aged below 24, which conforms to the general Muslim population, which brackets 36.6% in the ages 5 - 23 category (Ali, 2015).

Age		
	Frequency	Percent
Under 18	189	11
19 - 24	464	27
25 - 29	358	20.8
30 - 34	261	15.2
35 - 39	169	9.8
40 - 44	104	6
45-49	154	9
50 and above 50	21	1.2
Total	**1,720**	**100**

Table 7: Age frequency

The younger profile of the Muslim community means that while Muslims form 4.8% of the population overall, 8.1% of all school-age children (5 to 15 year old age band) are Muslim (Ali, 2015). This can be seen as meaningful in particular in regard to issues of schooling which have been discussed above but also in this analysis and the recommendations.

Income and Work Status

Income Group		
	Frequency	Percent
Lower income group	599	36
Middle income group	945	56.9
Higher income group	118	7.1
Total	**1,662**	**100**

Table 8: Income group frequency

The profile of the British Muslim community is still one of a lower income majority (Ali, 2015), and issues around inequalities and their impact continue to cause concern (Ali, 2015). However according to Ali's analysis (2015) there has been marked improvement since the 2001 census in the situation of the Muslim community with higher educational achievement being a factor in this. There has been, according to Ali, a reduction in Muslims with no qualifications from 39% to 26%. Further:

"The proportion of Muslims in the 'Higher professional occupation' category is 5.5%, which is comparable to the overall population – 7.6%. There is greater comparability in the 'Small employers and own account workers' category – 9.7% in the Muslim population and 9.3% in the overall population.

"There are a number of London boroughs where the population of Muslims in the 'Higher managerial, administrative and professional occupations' category exceeds the number in the 'Never worked and Long-term unemployed' categories."

The respondents in this survey are mainly from the middle income group. In terms of work status, 12.1% stated they were unemployed, 14.8% self-employed and 45.7% employed.

Work Status		
	Frequency	Percent
Employed	779	45.7
Self Employed	253	14.8
Unemployed	206	12.1
Retired	33	1.9
Student	435	25.5
Total	**1,706**	**100**

Table 9: Work status frequency

Religiosity

Religiosity, as self-perceived, ranks highly amongst respondents, with 72% stating that they are practising Muslims and a further 15.6% stating that they are highly practising Muslims. Nevertheless, those claiming essentially ostensible but not conscientious Muslim affiliation made up 12.4% of the sample

Religiosity		
	Frequency	Percent
Originally Muslim but not religious	72	4.3
Secular Muslim	72	4.3
Non-practising Muslim	63	3.8
Practising Muslim	1,207	72
Highly practising Muslim	262	15.6
Total	**1,676**	**100**

Table 10: Religiosity frequency

Visibly Muslim

Visible Muslimness, as will be shown later, like religiosity, runs very high in this sample with 83.3% stating they are visibly Muslim, and a further 1.1% stating they were not Muslim but sometimes mistaken for being Muslims.

Visibly Muslim		
	Frequency	Percent
Visibly Muslim (hijab/beard/ niqab/turban/hat/etc.)	1,257	75.2
Visible in other way	118	7.1
Not visibly Muslim	278	16.6
Not a Muslim, but sometimes mistaken for one	19	1.1
Total	**1,672**	**100**

Table 11: Visible Muslimness frequency

Proportion of neighbourhood Muslim

Most of those surveyed (40.8%) said they lived in an area where Muslims numbered less than one third of the population. The second largest group was where more than two thirds of those living in the area were Muslim, with 22.8% living in areas where one to two thirds were Muslim. The impact of what Holden and Billings (2008) called "enclavisation" needs further study, but has some relevance to the recommendations that will follow, particularly but not solely in light of Holden and Billings' findings.

Proportion of the neighbourhood Muslim		
	Frequency	Percent
Less than one third (minority)	691	40.8
Between one and two thirds	387	22.8
More than two thirds (majority)	457	27
I don't know	159	9.4
Total	**1,694**	**100**

Table 12: Frequency of proportion of neighbourhood Muslim

Muslim experiences in the UK: Hatred as Normative Experience

...I believe that the hatred and violent tendencies... is manifested and then exacerbated by a culture that deems Muslims are deserving of hate

Female, 22, London

The overall experience of hatred by respondents in the 2014 survey was worse than the 2009-10 survey. In some cases the increase was dramatic and suggests what various IHRC studies have claimed (see e.g. Ameli et. al, 2004b, Ameli et al, 2011) that whilst there are spectacular rises in obvious cases of violent hatred after crisis situations, logged notably as not only 9-11, 7-7, the killing of Lee Rigby, but also heightened tensions caused by comments like those of Jack Straw in 2006 on niqab.

One understanding that can be inferred is that whilst flash crises bring Muslims under intense scrutiny and thus create a micro-climate of intense pressure within which there is a rise of anti-Muslim attacks, there is no subsidence back to pre-crisis levels (Shadjareh and Merali, 2002 and Ameli et. al, 2006b). Another understanding is of general decline in the stability of the environment created by structural forces, permeating the environment within which obvious acts of hatred e.g. verbal abuse or physical attacks, take place.

The Domination Hate Model of Intercultural Relations (DHMIR) argues that the environment as a carrier of the ideology of hatred through discourse and policy is culpable for such acts and indeed these acts could not be possible without this. This chapter turns first then to the pervasiveness of ideological hatred in the UK against Muslims.

Experience of Ideological Hatred

Hate Ideology – that is encoding of demeaning representations and ideas of Muslims in public, media, educational and political discourse, as well as witnessing them directed against someone, is key to understanding what type of hate environment exists. Is there a severity of such representation across the board and does that translate into witnessing positive acts of hate against others?

The questionnaire assessed this aspect of experience through responses to the following questions.

1. Witnessing or hearing about Islamophobia directed towards someone else.
2. Having religious beliefs challenged or denigrated by work colleagues / school / college peers.
3. Hearing Islamophobic comments made in particular by politicians or high ranking officials.
4. Seeing negative or insulting stereotypes of Muslim people in the media.
5. Witnessing politicians philosophise that Islam and Muslims are innately problematic.

Witnessing or hearing about Islamophobia directed towards someone else

Witnessing/hearing Islamophobia directed towards someone else		
	2,010	2014
Never	49.7	17.9
Rarely	10.3	22.1
Sometimes	8.2	32.1
Often	14.5	19.4
Always	17.3	8.5
Total	100	100

Table 13: Frequency of Witnessing/hearing Islamophobia directed towards someone else in 2010 and 2014

The number of people stating they had never witnessed Islamophobia against someone has decreased drastically since 2010 from almost half never seeing such a thing to just under 18% in 2014. There is a concurrent dramatic rise in the rarely, sometimes and often categories, with a drop in the always category.

Having religious beliefs challenged or denigrated by work colleagues / school / college peers

Religious beliefs being challenged by work colleagues/school/college peers		
	2,010	2014
Never	63.5	31.9
Rarely	5.7	24.9
Sometimes	6.7	25.9
Often	13.4	11.8
Always	10.7	5.5
Total	**100**	**100**

Table 14: Having religious beliefs challenged or denigrated by work colleagues / school / college peers in 2010 and 2014

An identical pattern can be observed in the experience of having belief challenged by peers. Whilst highly frequent experiences (i.e. always) are down in number those reporting never having this experience is also much reduced (by almost half).

Hearing Islamophobic comments by politicians

Hearing Islamophobic comments by politicians		
	2010	2014
Never	40.8	16.8
Rarely	14.6	17.4
Sometimes	9.5	28
Often	16.7	22.6
Always	18.4	15.2
Total	**100**	**100**

Table 15: Percentage of respondents experiencing hearing Islamophobic comments by politicians

Likewise, similar patterns are established between the 2010 and 2014 results in this category. Significantly the 'sometimes' experience has trebled and the 'never hearing such comments' has reduced by over half.

Blame appears to cross party lines, with leaders in particular being blamed regardless of party.

Considering the political implications of events such as young British Muslims travelling to join the war in Syria, it has resulted in politicians such as Nick Clegg and Tony Blair to suggest a wave of Islamic extremism is growing in the UK.

Consequently, this promotes a negative image of Muslims in general.

Female, 22, London

Media

Politicians remarks against segregating and niqaab
Hate groups being given voices and a platform as legitimate
political parties

Female, 29, London

Some politicians like to highlight and politicise Islamic
issues to cause havoc and portray Islam in a negative
manner.

Male, 34, Bradford

The purpose of this is described as short term:

"Politicians openly use Islamophobia to gain votes or
notoriety and advance careers. This means policies and
behaviours that hinders the lives of Muslims."

Female, 31, London

Others highlighted the rise of far-right politics.   One
respondent from a Northern town where riots in the summer of
2001 were attributed in part to a response to police failures to
deal with the rise of the far-right (Bridges, 2011, Ahmed, Bodi et
al, 2001) states:

The presence of the BNP over the years and the far right
views of the EDL are a major cause in promoting what is a
weak 'cause/ideology. But the likes of UKIP certainly do
not help in easing a hostile atmosphere, backed by false
information/perceptions

Male, 18, Batley

However as will be discussed at the end of this section, many
see more long-term causality of ideological hatred.

Seeing negative stereotypes in the media

Seeing negative stereotypes in media		
	2010	2014
Never	30.1	6.7
Rarely	30.4	7.3
Sometimes	11.7	19.8
Often	17.7	26.8
Always	10.1	39.4
Total	100	100

Table 16: Percentage of respondents seeing negative or insulting stereotypes of Muslim people in the media.

One of the most pervasive experiences reported in 2010 (Ameli et al, 2011), the prevalence of Islamophobic tropes in the media, has not abated. Significantly not only has the experience of never seeing stereotypes in the media dropped from 30.1% to 6.7%, the experience of always seeing such stereotypes has risen from 10.1% to 39.4% of the sample. Not only is this a four-fold increase in experience, the 'always' experience in 2014 is the largest experience. As the discussion in Chapter 2 has developed in detail the role of media in perpetuating / fomenting / creating an environment of hate is key to the operation of structural prejudice and the resultant societal ills of hate crime and discrimination. With 93.3% of the 2014 sample saying they have at some time seen such stereotypes it appears that media discourse on Muslims has degenerated not simply in content but also by loss of nuance, ethical standards and aspirations towards balance. Whilst in 2010, and previously 2004 and 2006 (as reported in Ameli et. al, 2007), there was seen in the qualitative responses an understanding of institutional racism, (meaning that a level of ignorance rather than malice informs individual practitioners within an institution in this case the media establishment), such patience is fairly exhausted in the 2014 open-ended part of the survey.

> *Muslims are constantly blamed for Islamophobia because the perpetrators of 9/11 and 7/7 and Woolwich 'were Muslim' and acted 'in the name of Islam'. The role of Western foreign policy is entirely disregarded in the process of radicalisation and what is known as 'home grown terrorism' - instead, extremist Islamic ideology is categorically blamed for it. This despite the fact that 7/7 and Woolwich perpetrators directly cited Western foreign invasions and killings of Muslims abroad as the reason for their actions. The concept of 'radical Islamism' suggests that the more strictly you follow Islam, the more socially and morally deviant you become. There is also a real double standard when it comes to the reporting of terrorism in the media - Woolwich was reported as a terrorist attack but Pavlo Lapshyn's murder of Mohammed Saleem in Birmingham was not given anywhere near the same amount of attention from media and politicians. Anders Breivik was consistently referred to as a murderer or killer, never a terrorist, and certainly never a "Christianist".*
>
> Female, 31, Birmingham

In responses from those believing that a hostile climate for Muslims existed, to those responding to questions on the causes of that atmosphere and to causality regarding acts of aggression, respondents were bleak.

> *"Media blaming Muslims for various evil acts, other criminals are unlikely to have religion mentioned. Israel and the ongoing issues in Palestine."*
>
> Female, 44, Edinburgh

"Too much negative & reactionary propaganda, lack of hard facts or balanced reporting."

Male, 25+, Glasgow

"Crimes committed by Muslims are portrayed differently by the media. I'm not implying that they shouldn't be portrayed as wrong but a crime committed by a Muslim is then extrapolated to look like a crime committed in the name of Islam. One Muslim perpetrating a violent act is representative of all Muslims. This would not be the case with someone white/Christian/atheist etc. Images of Muslims in the media are almost always associated with violence, etc. Many see 'terrorist' and 'Muslim' as interchangeable and the government encourages this through policy too"

Female, 22, London

"In the movies which are representations of our societal norms Muslims are typically portrayed as terrorists and you will commonly hear 'Allah Akbar' play in the background right before something bad happens in the movie."

Female, 25, Canterbury

"Biased news reports"

Female, 24, Hertfordshire

"Islamophobia derives from people's misunderstanding and misinformation about Muslims and Islam which is promoted by the media...The media is the main culprit of Islamophobia. Whenever something negative happens and it involves Muslims, it is shown as an 'Islamist' stunt."

Female, 22, London

"Media focus on immigration Terrorism always linked to Islam with or without evidence e.g. virgin plane grounded in goa wad immediately linked to islamic terrorism with terrorism experts interviewed etc. Confirmed later that plane was grounded because of a drunk tourist causing disruption on the plane."

Female, 37, Watford

*"Muslims are the new 'bogeyman' of the western media.
There are never any positive stories in the press about
muslims/islam.*

*The press are currently having a field day with the halaal
chicken (non)story. The hypocrisy of the public in their so-
called outrage at the welfare of the chickens is clear when
they have no qualms about the miserable life of said
chicken stuck in a cage, in its own faeces, force -fed GM
food to gain weight and mature faster but they are very
concerned about the method of the slaughter of the
chickens.*

This is just an excuse to demonise islam."
Male, 41, London

Even those who are not Muslim who completed the survey
highlighted media as a key cause if not the cause for
Islamophobia.

*"As above, fear, ignorance and misinformation and highly
selective and manipulative information generated largely
by the media… The contribution of the media is clear for
all to see who look."*
Female, 64 (Not Muslim)

*"I believe it is on a continuum from the media, to
individual behaviour, to how the dialogue which is
reported is controlled - i.e. who is given voice and who
isn't, news stories of attacks by 'muslim groups' given
more coverage that hate attacks on muslims."*
Female, 24, Edinburgh
(Not Muslim but sometimes Mistaken for One)

A respondent who is a Muslim and who saw the situation with
the media as improved, however still saw the media's role as
overwhelmingly negative as to the cause of a hostile
atmosphere:

"1) I think it comes from top-down.
"2) Media has often portrayed Muslims very negatively
though they have been a little improved now.
3) News and other programmes do not provide a balanced
view of their reporting of Muslims and 'other' which
shows Muslims as always being in a state of fight and
'others' as in a state of defending themselves."

Female, 44, Edinburgh

Witnessing politicians philosophise that Islam and Muslims are innately problematic

		Witnessing politicians philosophise that Islam is problematic					Total
		Never	Rarely	Some-times	Often	Always	
Religiosity	Originally Muslim but not religious	1.50%	0.30%	0.60%	1.00%	0.70%	**3.90%**
	Secular Muslim	0.90%	0.90%	1.20%	0.80%	0.40%	**4.20%**
	Non-practising Muslim	0.40%	0.60%	0.70%	1.30%	0.80%	**3.70%**
	Practising Muslim	6.10%	7.20%	16.90%	21.00%	21.30%	**72.40%**
	Highly practising Muslim	1.70%	2.00%	2.20%	4.40%	5.50%	**15.70%**
Total		10.50%	10.90%	21.60%	28.40%	28.60%	100.00%

Table 17: Effect of religiosity on witnessing politicians philosophise that Muslims and Islam are problematic

The correlation in 2014 between religiosity and hearing politicians philosophise that Islam and Muslims are innately problematic shares similarities with the results above on media. Again the 'always' category is the largest.

Those stating that they often saw such behaviour from politicians was almost identical in size. The greater the religiosity, the more they were likely to say that they always or often saw this (although there is some parity with non-practising Muslims).

This indicates that the tone of the debate is felt keenly by those professing and adhering to the faith and further suggests that the political discourse is set around targeting the Islamic faith in particular and its tenets. Given the slide in discourse from arguments around radicalisation to religious conservatism with incidents like that of Trojan Horse / Hoax outlined in Chapter 3, as well as facets of the PREVENT strategy, this can be seen as the observable outcome of this practice by politicians.

"Recent comments by Cameron about Britain as a Christian country. when previously with the Rushdie Affair Muslims were criticised for not complying with 'secular British ideals', have led to further marginalisation of Muslims as a minority."

Female, 31, Birmingham

| | Witnessing politicians philosophise that Islam is problematic | | | | | Total |
	Never	Rarely	Some-times	Often	Always	
Employed	4.00%	4.20%	8.80%	13.60%	15.00%	**45.60%**
Self Employed	1.70%	1.40%	3.70%	4.20%	4.10%	**15.20%**
Unemployed	1.40%	1.40%	2.50%	3.10%	3.40%	**11.80%**
Retired	0.10%	0.30%	0.40%	0.50%	0.20%	**1.40%**
Student	4.10%	3.90%	6.20%	6.40%	5.30%	**26.00%**
Total	**11.30%**	**11.20%**	**21.60%**	**27.80%**	**28.10%**	**100.00%**

Work status

Table 18: Correlation between work status and witnessing politicians philosophise that Islam and Muslims are problematic

Notably work status and seeing politicians philosophise that Islam is problematic is significant with a third of all those employed. This is at a higher rate than those unemployed or self-employed. This suggests that political discourse is impacting negatively in employment spaces, which will be discussed further below.

*****

Contextualising the 2014 results on ideological hatred, respondents to the qualitative questionnaire observed that there was a longer history and a particular (often geo-political purpose) to the ideology of hatred, seen alternately and sometimes in combination between the media and government, as well as expressed at street level. This history was from the relatively recent 'War on Terror', the slightly longer frame of decolonisation and also the fall of communism, all the way to the discussions of the longue durée (see Grosfoguel and Mielants, 2006) and even the Crusades.

> "The media defines Muslims as the other and in so doing defines its people as superior therefore the change must happen in the media, and yes media has contributed massively. People, especially those in areas of a minority of Muslims will more likely believe it and those that want to be aggressive or place blame towards another will believe it."
>
> Female, 24, London

> "Muslims believed to be terrorists, shariah deemed to be backwards, women seen to be oppressed, die to representative in media and justification for wars"
>
> Female, 29, London

> "The media- includes journalistic and pop culture. A long standing 'othering' of Muslims/Arabs Entrenched racism
>
> Long held views about women of colour Political parties and public figures"
>
> Female, 31, London

> "Islamophobia is constantly endorsed by politicians and the media. The good Muslim/bad Muslim dichotomy has led to a justification of Islamophobia on a mass scale, i.e. it is justified to hate/fear "bad Muslims" (Islamists/radicals/terrorists). The difference in legal protection between religious and racial minorities has also disproportionately affected Muslims as a racially diverse religious minority. It has meant that people can say what they like about Islam as a faith, which has resulted in a widespread perpetuation of the concept of ISLAM as evil/deviant/abhorrent, yet this isn't deemed hate speech because it is directed at Islam, not Muslims, ignoring the fact that such rhetoric directly reinforces, encourages and justifies Islamophobia. Anti- terror policies

disproportionately target Muslims. The term 'Islamist' regularly employed by politicians reinforces an inseparable association between Islam and terrorism. Regular criticism, hysteria and 'public debates' about Muslim practices e.g. niqab, segregated seating and halal meat, all endorsed by leading politicians and fanned by the media, have led to a widespread belief of Muslims as 'the Other' and Islam as being fundamentally incompatible with British values....

"The root cause lies in Western imperialism and white supremacy, which has resulted in a common perception of Western ideology and Western civilisation as superior and all others as inferior."

Female, 31, Birmingham

"Colonial discourses which inevitably inferiorize Muslims are hegemonic in government and media; and society."

Male, 25, London

Whilst a few did also blame Muslims and in particular excesses committed by a few Muslims, they linked this generally with other factors including media and government e.g.

"The idiots that are rotten apples who make the headlines give all muslims a bad name they have personal political ideological aims that conflate with islam and due to their negative activities - bombings et al all muslims are tarnished and made out to be the the 'fifth column'

The west and various lobby groups - neo cons, zionists xenaphobes etc also have their own personal agendas and use their media machine to influence negative and incorrect conceptions of islam and muslims - they need a 'bogey man' so their society can function - with the fall of communism 'islam' replaced this bogey man."

Female, 32, London

"government need a scapegoat, it's a vote winner for politicians who hide behind 'war on terror'"

Male, 41, London

It would be surprising if they didn't after 10+ centuries of vicious anti-Muslim wars and propaganda disinformation to justify them. This is beginning to change, but things are getting worse with the rise of right-wingers across Europe, including here in the UK

Female, 68, London

Discrimination and Double Discrimination

Discrimination and Double Discrimination is a term in intercultural communication literature (Ameli et al. 2004b: 27) and happens when a person of a certain group is subjected to discrimination by formal structures like police and legal and bureaucratic systems (Ameli, et.al. 2013). Responses were analysed according to the frequency of the following experiences:

1. Job discrimination based on religion
2. Discrimination in educational setting based on religion
3. Failure to complain about discrimination based on the belief that those in authority do not care about Muslims (Ameli and Merali, 2014)

Correlations between demographic variable and the questions show that age and work status impact on job discrimination based on religion, but not on any question in 2014.

Job discrimination

		Experienced job discrimination					Total
		Never	Rarely	Some-times	Often	Always	
Age	Under 18	9.20%	1.10%	0.60%	0.10%	0.20%	**11.20%**
	19 - 24	17.80%	4.60%	2.80%	1.30%	0.50%	**27.10%**
	25 - 29	11.90%	3.70%	3.60%	1.50%	0.60%	**21.30%**
	30 - 34	7.30%	3.70%	2.70%	1.30%	0.30%	**15.40%**
	35 - 39	4.40%	1.70%	1.70%	1.30%	0.40%	**9.60%**
	40 - 44	3.20%	1.30%	0.70%	0.60%	0.10%	**5.90%**
	45-49	4.60%	1.40%	1.30%	0.80%	0.30%	**8.40%**
	50 and above 50	0.80%	0.30%	0.10%	0.10%	0%	**1.20%**
Total		**59.10%**	**17.80%**	**13.60%**	**7.10%**	**2.40%**	**100.00%**

Table 19: Effect of age on Experience of job discrimination

The experience of discrimination at work ran at 40.9%, with the largest group of 17.8% stating they experienced discrimination rarely. Whilst those claiming discrimination always happens was low (never over 0.6% of the total sample in any age range) it nevertheless bodes ill for those employed (as opposed to self-employed) that such a significant group experience this.

In terms of age it is the age range of 30 – 44 where the experience is highest with more than half 30 -34 year olds and 35 – 39 year olds experiencing job discrimination of some sort.

Experiencing discrimination at work 2010 and 2014		
	2010	**2014**
Never	71.9	59.1
Rarely	6.2	17.8
Sometimes	6.5	13.6
Often	4.5	7.1
Always	10.9	2.4
Total	**100**	**100**

Table 20: Frequency of experiencing discrimination at work 2010 and 2014

Every category sees an increase in experience except those experiencing it 'always'.

Work status was also a significant variable in this regard.

		Experienced job discrimination					Total
		Never	Rarely	Some-times	Often	Always	
Work status	Employed	24.20%	8.80%	7.90%	3.90%	1.20%	**46.00%**
	Self Em-ployed	8.40%	3.20%	2.00%	1.20%	0.30%	**15.10%**
	Unem-ployed	6.70%	1.70%	1.80%	1.10%	0.40%	**11.80%**
	Retired	0.90%	0.10%	0.20%	0.10%	0.10%	**1.40%**
	Student	18.70%	4.10%	1.80%	0.60%	0.50%	**25.70%**
Total		**58.90%**	**17.90%**	**13.70%**	**7.00%**	**2.50%**	**100.00%**

Table 21: Correlation between work status and experience of discrimination at work

Just under or over half of all respondents who were employed, self-employed or unemployed felt they had experienced work-related discrimination. Whilst the largest category (or near largest category) of each variable was the 'rarely' experience, it is notable that those who stated they were employed were more likely to say 'sometimes' than in other categories, suggesting again like the findings above, that for those employed the workplace is a problematic arena.

Experiences proffered by respondents of both discrimination and complaining about it highlight the problematics of systems where anti-Muslim hatred is not recognised or is reproduced upon a victim complaining:

> *"-being told I cannot work at my place of work if I wore the hijab because parents wouldn't feel safe leaving their children with a hijabi.*
> *"...- the work scenario I said that it is discrimination but I didn't put on hijab until 1.5 years later and there is a possibility I will have to look for a new job and relocate because of it (I work with children who have Autism)*
> Female, 25, Canterbury

> *"In the work place being left out and shunned and spoken over the top of by colleagues...*
> *"I did not complain about individual instances because I was not aware racism was a criminal offence. I also have no confidence in institutions and perceive them to contain racists at various levels including management and director."*
> Male, Rainham

> *"Subtle / indirectly when applying for jobs, using services, dwp..*
> *"No formal complaints"*
> Male, 25+, Glasgow

> *"...I went for a few job interviews after I became Muslim and was rejected outright because of my hijab (even after having a phone interview and being given the job over the phone.)*

"No, I've never complained against anyone because I feel sorry for their ignorance."

Female, 28, Houston

Double discrimination, as defined by Ameli et al (2004b; 2013a) works in two ways. Firstly, it can:

> "… characterise the additive and adverse effects of multiple factors…. Firstly when conflating two indicators or signifiers of social exclusion and discrimination, such as ethnicity and gender (Tang, 1997) or religion and ethnicity (EUMAP, 2005); and secondly, when describing processes of discrimination, for example, where a victim of a crime reports it to the police and experiences further discrimination at the hands of the police."

Those experiencing discrimination in a school or educational setting also rose between the 2010 and 2014 survey.

Experienced educational discrimination		
	Frequency	Percent
Never	1,046	64.2
Rarely	318	19.5
Sometimes	170	10.4
Often	73	4.5
Always	23	1.4
Total	**1,630**	**100**

Table 22: Frequency of experiencing discrimination in an educational setting, 2014

Of those answering this question in 2014, 35.8% said they had experienced some sort of discrimination in the educational space.

As with other experiences of discrimination cited already, it appears in qualitative responses that the hijab (an Islamic head covering) elicits strong responses:

> *I attended Middlesex university where I studied bachelors and masters in photography. A couple of my tutors were very anti Islam and made me feel very uncomfortable throughout my MA to the extent of breaking promises and assurances that they had made to me regarding employment at the university. I experience hatred on a regular basis in conversation with people when trying to dispel the myths and stereotypes they harbour.*
>
> Male, 39, London

> *"Had a lecturer at university who not only spoke to me in a derogatory manner but I could be a metre away from him and if he had to hand me a book he would throw it to the ground and have me pick it up as opposed to handing it me. My non hijabi friends did not always have their books handed to them."*
>
> Female, 25, London

It can be argued that whilst visible Muslimness has not been a significant variable in this category, the prevalence of hijab-related responses across the qualitative survey as a whole indicates that there is an issue related to female visible Muslimness. As other respondents already cited have stated, this can involve hijab, but goes beyond that to the idea of gender and Muslimness. In this scenario, we can see the stereotypes of veil and unveiled set aside for a more pervasive one of demonised Muslim femininity that encompasses Victorian era and preceding tropes of Muslim licentiousness with more recent tropes of Muslim puritanism. Whilst ostensibly contradictory, as we have seen in Chapter 3 both stereotypes come from the same obsession with 'Oriental' sexuality that in the current era of power dynamics, objectifies the Muslim subject, and in particular the Muslim female subject, as once more desirable but inferior. Being seen (ie unveiled) is not then an ideology of liberation, as many media and political discourses contend, but being made the object of the gaze (Mulvey, 1975 and Ameli and Merali, 2004), in this case the European male gaze analogous to Berger's description of Renaissance art until the current time:

> "Berger adds that at least from the seventeenth century, paintings of female nudes reflected the woman's submission to 'the owner of both woman and painting' (*ibid.*,52). He noted that 'almost all post-Renaissance European sexual imagery is frontal - either literally or metaphorically - because the sexual protagonist is the spectator-owner looking at it' (*ibid.*, 56). He advanced the idea that the realistic, 'highly tactile' depiction of things in oil paintings and later in colour photography (in particular where they were portrayed as 'within touching distance'), represented a desire to *possess* the things (or the lifestyle) depicted (*ibid.*, 83ff). This also applied to women depicted in this way (*ibid.*, 92)." (Chandler, 2014).

Unveiling, whether by force in a hate attack on the street, by school policies or political and media rhetoric, can be argued to conform to this idea of being put within touching distance. As the attacks related in Chapters 2 and 3 highlight, the idea that Muslim women wearing headscarves and those wearing face-veils must be touched and taught a lesson by doing so, appears to be a prevailing motivation of attacks. Such attacks may have no sexual motivation whatsoever yet their genesis is rooted in a sexualised discourse of touching and owning.

It is worth highlighting a case reported to IHRC in 2014 regarding a school involved in the Trojan Horse / Hoax debacle. Parents at the school were concerned at rumours that the new administration of the school imposed by the local authority were considering changing the uniform rules and would ban headscarves. When attempting to complain to the headteacher certain parents were told by form teachers that they had been advised that should any parent express this concern they were to be reported to the PREVENT office at the local police station for extremism. The desire to veil in an educational setting is now set in this scenario to be not just discriminated against but effectively criminalised.

The experience of double discrimination is not as intense as that of ideological hatred, which is a phenomenon observed in previous studies (see Ameli and Merali, 2014). However it is clear that this experience has risen. Concurrently a lack of trust in those who should be complained to is evident not just in the qualitative responses but also in cases like the one above regarding the reporting of complaining parents to the police as potential extremists / terrorist sympathisers.

When asked if they had complained about incidents, of those responding many simply said no. Others claimed they did not because they felt it would not be taken seriously whether due to malice or ignorance on the part of those complained to, others that they feared reprisals.

There were also some responses that indicated that whilst managers understood there to be problems with the treatment that staff receive from clients, they prioritised the need of the client (or the need to have the client) over the welfare or well-being of employees. This counters the trend of finding positive examples e.g. in Ameli and Merali, 2004, where an optometrist was abused by a client. The longstanding client was then turned away by the manager as a result of his behaviour. There were no such reports in this sample.

"I have not expressed my concerns to anyone. I think more so because these have often been low-level and I don't think they will be considered serious enough to warrant any attention."
Female, 44, Edinburgh

"I complained but managers think that customers are god, they refused to block customers' account because he was just too rich. I did not complain against colleagues, just stopped talking to them on religion."
Female, 32, Newham

"No one cares. The majority of people happily agree with the stereotypes they're fed."
Male, 39, London

"I have not complained. These have been random acts which have occurred outside on the street and I do not believe that

the British authorities would do anything about it. Much worse has happened to others and the authorities have been slow to act and usually do not acknowledge certain crimes as being islamophobic"

Female, 39, London

"Mostly, forgive and forget in the hope of some long term benefit from Allah."

Male, 35, Wakefield

"No I have not because we get further victimised"

Female, 37, Watford

"who do you tell?
what mechanism is there? none
you make a complaint and you are ostracised or made to feel like who do u think you are - you are being tolerated in this country - put up and shut up"

Female, 32, London

"Not normally as I have never had any ACTION taken - they simply say we can not provide for all different people and sometimes apologise."

Male, 71, Durham

Even those who hold positions within society thought to be of note or power, e.g. commentators or journalists have responded that being Muslim has made a difference in how they pursue matters, in this case, a lack of trust in the police, and a lack of expectation that anything will be done:

"I did not complain about the comments made in response to my articles, because I wasn't aware of the mechanism for complaints on HuffPost UK and did not think it merited a police complaint (or even if it did, I dislike the police to the extent that I would not want to get them involved in my affairs to begin with). I blocked the trolls on Twitter - can't recall if I reported them too, but if I did report them I certainly haven't heard anything back from Twitter about it."

Female, 31, Birmingham

Whilst some of this experience falls in line with general 'troll' behaviours on Twitter, Awan (2014) studied the phenomenon of anti-Muslim trolling on Twitter and called for government and law enforcement to deal with the matter, highlighting that it can fall under the Malicious Communications Act.

One response in particular underlined the continuing failure of implementing the recommendations of the McPherson report on perception (McPherson, 1999). As Ameli et. al. (2006b) have discussed previously, the idea that the perception of an incident as racist by a victim is sufficient for authorities to accept it as such needs to be seriously understood and acted upon. As this respondent states:

> "Police council and councillors and many other local organisations.
> "Very much so also a lack of understanding and inability to verify what they hear."

Male, 34, Bradford

The fear of double discrimination has been reported by IHRC since its early days and notably by Ameli et. al (2004b). The frequency of this in 2014 was high:

Experienced discrimination, did not complain because those would complain to, do not care	Frequency	Percent
Never	861	53.1
Rarely	283	17.4
Sometimes	234	14.4
Often	151	9.3
Always	93	5.7
Total	1,622	100

Table 23: Frequency of not complaining about suffering discrimination because people do not care

Some 46.9% (almost half) of respondents who had suffered some sort of discrimination did not complain at some time after an incident.

There appears to be not only no improvement in this situation but as we have seen in Chapters 2 and 3, concerted attempts to move away from cultures of accountability and recommendations to overhaul institutional racism. Indeed, as the example of perception has shown (Chapter 2 above) the arguments against it have grown apace with reasons cited for ignoring it being linked to the idea of Muslim grievance and giving Muslims a greater role in public space and discourse. Athwal and Burnett (2014) argue that:

> "The Macpherson report was the catalyst for a multitude of changes in the way the police and criminal justice system respond to racial violence. But as this investigation shows, racial motivation is often still ignored, downplayed or not acknowledged by criminal justice agencies."

Looking specifically at Muslim experiences Choudhury and Fenwick (2011) found from their focus groups that Muslims did not feel the police took hate crime seriously and that this further undermined their trust in the police. They recorded, not only instances where members of the focus group related going to the police to report hate crimes and not being taken seriously as well as being bullied or abused by the police when going to report such.

This shift away from a culture that acknowledged institutional racism to one which effectively implements it consciously and in some cases applauds it is one of the most shocking conclusions drawn from this study.

From ignorance to knowing: cross cultural schemata and intercultural sensitivity

As the authors have already explained, many studies, including those undertaken by IHRC (see Ameli et al, 2004a and 2007 in particular) have found that respondents often feel that better understanding on the part of individuals, organisations and institutions is the key to alleviating a hate environment. As a result of these repeated findings, respondents in this study were specifically asked their thoughts on intercultural sensitivity and cross-cultural schemata. According to Shahghasemi and Heisey (2009) cross-cultural schemata are: "abstract mental structures that one makes according to his/her past experiences or shared knowledge about the members of other cultures and thus makes them more understandable."

Intercultural sensitivity using Bennet's Developmental Model for Intercultural Competence and Sensitivity (Bennett, 1993) is the ability to discriminate and experience relevant cultural differences. Ameli (2011, 2012 and 2013) argues that: "Intercultural schemas and intercultural sensitivity... are highly rooted in dogma and values, which are created by social norms and social and political values represented in media production." (Ameli et al, 2013:80) This is one of the four elements that forms the Domination Hate Model of Intercultural Relations together with Domination Policy, Xenophobia Policy and Social Structure (See Chapter 4). These four elements underpin the four concepts of Hate for the model i.e. Hate ideology (experiences of which are discussed above), Hate Policy, Hate Representation and Hate Practice. These four concepts mutually constitute a hate environment.

Correlation tests with the demographic variables showed that no variable had greater significance than others. Experiences however are consistent with previous findings in the UK and other countries, in that respondents still feel that a better understanding on the part of those who discriminate against them would lead to a reduction if not elimination of these outcomes.   As with the decoding of media discourse, respondents feel that media content is a huge driver of Islamophobia.

In relation to understanding respondents' ideas regarding Hate Representation through the lens of cross-cultural schemata and intercultural sensitivity the following ideas were proposed:

Those who discriminate against us have an authentic picture about us and our religion

: Frequency of agreeing that those who discriminate against us have an authentic picture about us and our religion		
	Frequency	Percent
Strongly disagree	692	42.6
Disagree	245	15.1
Agree nor disagree	169	10.4
Agree	337	20.7
Strongly agree	182	11.2
Total	**1,625**	**100**

Table 24: Frequency of agreeing that those who discriminate against us have an authentic picture about us and our religion

57.7% felt that this was not a correct assertion, and many respondents cited ignorance as the cause of attacks and discrimination.

Those who discriminate against us are highly driven by media content.

Those who discriminate against us are highly driven by media content		
	Frequency	Percent
Strongly disagree	54	3.3
Disagree	35	2.1
Agree nor disagree	113	6.9
Agree	503	30.9
Strongly agree	924	56.7
Total	**1,629**	**100**

Table 25: Frequency of agreeing that those who discriminate against us are highly driven by media content

87.7% agreed with this contention, which bears out the findings above and serves to underline the findings recorded earlier in this chapter regarding the role of media in creating a hate environment.

I think if people know more about us, they would act much better than the way they do now.

If people know more about us they would act much better		
	Frequency	Percent
Strongly disagree	60	3.7
Disagree	56	3.4
Agree nor disagree	132	8.1
Agree	517	31.7
Strongly agree	865	53.1
Total	**1,630**	**100**

Table 26: Frequency of agreeing that if people knew more about us, they would act much better than the way they do now

84.8% of respondents agreed that this would be the case, and this forms part of the basis of community recommendations at the end of this study. This finding also highlights a sense of hope on the part of respondents, year in and year out, from the various studies the authors have been involved in, that the lifting of ignorance will be a panacea for the social ills they suffer.

Muslims as a hated society (Ameli et. al., 2012) are portrayed by the hating society (Ameli et. al. 2013) as being separatist minded only to hate the 'other' i.e. the idea of a homogenised majority 'non-Muslim' rather than the victims of subalternisation. These findings show a desire, indeed a belief in the processes of intercultural sensitivity that work on a scale towards harmony and away from discord. This is an important and repeated finding of these works, and it is one that policy makers must acknowledge.

The everyday and the feeling of being a member of a Hated Society

Eight questions were asked in order to understand the everyday experience of being Muslim. What were the levels of:

- Experiences of physical assault

- Being stared at by strangers

- Hearing or being told an offensive joke or comment concerning Muslim people or about Islam

- Being treated in an overly superficial manner

- Being talked down to or treated as if you were stupid; having your opinions minimised or devalued; others expecting you to be less competent

- Being treated with suspicion or being wrongly accused of something

- Being overlooked, ignored or denied service in a shop, restaurant or public office/transport

- Verbal abuse

Analysis of the eight questions above provided indicators as to the ubiquity or otherwise of the experience of feeling a member of a hated society. Assessing everyday experiences, as outlined in the diagram above, provides indicators regarding the perception of being a member of a hated society (Ameli and Merali, 2014).

A female respondent who describes herself as not Muslim, aged 24, from Edinburgh explains her experience:

> *I feel that there is a growing climate of Islamaphobia. I grew up with racial insults and have found over the years these have become increasingly islamaphobic - where I used to get told to 'go back home' my younger brother is told by school bullies 'you're a terrorist', do you and your dad have an AK47 at home', etc. I think what is disturbing is that this islamaphobia is now being reflected in government legislation and policy - most recently in the proposals to 'ban the burka' which predominant discussion around this issue being facism [sic] disguised as concern for women, translating into a proposition that would legislate on what muslim women can wear and thus restrict their freedom and access to public space.*

Another female, aged 21, from Bishops Stortford describes her experience of name-calling at school and the response when she complained thus:

> *Been called a Osama bitch, paki, bullied at school. Where I live people are not accepting of muslims...*
> *I did tell the school but it didn't stop the bullies.*

Experiences of physical assault

This experience has increased since 2010.
In 2010 the experience was 13.9% in total whereas in 2014 it was 17.8%.

Physical assault	
	Percent
Never	82.2
Rarely	13.3
Sometimes	3.5
Often	0.7
Always	0.3
Total	**100**

Table 27: Frequency of experiencing physical assault

Whilst this can be argued to be an incremental climb at 1% per year, the nature of attacks outlined in Chapters 2 and 3 above show the intensity of attacks as becoming extraordinarily violent. A respondent in the survey did relate some physical abuse:

> *"pushed whilst on a bus to the ground - bus driver ignored me and carried on"*
>
> Female, 37, Watford

Her experience of being left and ignored in a public space has been highlighted in Chapters 2 and 3 above as a frequent complaint by victims.

Threat as a form of physical assault needs to be looked at in more detail. Verbal abuse or damage to property threat itself can be argued to be an assault. One respondent highlighted how this operates:

"I was hit by an egg once in Mayfair, and have had to fend off angry men about three times, mostly in connection with anxiety about my car's nearness to their cars, but one did say negative things about Muslims."

Female, 68, London

Incidents in the chapters above also attest to the levels of violence inflicted. Whilst the collection of reports and monitoring of new media in this way is more anecdotal, it is notable that the scenario after an extreme case such as 9-11 and the foregoing bear marked similarities:

Physical violence

• 52 incidents reported

This has ranged from pushing, shoving and being spat at, to violent attacks leaving victims hospitalised and in one case paralysed. A large number of reported incidents involved victims being spat at. One case involved rotten fruit being thrown at two Muslim women as they walked out of college.

Many cases have been reported of Muslim women having their scarves forcibly pulled off. These types of incidents are serious assaults in themselves but have an added element. They have a particularly humiliating aspect to them involving both the removal of essential clothing and dousing in a liquid that is considered impure in Islamic teaching. In another incident a schoolgirl had her scarf pulled off by a female adult at her school gates. IHRC has received direct reports of serious physical assaults. It has also monitored press coverage of attacks. Amongst the more severe assaults, there have been at least three clubbings with bats, an attack on a child with pepper spray, and a Muslim being deliberately run over with a car. Additionally there have been several cases involving beatings and kickings. Reports of three rape cases are currently circulating. Whilst there has yet to be an official recognition that these cases may have an anti-Muslim component there is a strong feeling amongst those communities from which the victims hail that this component is part of these attacks." (IHRC, 2001)

The above was taken from a report overviewing reporting and monitoring in the wake of 9-11 until the end of October that year, a seven-week period. The intensity and nature of the attacks is not simply mirrored by the foregoing, there appears to be significant deterioration, particularly in terms of the severity of attacks, at a time when for the most part there have not been any crises to 'provoke' an upsurge of attacks.

At the time of writing, 81 year old Mushin Ahmed was assaulted in an area just off Fitzwilliam Road, Rotherham in the early hours of Monday 10 August whilst he was on his way to the mosque. He subsequently died. Research by the Institute of Race Relations had documented racist killings in the UK putting them at a minimum of 93 since the McPherson report of 1999 (IRR, Athwal and Burnett, 2014):

- There have been at least ninety-three deaths with a known or suspected racial element since February 1999. Of these, 97 per cent of the victims were from BME communities (including those from Gypsy or Traveller communities and European migrant workers).

- In 84 per cent of cases there was a conviction of some kind – though not necessarily for murder or manslaughter. In only a quarter of the cases was the allegation of racism accepted and prosecuted as such; with racial motivation factored into the sentencing of the perpetrator(s).

- If the relevant authorities, including the police, had on occasion intervened earlier when persistent harassment and low-level abuse was being reported by victims, some deaths could have been prevented.

- Where there are convictions, the racially motivated aspect of cases is being filtered out by the police, the CPS and the judiciary, through a failure to understand the broader context within which racist attacks are carried out, an unwillingness to recognise racial motivation and the reclassifying of racist attacks as disputes, robberies or other forms of hostility.

• The over-strict interpretation of the legal definition of racial motivation may inhibit the charging of perpetrators by removing the racial basis of a crime from the courtroom.

• Families still have to resort to challenging the decisions of the police, mobilising the media, exerting pressure to ensure the recognition of racial harassment and, ultimately, challenging the criminal justice system. (IRR News, January 23, 2014)

At the time of the Lee Rigby killing in 2013, it was noted by many Muslims that an attack three weeks earlier on another elderly Muslim man going home from the mosque was motivated by anti-Muslim hatred, yet it received little media attention, and indeed was not initially treated as a hate crime by police. The extremes of racist violence as a factor of everyday experience that includes murder is clearly a facet of Muslim experience.

The fact that any number of attacks are being perpetrated around mosques is clearly a phenomenon that law enforcement agencies must look at post haste.

Hearing or being told an offensive joke or comment concerning Muslim people or about Islam

Hearing or being told an offensive joke		
	Frequency	Percent
Never	376	22.9
Rarely	452	27.5
Sometimes	503	30.7
Often	237	14.4
Always	73	4.4
Total	**1,641**	**100**

Table 28: Frequency of hearing or being told an offensive joke

28.8%, more than a quarter of respondents had this experience often or always. In total 81.1% had this experience. It should be noted that this survey took place before the attacks on the Charlie Hebdo offices in Paris in 2015, after which there were several 'cartoon' campaigns lampooning the Prophet of Islam (peace and blessings be upon him). This experience, already running at such a high rate, predates that event.

One respondent gives an example which highlights once more the role of the veil, and the idea of being in touching distance as a cultural trope that this becoming a motivator for attacks:

> It's happened to me many times that men have made advances towards me as a joke for themselves and make me feel uncomfortable,...
>
> Female, 28, Houston

Being treated in an overly superficial manner

Being treated in an overly superficial manner		
	Frequency	Percent
Never	635	39.2
Rarely	459	28.3
Sometimes	356	22
Often	141	8.7
Always	30	1.9
Total	1,621	100

Table 29: Frequency of being treated in an overly superficial manner

Whilst the largest response to this was 'never' at 39.2%, it belies a major increase in this experience since 2010, when the 'never' response was nearly three quarters of all respondents at 71.3%. This increase can be seen in all the categories except for 'always', where there has been a drop. This is not in itself positive in that the frequency of experience has become much more pervasive.

Being treated in an overly superficial manner		
	2010	2014
Never	71.3	39.2
Rarely	6.7	28.3
Sometimes	7	22
Often	6	8.7
Always	8.9	1.9
Total	**100**	**100**

Table 30: Frequency of being treated in an overly superficial manner in 2010 and 2014

Being talked down to or treated as if you were stupid; having your opinions minimised or devalued; others expecting you to be less competent

Being talked down to or treated as if you were stupid; having your opinions minimised or devalued; others expecting you to be less competent		
	Frequency	Percent
Never	609	37.1
Rarely	446	27.1
Sometimes	371	22.6
Often	188	11.4
Always	29	1.8
Total	**1,643**	**100**

Table 31: Frequency of being talked down to or treated as if you were stupid; having your opinions minimised or devalued; others expecting you to be less competent

One male respondent, aged 71, from Durham described being 'kept out of the loop' as a hateful act that he experienced, although he did state that it was not an overt act:

"…but feeling that I am not 'one of us' inspite of having lived in the UK since 1962"

This is another data set where there has been significant change from 2010.

Being talked down to or treated as stupid		
	2010	2014
Never	61.7	37.1
Rarely	9.6	27.1
Sometimes	4.1	22.6
Often	13.3	11.4
Always	11.3	1.8

Table 32: Frequency of Experience of being talked down to etc. 2010 and 2014

There has been a significantly large increase in the number of people who have had some sort of experience, with 38.3% having such an experience in 2010, now rising to 62.9%.

Being treated with suspicion or being wrongly accused of something

Being treated with suspicion or wrongly accused of something		
	Frequency	Percent
Never	693	42
Rarely	467	28.3
Sometimes	342	20.7
Often	128	7.8
Always	20	1.2
Total	**1,650**	**100**

Table 33: Frequency of being treated with suspicion or being wrongly accused of something

More than half (58%) felt they had experienced this.

One respondent highlighted how suspiciousness feeds into the psyche of violence, and contributes to an underlying violence in the environment in the way Muslims are perceived:

> "I believe that the hatred and violent tendencies present within individuals is manifested and then exacerbated by a culture that deems Muslims are deserving of hate (or at the very least: suspicion and wariness)"
>
> Female, 22, London

Another feels judged:
> "People judge you often on the streets"
>
> Female, 50, Surrey

The operation of suspicions with regard to terrorism is seen as the result of government policies leaving visible Muslims stigmatised:

"war on terror is used as excuse for limiting freedom
"yes, freedom of religious expression is curtailed so women
who wear a scarf feel/ men with beards feel stigmatised"

Male, 41, London

Being overlooked, ignored or denied service in a shop, restaurant or public office/transport

Being overlooked, ignored or denied service		
	Frequency	Percent
Never	778	47
Rarely	458	27.7
Sometimes	322	19.5
Often	81	4.9
Always	15	0.9
Total	**1,654**	**100**

Table 34: Frequency of being overlooked, ignored or denied service in a shop, restaurant or public office/transport

The unobvious nature of this is picked up by one respondent who highlighted that this is subtle and therefore often unacknowledged:

"Subtle / indirectly when applying for jobs, using services, dwp."

Male, 25+, Glasgow

There was a significant rise in the experience of this compared to 2010, with a 20% reduction in those never experiencing it. 53% of the sample stated they had experienced this in 2014. The largest category of experience in 2014 was 'rarely' with 27.7%.However this is not as it would appear a positive finding in that it does not reflect a reduction in the frequent experience of this, but rather a rise in the experience of this since 2010.

Being overlooked, ignored or denied service		
	UK 2011	UK 2014
Never	67.6	47
Rarely	5.2	27.7
Sometimes	2.8	19.5
Often	12.1	4.9
Always	12.4	0.9
Total	100	100

Table 35: Frequency of being overlooked, ignored or denied service in a shop, restaurant or public office/transport in 2010 and 2014

Being stared at by strangers

Hussain and Bagguley (2012) argue that "funny looks' captures quite cogently the subtle shift in everyday behavioural Islamophobia or racism since the 7/7 bombings.' They argue that after 7-7 there has been a shift in the 'racist self' referencing Picca and Feagin (2007) and their use of Goffman's analogy that racist behaviour had previously been moved backstage to white spaces. Citing Poynting and Mason (2006), they say that the 7-7 bombings allowed racism to move front stage again with the political and media response to events giving people 'permission to hate'.

Being stared at by strangers		
	2010	2014
Never	40.3	24.8
Rarely	19	24.4
Sometimes	11.6	27.5
Often	15.3	15.9
Always	13.7	7.4
Total	**100**	**100**

Table 36: Frequency of being stared at by strangers

Correlation analysis shows that factors affecting being a member of a hated society in research on Muslims in the UK are gender and visible Muslimness when it comes to being stared at by strangers

		Being stared					Total
		Never	Rarely	Some-times	Often	Always	
Gender	Male	16.30%	13.70%	13.70%	6.90%	2.90%	**53.40%**
	Female	8.80%	10.50%	13.90%	8.70%	4.70%	**46.60%**
Total		**25.20%**	**24.20%**	**27.50%**	**15.60%**	**7.60%**	**100.00%**

Table 37: Effect of Gender on being stared at by strangers

Women have a greater experience than men, and this added to the factor that greater visible Muslimness is a significant variable, suggests once more that the wearing of hijab or other 'Muslim' associated dress by women is becoming a lightning rod for hatred.

Hussain and Bagguley (2013) found 'evidence that Pakistani Muslims are now seen as strangers (Bauman, 1991), as familiar but threatening, as physically close, but spiritually distant. Women especially have been subject to this gaze (Fortier, 2008, cited in Hussain and Bagguley).

		Being stared at by strangers					Total
		Never	Rarely	Some-times	Often	Always	
Visibly Muslim	Visibly Muslim (hijab/beard/niqab/turban/hat/etc)	14.90%	17.40%	21.90%	14.70%	6.90%	**75.70%**
	Visible in other way	2.10%	2.10%	2.20%	0.60%	0.30%	**7.30%**
	Not visibly Muslim	6.70%	5.10%	3.10%	1.00%	0.20%	**16.00%**
	Not a Muslim, but sometimes mistaken for one	0.30%	0.30%	0.20%	0.10%	0.10%	**1.00%**
Total		24.00%	24.80%	27.40%	16.30%	7.50%	100.00%

Table 38: Effect of the experience of being stared at by strangers correlated with visible Muslimness

Being visibly Muslim means there is a greater chance of being stared at.

The experience of being stared at is often associated with other acts, particularly name calling.

"Being spat at, verbally attacked and stared at and mocked"
Female, 39, London

"When I am out an about I get the long stare and have had people abuse me calling me terrorist and other names also being aggressive towards me."

Male, 34, Bradford

. As Athwal and Burnett (2014) point out, lower level incidents can escalate if left unchecked, and the failure of authorities to take this seriously can allow, particularly in the present climate, situations to spiral out of control.

Verbal abuse

Many of the responses given above highlight the operation of verbal abuse in various situations, and as such it is arguable that this is not a discrete category. Having refined the questionnaire after the 2010 pilot project to remove this experience, the authors decided to reinstate it for the 2014 survey. As a result it is possible to compare this category from the quantitative responses in 2010 with 2014. This is one of the questions where there has been a significant rise in experience:

Verbal abuse		
	2010	2014
Never	68.1	44
Rarely	6.4	31.8
Sometimes	4.6	17.8
Often	8.8	4.8
Always	12	1.6
Total	**100**	**100**

Table 39: Frequency of experiencing verbal abuse in 2010 and 2014

Whilst the experience of often and always in 2010 was much higher than in 2014 (20.8% compared to 6.4%), this masks the overall rise in experience with those stating 'rarely' and 'sometimes' rising from 11% to 49.6% (nearly half of everyone surveyed). In 2010 the overall experience ran at 38.9%, in 2014 it ran at 66%.

The drop in 'often' and 'always' experiences in 2014 may not necessarily indicate that verbal abuse at that level of frequency has dropped. It may be, as the foregoing examples have shown, that the experience of verbal abuse is combined with other hateful attacks e.g. assaults, and are recorded and assigned significance by respondents elsewhere.

Policy, Political Discourse and the Law

Four propositions were presented to the respondents to rate whether they had:

1. Seen political policies (local or national) that negatively affected Muslim people

2. Seen policies or practices at work, school or business that excluded or negatively affected Muslim people

3. Felt that politicians did not care about Muslims

4. Felt that politicians condoned discriminatory acts against Muslims.

Seeing political policies (local or national) that negatively affected Muslim people

Only 14.7% of the sample disagreed with this contention. A number of policies on immigration, extremism (in particular, double standards over the far right and Muslims), as well as lack of policy in combating racism and Islamophobia were given as examples.

Seen political policies that negatively affected Muslims		
	Frequency	Percent
Strongly disagree	65	4
Disagree	173	10.7
Agree nor disagree	421	26.1
Agree	610	37.7
Strongly agree	347	21.5
Total	**1,616**	**100**

Table 40: Frequency of seeing political policies that negatively affected Muslims

" Wrong policy ineffectiveness to deal with extremist groups of any religion...
...Inability to deal quickly to stop extremist groups especially non Muslim extremists like bnp. Edl. Britain first."

Male, 34, Bradford

"government policy - directly and indirectly demonising minorities and immigrants and muslims"

Female, 32, London

"Muslims are the ultimate 'other'. We are seen as foreign, dangerous, different, and are easily and too often demonised and dehumanised by government policy directly....
"...use the certain issues to increase their influence of readership as well as serving a certain subset of society (affluent white middle/upper class). Policies, stories, wording, timing to make certain claims, not condemning racism and Islamophobia enough..."

Female, 31, London

The government's foreign policy and its overseas interests contribute toward the image of Muslims as 'the enemy' that must be defeated

Female, 22, London

The experience of this has increased since 2010:

Have seen political policies that negatively affected Muslim people		
	2010	2014
Strongly disagree	41.3	4
Disagree	15.4	10.7
Agree nor disagree	9.1	26.1
Agree	19.4	37.7
Strongly agree	14.8	21.5
Total	100	100

Table 41: Frequency of seeing political policies that negatively affected Muslim people in 2010 and 2014

Whereas in 2010, an already low figure of 56.7% disagreed with the proposition that they had seen such a thing, in 2014 only 14.7% gave the same answer. This is a noticeable shift. Where before the media (Ameli et. al., 2011) was blamed as the main culprit in creating an Islamophobic climate, the government and political class now seems to be much more at the forefront of Muslim attention. In 2010, 34.2% agreed or strongly agreed that they had seen such policies but in 2014 this had increased to 59.2%.

Seen policies or practices at work, school or business that excluded or negatively affected Muslim people

Counter-terrorism policies and an obsession about the face-veil may account for the severity of the findings in this category, with 44.4% stating they have seen practices that exclude or negatively affect Muslim people.

Practices that excluded or negatively affected Muslim people	
	Percent
Strongly disagree	7.7
Disagree	17.4
Agree nor disagree	29.5
Agree	31.3
Strongly agree	14.1
Total	**100**

Table 42: Frequency of seeing practices that excluded or negatively affected Muslim people

-Niqab bans - movies
-lack of info counteracting Muslim stereotypes

Female, 25, Canterbury

Security / 'Intelligence' establishment targets Muslims particularly and pushes out negative propaganda about Muslims.

Female, 68, London

There is a constant need to categorise Muslims into boxes that coincide with the government's view of the necessary integration of Muslim communities. The problem is that the govt & its institutions do not understand who the Muslim community are and what part its religiosity and attitude towards Islam plays in its identity. It is problematic to properly formulate coherent policy towards a community you do not understand and this is evident in the govt attitude towards counter-terrorism and the consistent conflation between practising Muslims & "Islamists" (again a term that has been hijacked & used in a haphazard, undefined & very broad way in accordance to the political needs of the occasion). This public confusion and stigmatisation by the govt naturally has an impact on the view that society takes of Muslims and 'what they are about'.

It is partly due to the political pandering of the government as they wish to be seen as taking strong action against an easy & open enemy. Terrorist acts provoke strong emotions in an electorate and so the governance take a strong & often arbitrary and ineffective approach to tackle it. Despite flaccid attempts to include 'far-right extremism' in the same battle, the unintelligent approach means that the average Muslim (who has nothing to do with extremist groups) is unjustly affected in a way that the average Englishman (who is as uninvolved in far-right groups) is not.

The war on terror has allowed incremental broaches upon the personal freedoms and daily grind of Muslims, in stigmatising them so that they face implicit challenges in the face of those who are affected by the media/governmental outlook and also in the changes in policy and law that has led to practical curtailment to their freedom of movement (also leading to further stigma).

Female, 25, Nottingham

According to Choudhury and Fenwick (2011) " the impact of counter-terrorism laws, policies and practices on community cohesion, equality and human rights is critical. Concerns have been raised that counter-terrorism laws and policies are increasingly alienating Muslims, especially young people…"

Such policies include: specific counter-terrorism laws, policies and practices including stop and search powers (which a few respondents mentioned experiencing), PREVENT, control orders, regulations directed at the financing of terrorism, stops at ports and airports, arrests, pre-charge detention, indirect incitement (including glorification of terrorism) and banning of organisations. This list as set out gives an overview of the pervading nature of the security state in a legal and policy regime that effectively targets Muslims (see Ansari, 2006 and Kundnani, 2011).

In 2015 a campaign was launched calling for the abolition of all anti-terror laws in the UK on the grounds that sufficient criminal laws already existed to prosecute perpetrators of any criminal acts of political violence. Launched by way of a letter to The Guardian and followed by a conference on PREVENT, it was co-organised by IHRC and CAMPACC. The launch letter reads as follows:

Yes, the counter-terrorism and security bill is "ideological extremism masquerading as British values", especially by conflating extremism with dissent against unjust western policies (Karma Nabulsi, Opinion, 4 February). In a familiar pattern, every terrorist act is exploited for strengthening executive powers, extending punishment without trial, widening powers of the security services, eroding fundamental freedoms, and further targeting Muslim communities. Moreover, the government's latest bill would require public institutions to monitor and suppress "extremist" voices – supposedly to prevent terrorism.

All anti-terror powers are based on the Terrorism Act 2000. It redefined terrorism, blurring any distinction between violent acts and political dissent, thus criminalising vague association and speech acts. Anti-terror powers are about protecting UK foreign policy from dissent, rather than protecting the public from violence.

This political agenda explains the discriminatory application of anti-terrorism laws. For example, schedule 7 of the act, which authorises border officials to detain and question individuals, has disproportionately targeted Muslims and ethnic minorities. Since 2001, some 70% of all arrests under anti-terrorism legislation have been of non-whites. Such practices serve a politics of fear – marginalising Muslim and migrant communities, making others fear them, creating mutual mistrust and increasing risks of violent attack. This Orwellian agenda makes our society more dangerous, not safer.

Ordinary criminal law remains adequate to protect the public from violence; terrorist attacks have resulted from inadequately using intelligence and available powers, not from inadequate powers. Therefore we advocate the repeal of all anti-terrorism legislation since the Terrorism Act 2000.

Lady Jones *Green Party*
Shahrar Ali *Deputy leader, Green Party*
Les Levidow *Campaign Against Criminalising Communities*
Arzu Merali *Islamic Human Rights Commission*
Hanne Stevens *Director, Rights Watch (UK)*
Asim Qureshi *Cage-UK*
Malia Bouattia *NUS Black Students' Officer*
Zarah Sultana *NUS National Executive Council*
Zekarias Negussue *NEC representative, NUS Black Students' Campaign*
Arwa Almari *West Yorkshire Racial Justice Network*

The charge of entryism, discussed in previous chapters, to describe political participation of Muslims, which undertaken by anyone else would pass unnoticed, highlights how Muslim identity, rather than being forced onto society at large is being forced into the spotlight as a precursor to exclusion. This actually sets a precedent for curtailing political participation per se, but the Muslim specificity of this type of exclusion can be seen at different levels and intersects with the counter-terror regime. The case of Muslim tourist Nasser Al-Ansari highlights the absurdity and horror of it. Al-Ansari was arrested under the Terrorism Act in July 2015 for recording a selfie video of himself outside a Brighton shopping mall, an ordinary event that would have gone unnoticed had he not been a Muslim.

Some respondents picked up on the anti-immigration discourse and policies that interchange with similar discourses and policies on Muslims:

This is further influenced by government focus on immigration, David Cameron's latest 'we are a Christian country' stuff, proposals to legislate against what muslim

*women can wear, and the lack of visibility of muslim people
- in particular muslim women - in government and public
discourse.*

Female, 24, Edinburgh

*Government, politics like UKIP are adding to the fact that
they want all cultures to stop coming into the UK.*

Female, 21, Bishops Stortford

Felt that politicians did not care about Muslims

Politicians do not care about Muslims		
	Frequency	Percent
Strongly disagree	43	2.7
Disagree	159	9.8
Agree nor disagree	394	24.4
Agree	609	37.7
Strongly agree	412	25.5
Total	**1,617**	**100**

Table 43: Frequency of feeling politicians did not care about Muslims

*On a national level governments/politicans certainly do
not understand muslims, nothing beyond the basic level of
knowledge they are drip fed to 'appeal' to Muslims.*

Male, 18, Batley

*They perpetuate the colonial, white god-complex, Muslim-
inferiorizing discourses...
... Racism (White Supremacy) / Islamophobia is intrinsic
to the constitution and standard operating procedures of
the modern state, especially 'Western' states.*

Male, 25, London

There are some whoever who do disagree:

> "...The government is not to blame in my opinion. If the government of the UK or other western countries were against Muslims, they would not have allowed millions of Muslims to migrate to these countries for a better lifestyle. Muslims are also allowed to exercise their free speech. They are allowed to become citizens and marry local people. However, if a foreign Muslim migrates to a country such as the UAE, or Saudi Arabia, he cannot become a citizen, and is not allowed to marry a local person. Thus, Muslims should be thankful that they have such rights in non-Muslim countries which treat them better as opposed to Muslim countries that treat them worse than third class citizens..."
>
> Male, 19, Canterbury

Felt that politicians condoned discriminatory acts against Muslims.

Discriminatory acts are condoned by politicians	
	Percent
Strongly disagree	8.3
Disagree	14
Agree nor disagree	27.6
Agree	34.7
Strongly agree	15.4
Total	**100**

Table 44: Frequency of feeling that politicians condone discriminatory acts against Muslims

51.1% of the sample – just over half – believe that politicians condone discriminatory acts against Muslims. This perception indicates that the level of political discourse is seen to be poisonous and one of attribution of blame to Muslims. As one respondent claimed:

> *I believe that the hatred and violent tendencies present within individuals is manifested and then exacerbated by a culture that deems Muslims are deserving of hate (or at the very least: suspicion and wariness)*
>
> Female, 22, London

This response was already cited in the section on being treated with suspicion, but informs many parts of this report in that it encapsulates an understanding of DHMIR and the connection between hate acts and crimes, the hate environment and the causality of that environment, in this case a culture that deems Muslims to be deserving of hate.

> *Some politicians like to highlight and politicise Islamic issues to cause havoc and portray Islam in a negative manner.*
>
> Male, 34, Bradford

> *The government is extreme in its view and representation of Islam. They work very hard alongside the media to insure that the general public have a false and negative view towards Islam and Muslims.*
>
> Male, 39, London

> *The Government making no effort to differentiate Muslims from extremists, they are happy to allow people to think extremists "misinterpret" the Quran when in fact they deliberately distort it to justify their evil actions and hope people fall for this so Islam is blamed and not them.*

> *Common terms such as "Islamist", "jihadist", Muslim extremists or terrorists, being made as acceptable norms when they are offensive and generalise terrorist acts as associated with Islam and Muslims. This makes no sense as I previously stated Muslims are the number one victims of extremist attacks.*
>
> Male, Rainham

Impact of the Hate Environment

Some politicians like to highlight and politicise Islamic issues to cause havoc and portray Islam in a negative manner.

Male, 34, Bradford

Creating havoc

The idea of havoc or social breakdown is a key theme in many responses to the qualitative questionnaire. With regard to the experience of a hateful act, some 22 respondents felt they had experienced one, with 8 unsure and 19 stating they had not.

Nevertheless, when asked if they thought there was a racist or Islamophobic culture, some 31 said yes, 8 were unsure and only 2 thought there was not.

The impact of this culture was seen by respondents as manifested in a variety of ways. Social ills such as the hate attacks described above were cited, but also intra-community ills such as crime and institutional racism in the legal system come to the fore, as does the rise of the far right:

Muslims hugely over-represented in the prison population. The Rise of UKIP as a cover for racists and right wingers, as BNP loses momentum. Rise of other rightist parties across Europe.

Female, 68, London

When asked if Muslims were under pressure to change their behaviour 26 said yes, 5 were unsure and 9 said no.

One respondent, a female aged 25 from Canterbury stated that:

I think Muslims should change their behaviour as a result of the culture they have chosen to submerge themselves into. If

they were more accepting of the culture around them then
people most likely will be more accepting of them.

This admonition of Muslim exclusivism however is the only one in response to this question.

Various examples of the types of change were given and included acts that effectively reduced or erased Muslim visibility, as individuals, but also as a community of confession, or as individual actors or groupings in political and civil society arenas:

1. Muting of beliefs, whether religious or political
2. Removing visible expression of faith e.g. shaving off beards or removing hijab and niqab
3. Denunciation of terrorism, 'extremism' and various acts that are unrelated to Muslims either as individuals or communities
4. The requirement to perform or be vocal in the performance of normative citizenship. This in particular seems to have been picked us as pressure on those Muslims in leadership positions
5. Socialising to supposed majority norms
6. Assimilating to supposed cultural norms e.g. consuming alcohol

Additionally many responses intimated or stated clearly that a climate of fear amongst Muslims is already, or will in the future, prevail causing insularity and more of the above.

Finally, the political pressures are seen as a way to socially engineer the acceptance of a depoliticised and secular 'Islam' amongst Muslims in the UK.

The muting that the expectations of Muslims to hide their beliefs and views, is a form of violence and bodes ill for the future.

we have to denounce 'terrorist activities' etc
it feels like we are all under a permanent 'mcarthy trial' big
brother is watching and we better watch out

Female, 25, London

Ahmed (2011) argues that the counter-terrorism laws foster Islamophobia in two ways, firstly in the rise of general discrimination against Muslims, but secondly by requiring Muslims to distance themselves from Islamic practice.

> *I hear some have. They try not to speak to much about religion when around non Muslims*
>
> Female, 21, Hertfordshire

> *I think that many people will become increasingly insular and isolated out of fear.*
>
> Female, 24, Edinburgh

This pressure was seen to extend to civil society figures as well as grassroots figures.

> *We are divided into 'good Muslims, i.e. 'moderate/liberal/'secular' Muslims who are happy to conform to the status quo, and 'bad Muslims' i.e. conservative/ultra-conservative/radical Muslims who either pose a constant terrorist threat to British society or constantly ruffle feathers because of their refusal to 'integrate' and 'adapt' to British culture.*
>
> Female, 31, Birmingham

> *To embrace an assimilationist, secularized, depoliticised understanding of Islam.*
>
> Male, 45, London

> *I think Muslims in certain positions may feel pressured to behave 'more moderately' or pressured to behave in a way that's more Westernised. For example, the 'Happy Muslims' video; from an Islamic perspective I don't think a video as such pertains to what Islam is. It was disappointing to see renown faces such as Myriam Francois Cerrah, Raheem Jung and Adam Deen partaking in the video. Muslims should be able to express their happiness in a way that is permissible. Some people may view this as a radical opinion and will tell me to 'lighten up'. However*

Muslims should ask themselves: would Prophet Mohammad (peace and blessings be upon him) applaud at the video? I am sure the intention was a good and positive one however it seemed to me as an attempt to show people how liberal Muslims are.

Female, 22, London

Indeed they do the most recent and ludicrous example of it was the happy Muslim video clip.

Male, 35, Durham

The need to prove one's worthiness and liberal stance at the civil society level extends at the grassroots level to the pressure to reduce visible Muslimness whether that is through dress or through the discussion of views deemed 'Muslim' be they political or religious:

...be less visibly muslim

Female, 44, Edinburgh

As a fellow Muslim I took of my hijab because I was bullied so much. Till this day I regret doing so but in such a racist environment I find it very difficult to even fit in with the colour of my skin

Female, 21, Bishops Stortford

I would hate to think that Muslims living in the UK try to "integrate" by giving up their religious traditions and copying the "West" but I fear it may be happening. the pressure must be enormous and growing all the time.

Female, 64 (Not Muslim)

Stop from growing beard and not sticking to prayer times.

Male, 71, Durham

I do sometimes feel that Muslims are forced to assimilate and cannot simply be themselves as they wish. Examples of this include outward appearance but also the need to apologise for something I have not done/have had nothing to do with.

Female, 22, London

*Yes, stop wearing the niqaab/ head scarf/ cut the beards.
Stop voicing your concerns/ issues*

Female, 44, Edinburgh

*Women stop observing Hijab/Islamic dress code. So do men
as well as clean shaving their beards. Muslims stay at home
when possible and don't go out due to fear. Some Muslims
become less practising and go to pubs and clubs to fit in.
Muslims be become apologetic for even existing, being in
Britain even though they may have been born here, been a
productive member of society and their country of ethnicity
had its wealthy and natural resources stolen from Britain
and the people used as soldiers to fight for Britain in World
War 2 and their parents came to Britain to help the
economy due to massive skills shortage!*

Male, Rainham

*Some think they have to confirm or feel that they may not
be able to express their beliefs.*

Male, 39, London

The slide from the display of liberal values to the
performance of Britishness comes in increasingly direct forms.
In early October 2014, the front page of the UK's best-selling
newspaper The Sun, pictured the profile photograph of a
supposedly Muslim young woman wearing a union flag hijab
under the campaigning headline 'Unite against ISIS'.

'Unite against ISIS'

Alongside the headline, The Sun included inside its edition
a cut-out flag with 'United Against ISIS' written on it to be
displayed in windows across the national. According to Malik (8
October 2014):

"The implications of this stunt are clear. Even though the
editors shoehorned in an appeal to "Brits of all faiths", this can
only be a figleaf as the image clearly screams "Muslims".

"What the Sun says is that Muslims have to prove their British credentials with a display of loyalty – that their Britishness is not taken for granted until they do so. You are a shady Muslim first, and a citizen second. It may be masquerading as a jolly exercise in solidarity of the "Keep calm and carry on" type. But the subtext is pretty clear: "We are united against IS, Are they?"

"The most charitable explanation is that this is just a well-meaning campaign that was badly implemented. But then ask yourself, who is it for exactly? Does the Sun genuinely think Muslims are going to react to this by scrambling to prove that they are not Isis-huggers and harbourers; by continuously and never-endingly condemning all random acts of Islamic extremism everywhere? More probably, it is a way to sneak into plain sight an increasingly popular view that Muslims are an enemy within, and, as Islamic State allegedly reaches British shores, the idea that British Muslims are their allies.

"In any case, if the past few months are anything to go by, people are deaf to Muslim condemnation of extremism… that's not what this is about. It's a hollow demand that is a proxy for bigotry. It is the politically correct way of airing a suspicion that all Muslims are basically terrorist sympathisers, not a genuine request.

"Which is not to say that Muslims should not condemn Islamic State. Many do, and have. But to have it demanded of you is different. And to have it linked to your nationality via the Union Jack is a threat. It attaches conditions to that nationality that others do not have to meet.

"So, this "campaign" is disingenuous and pointless. But it is also dangerously counterproductive. It represents yet another chapter in the mainstreaming of intolerance. It increases the feeling of being under siege, of Muslims' religion rendering their loyalties suspect. These messages are no longer subliminal but overt. Imagine being subjected to this every single day, having national institutions arch a sceptical eyebrow at you just for being Muslim – whatever that might mean to you."

Thus threat comes via the front-page of national newspapers. Ameli et. al, (2004 b and 2007) highlighted the prevalence of anti-Muslim front pages even a decade ago, in particular The Daily Express, which had a particular fetish for burqa related stories. Again we see then and now a criminal association being made with female Muslim dress.

Being forced to socialise with assumed majority norms

Yes we are expected to act and live like English people and forget our religious values which do not fit with their values.

Male, 34, Bradford

Young Muslims often feel pressured to 'integrate' by abandoning their Islamic values and practices and adopting the local culture, often of crime, alcohol drugs, or money. Older ones too can remain hostile or skeptical towards Islam for the rest of their lives.

Female, 68, London

Muslims feel that they cannot practise their faith as they choose for fear of being labelled an extremist, eg: long beard, niqaab,not shaking hands of opposite sex etc

Female, 39, London

I feel nervous when I need to pray discretely in public eg in motorway stations in case I am attacked I do not get involved In political discussions in case I am misunderstood

Female, 37, Watford

Muslims are constantly under pressure to conform to British ideals. They feel the need to condemn acts of terrorism supposedly committed in the name of Islam. They feel the need to publicly confirm, "yes, Britain is a Christian country". They feel the need to show their support for symbols of British patriotism such as the

Remembrance Day poppy and royal family, without questioning the moral implications of either. The feel the need to condemn/criticise/dismiss the practice of wearing niqab because in fact "it isn't an Islamic requirement" and "it further alienates Muslim women" and "it prohibits communication and integration" and "it denies Muslim women opportunities".

Female, 31, Birmingham

There is a need for Muslims to defend themselves, prove themselves the 'good' type of Muslim, to mitigate their Muslim-ness...

Female, 31, London

It appears from the findings that Muslims in the UK feel targeted by media and political institutions, which in their understanding contribute heavily towards a deteriorating climate of fear, a rise in far-right groups and a rise of anti-Muslim racism per se. As a result they feel pressured to modify their behaviour and in some instances feel that this is the deliberate goal of government and the political classes. This latter feeling is something more evident in 2014 than it was in 2010, when the operation of institutional (and what was understood to be often ignorant) reproduction of stereotypes by the media was seen to be the primary cause of an anti-Muslim culture.

The findings above suggest that there has been an alarming rise in the level of hate experiences, which suggests that most Muslims now feel they are hated, and that something akin to the feeling of being a 'hated society' as was found in the survey sample in France in the same period (Ameli et. al., 2012) can now be found in the UK.

Part of the feeling of being a 'hated society' comes from the push of government to socially engineer a Muslim condition, and that seems to be a major outcome of the hate environment, with respondents largely agreeing that Muslims in the current climate feel the need to modify their behaviour out of pressure and fear. This situation is clearly a violation of the norms and demands of citizenship, and a violation of minority rights, whether envisaged as individual or communal (Ameli et. al. 2006b). The following chapter looks at ways to overcome what seems to be a crisis of citizenship and the social contract set against the deliberate undermining of the notion of the multicultural and plural in favour of monocultural hegemony and hierarchical social structuring.

Chapter 6

Discussion and Recommendations: Hopelessness or Beginning Something Good

This chapter will set out recommendations from respondents, as well as the authors' own recommendations based on this, previous and various projects.

Respondents were asked how they felt the problem of Islamophobia could be dealt with.

They identified 11 key possibilities:

1. Education
2. The need for Muslims to condemn atrocities
3. Better public relations and awareness raising
4. Integration
5. Prayer, calling to Islam, love, Islamic behaviour and positivity
6. Action from the government and law enforcement
7. Action from the media
8. Action from wider society
9. Action from other actors
10. Dialogue
11. Nothing can be done

However certain cross-cutting themes come through. Whether railing against state or social injustice or calling for Muslim introspection, respondents conveyed a sense of fear, and a type of betrayal of loyalty. Very few respondents claim any sort of separatist identity, but rather felt that despite their desire and / or right to belong they were rejected by society and / or state.

To this end, one of the categories that is identified is one that didn't arise in the previous study on the UK and that is the category of hopelessness or near hopelessness that the situation can improve. This new expression of essentially raw emotion finds its opposite in the expression of hope in prayer, Islamic behaviour, love and positivity. Whilst the latter has been a feature of the findings of all previous surveys in this project, these suggestions are now being made with a sense of it being the right thing to do rather than something that will ultimately be successful. Responses in previous surveys e.g. Ameli et. al, 2004a and 2007 find respondents stating that e.g. outreach to government and media can help solve the problem, whereas now, the idea of outreach is as much about self-preservation or simply the need to do something regardless of and maybe despite the outcome. It would be wrong to characterise these responses as cynical; however they are in many cases the product of bad experiences.

Being truly known - education, education, education (and some PR) (and some dialogue and condemnation)

As with previous research in this project where respondents were asked this question (see Ameli et. al., 2011 for the UK), education was often cited, sometimes as simply a one word answer. When expressed as such it is hard to see whether what is meant is education of the state, the masses or of Muslims. However the bulk of responses indicated that a general education programme, often tied with public awareness campaigns was the route to follow.

A bottom up and top down approach.
- teaching children at a young age the importance of diversity
-teaching children the components of the religion (not with the intention to convert but with the intention to educate and teach that Islam is about peace and to counter the stereotypes)
- teach young children about stereotypes and how to find out if it's true or not
- have commercials that show Islam in a positive, peaceful light
- use humour in commercials to address stereotypes
- have people in Parliament speak positive about Muslims
- have awareness campaigns where the general public are encouraged to ask questions free of judgement
                                    Female, 44, Edinburgh

Education and campaigns to raise awareness
Male, 40, Kuala Lumpur

The role of government and its agencies in hampering the process of education was also remarked upon

> *Education is the only way that I can see (but that is a problem under the present government). And some sort of - we cannot say "control" of the Media but some sort of way of getting the Media to see that positive and accurate reporting are a responsibility of a free press! I have no present knowledge of how the legal and penal system's operate in relation to Muslims these days I fear they will not be fair.*
>
> Female, 64 (Not Muslim)

> *"Educating the people on mass [sic] Islam is to promote peace only.*
> *To crack down on those who promote religious hatred and stop them straight away instead of waiting for something g bad to happen."*
>
> Male, 34, Bradford

> *"Educating the public through the media and having programmes which focus on muslims that contribute to the country eg doctors professors teachers bankers lawyers"*
> Female, 37, Watford

The desire to be known in one's true sense by others in society, rather than through the mediated gaze of media or government discourse resonates with the quantitative findings which have found (as demonstrated above) both discourses to be troubling and the cause of Islamophobia.

This desire to be known is however a double-edged sword and can descend into the type of 'Unite Against ISIS' campaign proposed by The Sun i.e. to extract loud denunciations from Muslims as the condition of their acceptance in society. Just as Malik (8 October 2008) decried the demand, so too should there be concern when Muslims themselves call for this action as a prerequisite for societal acceptance and inclusion:

again, muslims should condemn any hate against any religion or group

Female, 50, Surrey

Through respect, learning, acquiring knowledge for the 'other'. Being kind, tolerant and willing to have a peaceful conversation.

Male, 30, London

Quit acting like misguided CLOWNS / heretics and people may like treat you like such...

Male, 47, Atlanta

As Malik says, this is not to criticise Muslims for condemning ISIS but to understand that the discourse of condemnation is an exclusionary one, and that by fulfilling the demand of condemnation, Muslims will still not be included but will be simply reinforcing their connection to something which they claim not to be connected with.

The idea of dialogue as part of the educative process is also raised and again carries with it the need for self-reflection but also the idea that condemnation is required to obviate the problems caused by demonised discourse:

Through challenging such views via well backed intellectual debates and discussions, but also a stronger sense of unity amongst those who follow the Islam we know to be peaceful where we can live side by side in whatever society, even if it means publicly banishing/condemning those who seemingly create their own ideologies and allegedly represent Islam.

Male, 18, Batley

Recommendation: More education and interfaith programmes from Muslim community groups

Any number of education programmes run by Muslim communities can be looked to as examples of how Muslims try to reach out. There have recently been local events that have become high profile for a variety of reasons. Two are noted here: one as a successful example of emergency outreach, and another as a salutary reminder of the authors' argument that such events, even when conducted on a large scale can be easily maligned when powerful actors become involved, reinforcing stereotypes and mutedness (Ameli et. al, 2006b).

Tea, biscuits, football, mosques and the EDL

In May 2013, six protestors arrived outside a Yorkshire mosque after an EDL forum called for a demonstration outside. Members of the mosque came outside offering tea and biscuits and inviting the protestors to come inside and also to join a game of football, which was accepted.

The action was loudly hailed as a great moment where huge tension was diffused.

According to the BBC (13 May 2013):

"Father Tim Jones, who went to the Bull Lane mosque, which is situated in his parish, said: "I've always known they were intelligent and compassionate people and I think this has demonstrated the extent to which they are people of courage - certainly physical courage and also a high degree of moral courage.

"I think the world can learn from what happened outside that ramshackle little mosque on Sunday."

> Hull Road ward councillor Neil Barnes said it had been a "proud moment for York".
>
> He said: "I don't think I'll ever forget the day that the York Mosque tackled anger and hatred with peace and warmth - and I won't forget the sight of a Muslim offering a protester tea and biscuits with absolute sincerity.""

More structured events with national reach include the Big Iftaar and Visit My Mosque Day. The former has seen key political figures take part in iftaar (breaking of fast) events across the UK in Ramadan, where local Muslim communities share their meal with members of the wider community. The latter was designed by the Muslim Council of Britain as 'a nationwide initiative...., in order to "reach out to fellow Britons following tensions around terrorism"' (Guardian, 2 February 2015). Events at the 2015 Visit My Mosque day in South London took a damaging turn after Channel 4 News presenter Cathy Newman, tweeted that she had been turned away from the South London Islamic Centre, as she believed, because she was a woman.

In looking at the MCB's description of the motivation for the event, as laudable as the event is, such wording arguably reinforces what Malik (8 October 2015) describes as the demand. Whilst Muslims rightly want to open their doors in an attempt to be known for who they really are, the process of opening these doors takes place in the context of a poisonous discourse that still holds sway during the event itself. Thus the event is still mediated by that discourse as 'Ushergate' (as the Cathy Newman event became colloquially known) exposed.

'Ushergate'

Having tweeted acerbically that she was turned away from the mosque because of her gender and 'ushered out' by a man, Newman went on to describe the warm welcome she received at a nearby mosque. During the course of the reporting of the incident (see e.g. Guardian, 2 February 2015) it was claimed that the mosque she entered was the wrong mosque and was not taking part in the event and was male only. In its initial defence the mosque offered profuse apologies and tried to clarify that it was not a men only mosque but that it had found out about the event too late to do anything for it. A spokesperson for the mosque then stated that he was sure she had been accosted by one of the 60% of the congregation who were Somali, "about half of whom do not speak English" and that some misunderstanding had ensued. The mosque spokesperson offered an unreserved apology and swore a full investigation would take place.

Demonised media coverage ensued, with the mosque in particular and Muslims in general being called out for anti-women practices. The mosque where Newman ended up also tweeted how appalling her treatment was, thus performing the function of good / liberal / acceptable Muslim, the South London Islamic Centre itself apologised without investigating and indeed blamed the incident on the idea of an unknown Somali male worshipper who cannot speak English, thus blaming an 'otherised' Muslim and creating once more a hierarchy of good Muslim citizen vs bad.

None of the apologia however prevented numerous threats and attacks on the mosques, including a death threat that even the police took seriously.

The investigation by the mosque however revealed that the incident as described by Newman did not actually take place. CCTV footage showed Newman leaving the centre without anyone else and also of her being given direction by a worshipper inside. The worshipper (not of Somali heritage and an English speaker) stated he had thought she was lost and tried to give her directions. As this news broke, some media outlets began reporting that the mosque was in fact open to everyone whether male or female and had good community links. Whilst this again conforms to ideas of good / bad Muslim, it is clear that there was only an interest in the nature of the centre once the centre itself had exposed the story against them.

The tweets of Cathy Newman were enough for the press and indeed the mosque itself, for her version of events, to be taken for granted. It took Newman and the editor of Channel 4 News a further week to apologise for 'Ushergate', however it appears that no sanction against Newman was taken by Channel 4 News. In a letter expressing disappointment at Newman's tweets the mosque stated:

> "In her apology, Cathy Newman laments her 'poorly chosen' words, which she believes 'caused offence'. We were not offended by her choice of words. We were deeply disappointed that her instinctive reaction to a confusing episode was to assume that she was being mistreated by Muslim men on account of her gender. It was this assumption, exacerbated by the hyperbole in her tweets, that caused the maelstrom of abuse and national controversy our Centre was subjected to. These were not merely poorly chosen words - they painted a picture of an incident that never occurred.
>
> "If any good can possibly come out of this incident, we hope that it will remind public figures of the need to be judicious not just in the language they use, but in considering how their view of our faith is tainted by the fog of Islamophobia, which is increasingly clouding our national dialogue." (Guardian, 8 February 2015)

There is a genuine and worthy call out from respondents for more events of large and small scale, as well as dialogue and other public awareness campaigns, with which the authors concur repeatedly (see Ameli and Merali, 2004a and Ameli et. al. 2004b). The authors argue that these measures cannot be the sole or main plank of any concerted effort to tackle Islamophobia.

If, as the authors argue, condemnation of practices or extreme groups, or performance of citizenship, are not to be called upon, how can there be further education?

As many respondents have highlighted, there has to be action from outside the Muslim community, from the centres of power, to change discourse. As one respondent argues above, it has to come from 'top down'.

Recommendation: Media Regulation and Media Self-Renewal

Regulation

This recommendation comes after the Leveson Enquiry Report (2012) called for the setting up of more a powerful independent press watchdog. Whilst the new watchdog, the Independent Press Standards Organisation, is indeed more powerful and has the ability to fine up to 1% of a newspaper's turnover (capped at £1million) and has interventionist investigatory powers, newspapers are free to opt out of the system.

As with its predecessor, the code it implements is vague if not exclusionary on issues of generalised demonisation. An individual who is maligned can bring a case, but what about the issues of stereotyping, encoded ideas of inferiority etc.?

The issue of dealing with structural inequalities and systemic racist discourse remains untouched, with regulatory mechanisms, such as they are, still working within the framework of a post-racial society, as opposed to dealing with issues of institutional racism.

This nuanced understanding is reflected in respondents' ideas on what can be done.

Education, accountability of the Media and Policy makers.
Male, 37, London

Through a more inclusive approach to reporting by the media
Female, 25, Nottingham

A positive image of Muslims A fair portrayal of Muslims...
A more equal balanced view of Muslims in the media.
STOP equating Muslims with terrorisms
Female, 44, Edinburgh

Media needs to have a more balanced view of Islam and the teachings behind it, knowledge is power
Female, 24, London

Education!! The news need to do their research properly. Stop highlighting terrorist attacks to be all Muslims
Female, 21, Bishops Stortford

Self-Renewal

Ameli et. al, (2007, 2012) have called for a sea change in the UK media that can only be internally driven. This is not simply a question of equal opportunities in terms of Muslim representation with the media as professionals. This involves a cultural shift in the thinking of media institutions.

Ameli et al (2007) argued with regard to the UK, a sea change in reporting and cultural activity has already transformed media practice on issues of anti-Semitism, anti-Catholic prejudice and sexuality, among other prejudices:

> "However... many would argue that the struggle with regard to racism is far from won, anti-Muslim prejudice – the specificity of Islamophobic representation – has become a recognisable theme in representation that has yet to result in ethical reevaluation at any serious level.
> "From a human rights perspective this is disappointing

and potentially disastrous. Demonised representation is one of the deepest and most effective anti-human rights practices, as it has the potential not just to libel or demonise a particular person, but it can demonise all members of the represented community e.g. all Muslims or all British Muslims. The potential for societal discord as a result is clear and as the research of this series shows, is in part understood to be having serious repercussions on the everyday lives of minorities, particularly Muslim minorities..."

Writing at the present time and post 2011 riots and 2015 general election, the authors raise concerns that rather than there being any move towards a cultural shift in the way Muslims are discursively represented, there has been a resurgence of anti-Semitic (see Chapter 2 above) and anti-Black racist discourse (Merali, 2016 forthcoming).

The media's role as an engine of hate practice has clearly been defined by respondents. The authors cite here adapted recommendations from previous work to media, but also other actors in terms of dealing with the issues raised by media (Ameli et. al. 2013 and Ameli and Merali, 2014).

Recommendation: Denunciation

Organisations that work on issues of anti-racism, community cohesion, faith relations and human rights need to be prepared to take a much stronger stand in speaking out against these ways of thinking and publicly denounce those who adopt such a discourse, even if, as is increasingly the case, those who do so are speaking from a position of sound 'liberal' or 'left-wing' credentials (Kundnani, cited in Ameli et al., 2007:94). Cases in point relate not only to the operation of stereotypes and misrepresentation in news media print, audio/visual and digital, but also the reproduction of demonised discourse in film and literature. Critiques of demonised discourse cannot exist in academia alone, and the implications of demonised representations of peoples and countries by filmmakers and writers perceived to be progressive must be denounced.

Recommendation: Community alliances

There ought to be stronger relationships between Muslim organisations... and groups that have campaigned against racism and prejudice in the media. Although such alliances will present challenges to both parties, they are a prerequisite to bringing about change (Kundnani cited in Ameli et al. 2007:94). This goes without saying, but much can be learned from past and ongoing campaigns.

Recommendation: Monitoring of Demonised Representation in the Media

This can and must work on a variety of levels, including in academic institutions, by community organisations and major civil society organisations (perhaps in partnership) and by media outlets themselves. This monitoring process should be done in earnest with a view to assessing the levels and ways Muslims are demonised in order to avoid innocent and negligent repetition of such tropes. As Joseph and D'Harlingue (2012), in their study on the Wall Street Journal's Op-eds, point out: "[G]iven the power of these representations on other fields, such as politics, we suggest that the WSJ, whether inadvertently or intentionally (investigating intentionality is not our subject), contributes to the demonization of Islam and Muslims. This is not an exercise in identifying what the WSJ "got wrong." Rather, the argument is that the paper's structure of representation participates in and contributes toward the production of politics, policy, rights, and citizenship."

This reference to Joseph and D'Harlingue is pertinent in particular (as this was their focus) to the writings of the commentariat. It can have wider application to 'simple' reporting e.g. in the case of Trojan Horse / Hoax, or the initial reports into 'Ushergate'.

Monitoring needs to work towards identifying how to transform that structure from one that participates in oppression to one that challenges it. While the initial onus of this must be on broadcasters and those responsible for media representation of Muslims, government needs to be involved in this process, commissioning studies if necessary or facilitating the requisite debate around alienation and the impact of media on the process, in the hope that this will generate more than just a superficial self-analysis by media producers (Ameli et al., 2007).

Recommendation: Community agitation for a fair media

Many such projects already exist, and the authors emphasise that the following actions: writing letters of complaint, letters to the editor, submitting alternative opinion pieces and such like, are essential components of this process. However, the authors contextualise such action as important thus:

• To foster a feeling of confidence among the community.
• To empower the community and its members to interact and protest at a time when immense pressure is put on Muslims and wider dissident voices to be silent.
• To ensure that media producers are aware that they are under scrutiny and that they are failing to meet the standards expected of them.

At the same time, it is important that community groups and organisations that run such campaigns also become familiar with and raise awareness of the structural issues that surround the media and its problematic role. They must not inadvertently foster an idea that the media is structurally sound and it is solely the lack of Muslim voices or interaction with the media that causes misrepresentation of Muslims to occur.

A related recommendation to civil society is to interact and seek training from organisations and academics that have a shared understanding about the structural issues involved. It is also important that organisations and activists target the way politicians, the judiciary and security and law enforcement agencies use the media.

Self-Renewal: Personnel and Product

In the wake of the Macpherson report's lambasting of institutional racism, the then BBC Director-General Greg Dyke claimed the organisation was 'hideously white'. In 2001 the union Bectu went further and claimed British television was institutionally racist (Doward and Wazir, 25 August, 2002).

The authors, here and previously, argue that this is not simply a question of personnel and ensuring that the faces of media institutions are more diverse. Representation in the media is both an issue of the substance of how and what is reported, whether fictionalised or variously portrayed, and as a matter of the demographic profile of those who work in the media.
As Hoskote (2007 in ed. Merali, 2008) notes:

> "The tendency to reduce Islam's richly variegated tradition to… bigotry … and violence…, the reflex of picturing it as a breeding-ground for fire-breathing *ayatollah* and kamikaze martyrs, obscures the fact that Islam was - for nearly a millennium – a vibrant cultural framework that linked South and West Asia with North Africa and West Europe, synthesising Arab, Greek, Persian, Indian, Turkish, Mongol and Chinese influences. During this millennium, civilization was embodied by the House of Islam (with its emphasis on the illumination of learning, urbane sophistication, social and geographical mobility, and a mercantile economy)…"

That tendency to reduce can only be tackled through serious reassessment of how representation is produced. It is not enough (though much needed) to simply refrain from negative stereotyping. There has to be the enrichment of representation that humanises all subjects, and in the cases of out-groups like Muslims, this can only come from the presentation of the idea of a 'House of Islam' that has historical context and civilisational meaning. As a male respondent from Rainham expressed it:

> ... a proper appreciation [must] be made of Muslim contribution to society and historically in science and fighting for Britain in World War 2.

This does not mean that Muslims and indeed Muslim history must not be challenged or critiqued, but that can only be done when there is (a) multiple levels of representation of the out-group including its histories, as well as (b) the levelling of the playing field in terms of interaction with the media. It is of no use claiming that free speech prevails when media production represents only certain ethnos, religions and class groupings to the exclusion of groups who cannot respond to or create a media with reach and the same audience.

The authors refer to their reference to the US Kerner Report (1967), which will be quoted here in part, which identified the issue of personnel and product. As has been noted elsewhere, at times the issue is portrayed as something that would be remedied if only there were a representative 'amount' of minority faces working within media organisations, without looking at how such measures can simply reproduce the same problem. The Kerner Report's recommendations are used as a basis for this report's recommendations below, in part because they still apply, as Gonzalez and Torres (2011) state, with respect to the subject of racist representation and its impact in general.

The racialisation of Muslims makes these recommendations pertinent to communities like Muslims in the UK (as well as the US, where the authors first cited these in Ameli et. al. 2013). The media needs to:

• (Adapted from Kerner, 1967) Expand coverage of Muslim community affairs and of race and Islamophobia problems through permanent assignment of reporters familiar with the issues around these affairs, and through establishment of more and better links with the Muslim community. The Muslim community is a diverse one, and the media needs to engage with that diversity and not promote or rely on sensationalist or apologetic voices that simply help propagate deeply held negative ideas.

• Integrate Muslims and Muslim activities into all aspects of coverage and content, including newspaper articles and television programming. The news media must publish newspapers and produce programmes that recognise the existence and activities of Muslims as a group within the community and as a part of the larger community (adapted from Kerner, 1967). Ameli et al (2004a and 2007) emphasise the idea that a dual space for minorities is essential for any society to foster a sense of citizenship among minorities. To do this, a space for minorities to call their own is essential and a media that is supported in the conceptual sense by dominant society is essentially a part of that. Likewise, the mainstream media must also show as a norm that Muslims are an integral part of society.

• Recruit more Muslims into journalism and broadcasting and promote those who are qualified to positions of significant responsibility. Recruitment should begin in high schools and continue through college; where necessary, aid for training should be provided.

• Accelerate efforts to ensure accurate and responsible reporting of news concerning Muslims and all minorities through adoption by all news gathering organisations of stringent internal staff guidelines.

• Cooperate in the establishment of and promotion of any existing privately organised and funded independent institute(s) to train and educate journalists in Muslim affairs, recruit and train more Muslim journalists, develop methods for improving police-press relations, review coverage of Muslim related issues, and support continuing research in these fields.

Towards love or broken-heartedness: Can there be change?

Injunctions to pray (make dua) or even to proselytise in some form the tenets of Islam, have been recurring themes in previous research and exist in responses from Muslims in this survey as to how best to deal with the problems being faced. This combined with a need for positivity and positive imaging of Islam, as well as good and Islamic behaviour can be found in many responses.

Anti-Muslim hate cannot be dealt with by spreading more hate and negativity. It should be dealt with how the Prophet Muhammad (pbuh) would have dealt with it. He was a tolerant, loving, gentle and kind-hearted man. His opponents were cruel and unjust to him and instead he prayed for them.
Dua is key.

Female, 22, London

Positive action.

Male, 25+, Glasgow

...personal good examples of Islamic behaviour by Muslims at all levels.

Female, 68, London

.. more initiatives taken by Muslim individuals and organisations themselves to become involved with local governance and be more vocal about their faith as formulating a positive foundation for their identity

Female, 25, Nottingham

we moslems must take the initiative to introduce real islam and gentle teachings to them

Male, 71, London

Through, respect, learning, acquiring knowledge for the 'other'. Being kind, tolerant and willing to have a peaceful conversation.

Male 39, London

Muslims need to start practising what they preach, we talk about love but don't act on it as much as we should.

Female, 24, London

Islam is peace. So, let's cultured and full of glory of Islam. Surely the world will be peaceful.

Male, 47, Jepara

However, these are tempered by a new state of disillusion:

I would have said by the promotion of a better understanding and awareness of Islam but this has not worked. I believe that the govt and media actively nurture anti-Muslim sentiment in Britain

Female, 39, London

I am not hopeful.

Female, 31, Birmingham

*with great difficulty not sure if it can
the people that set the agenda have to much vested interest
in making us the evil cretants that society perceives us as*

Female, 32, London

No solution

Male, 75, London

I think that unfortunately this will always be a problem. You can only try to be the best you can be and educate yourself. Deal with problems as they come along.

Female, 28, Houston

It is hard to focus recommendations that can encompass this range of emotion. Rather the authors seek a recognition from government and media in particular that this range of emotions from Muslims or any other out-group is acceptable. As far back as 2009, IHRC (2009b) submitted to the UK government:

> "IHRC wishes to remind Prime Minister Brown what the UN Special Rapporteur on Freedom of Religion or Belief, Asma Jahangir, said in her report on the UK in 2008: "The Special Rapporteur would like to emphasize that it is not the Government's role to look for the "true voices of Islam" or of any other religion or belief. Since religions or communities of belief are not homogenous entities it seems advisable to acknowledge and take into account the diversity of voices. The Special Rapporteur reiterates that the contents of a religion or belief should be defined by the worshippers themselves ..."

> "Rather than deal with those creatures of Government who will tell it what it wants to hear, the Government should engage with those groups and individuals with whom they may disagree but who will provide them with a more accurate and realistic viewpoint of how it is actually perceived at the grassroots. Over expensive and cosmetic projects may make good press but will not "prevent violent extremism" in any community."

This recognised that even then, (a) there was an intrusive discourse set to socially engineer a 'British Muslim' identity that violates the idea of citizens as free from government control in their religious and political affiliations; and (b) that Muslims were particularly targeted for this treatment.

Recommendation: The reimagining of citizenship and acceptable behaviours

The double standards that Muslims face in their treatment is a recurring theme of this research. From failures to address Islamophobia as a form of racism, to the failure to ban far right rallies or enact laws that effectively protect from discrimination, there is a litany of grievance being expressed, despite the demonisation of Muslim grievance.

Nevertheless, it is also noted that complaints about foreign policy in qualitative responses are reduced compared to previous years, and this begs the question as to whether the climate of fear induced by frequent anti-terror laws and ubiquitous praxis under PREVENT has resulted in more muting of Muslim complaints, beliefs or thoughts.

Whereas hate-filled newspaper inches, twitter feeds and multiple other platforms are justified under the aegis of the so-called British value of 'free speech', critique expressed otherwise by non-Muslims becomes 'dangerous' and in need of silencing if expressed by a Muslim.

This reimagining comes from law, but also government practice. De Menthon (for IHRC, 2013) recommends that:

> "It will be more productive for the government to build trust, and address the needs of the Muslim community in the interest of social justice, rather than through the lens of anti-terrorism.
> "In order to do this, Islamic grass root organizations must be involved in procedures implemented by the government. The government should prioritise addressing Islamophobia and Institutional anti-Muslim discrimination within mainstream agencies such as within central government, local authorities, health services, police and others. This will aid the ideological shift from branding Muslims as 'suspect' towards a

216 Environment of Hate:

cohesive society that tackles the threat of terrorism from a homogenous stand point. This will be more constructive and helpful in the fight against violent extremism and will get Muslims on board as equal partners."

As discussed in Chapter 5, the feeling of being suspect is part of the experience of being a member of a hated society that Muslims report. This feeling is a response to the effects of systemic racism and culture of inferiorisation based on racist assumptions and hierarchies (Grosfoguel, 2013).

The authors reiterate IHRC's (2009a) recommendation to the UK Home Office that:

"What Muslims in Britain do represent is a clarion call for change, in both domestic and foreign policy, a call that as of yet remains unrecognised and unheeded by the government. What is required is a radical re-think of government strategy attempting to deal with the problems facing Muslims in Britain. Keeping foreign policy and the detrimental effects of its anti-terror policies upon British Muslims off the agenda represents a fundamental flaw at the heart of the CONTEST strategy and is evidenced by the engagement of think tanks such as the Quilliam Foundation. It must be accepted, even if it is disliked in some quarters, that Muslims in Britain feel directly connected to the suffering of other Muslims across the world. A denial of this basic fact, based upon the desire to keep foreign policy out of the spotlight, will result only in further and more prominent discrimination against Muslims in Britain caused ostensibly by a misunderstanding and misrepresentation of what they truly stand for and against."

As some respondents noted, the solutions to this need to come from actors external to the Muslim community and cut across paradigms:

By replacing Racism (White Supremacy) with justice through constructive thought, speech and/or action in all major areas of activity included economics, education, entertainment, labour, language, law, politics, religions, sex and war.

Male, 45, London

The first step is to achieve widespread recognition and acknowledgement of the sheer pervasiveness of Islamophobic attitudes. The majority of the British public, as well as academia, seem to treat Islamophobia as a problem of the far-right when it is no such thing. The 2006 Act needs to be amended to provide equal protection for religious and racial minorities. There needs to be greater recognition of the concept of Islamophobia AS RACISM even though 'Islam is not a race'. And general understanding of what does and does not constitute Islamophobia needs to be much-improved, e.g. the term 'Islamist', the racial profiling of Muslims for anti-terrorism initiatives, and constant public hysteria over Muslim practices.

Female, 31, London

Other respondents highlighted the role of academia in working to change the climate through research. A combination of legal sanction against racism, a structural understanding or racism and a cross-cutting social movement to effect serious transformation to attitudes from 'top to bottom' is not so much a recommendation but in many ways a rallying cry.

The question that is begged by these findings is whether there is a listening ear that will respond to this cry. Without partners in the project of social transformation, can Muslims or indeed any out-group effect meaningful social change? In previous sets of recommendations the authors have highlighted the need for institutional partners for any meaningful social change to take place. Effectively the authors have argued that the muted group (Kraemerei, 1998 and Ameli et. al. 2006b) can only gain a voice if those that mute it decide to listen to rather than silence the muted group. This envisioning of the scenario unintentionally reinforces the power dynamic that leaves the muted group powerless, and reliant on the largesse and / or conscience of the powerful that silence it.

In arguing for new alliances, the authors suggest that new thinking is required to find partners to obviate the need for the powerful to act. In other words, can there be a peaceful mobilisation that can wrest social and political change without relying on, being socialised to, or being involved in institutional structures as they exist currently?

At the time of writing, a new leader of the main opposition party in the UK has been elected. A hitherto marginalised figure, not least because of his pro-Palestinian, anti-racist and environmental campaigning, his overwhelming victory has been attributed to the building of a grassroots movement rather than political manoeuvring of the traditional sense. This gives the authors a sense that the call for peaceful mobilisation is a realistic one – though not without challenges – but one which those suffering can look to with hope. The authors conclude with the call for hope over despair – indeed it is an Islamic injunction to believe this. In consciously ending with a 'religious' claim, the authors know they will be inviting criticism, not least the ire of an Islamophobic elite hell bent on silencing any type of 'Muslim' voice.

Bibliography

(2007) Young Black People and the Criminal Justice System, Second Report of Session 2006-07, Volume Two Oral and written evidence. House of Commons. London: The Stationery Office Limited.

(2009 inferred) Antisemitic incidents and threats to Jews arising from Gaza crisis – CST Protecting the Jewish community. [Online] Available at: http://www.ihrc.org.uk/attachments/4274_CST_briefing.pdf

(2009) *Hate Crime Laws, A Practical Guide.* OSCE Office for Democratic Institutions and Human Rights, Poland. PDF.

(2010) *Project Champion: Scrutiny Review into ANPR and CCTV Cameras, A report from Overview and Scrutiny,* Birmingham City Council. PDF.

(2012) *Challenge it, Report it, Stop it: The Government's Plan to Tackle Hate Crime.* HM Government. Home Office. London. PDF.

(2013) *An Overview of Hate Crime in England and Wales.* Home Office, Office for National Statistics and Ministry of Justice. PDF.

(2014) *Challenge It, Report It, Stop It: Delivering the Government's hate crime action plan.* HM Government. Home Office. London. PDF.

(2014) *Challenge It, Report It, Stop It: Delivering the Government's hate crime action plan.* HM Government. PDF.

(2014) *Hate Crime: Should the Current Offences Be Extended?* The Law Commission. Publication available at www.gov.uk/government/publications Accessed: 10.03.2015

(2014) *Hate speech, freedom of expression and freedom of religion: a dialogue.* Foreign and Commonwealth Office. Download at: https://www.gov.uk/government/publications/hate-speech-freedom-of-expression-and-freedom-of-religion-a-dialogue Accessed: 10.03.2015

(2014) Protecting all our children: Tackling Grooming, Safeguarding Children in all Communities. MCB Post-Conference Report 2014. London.

(2014) Statistical News Release: Hate Crimes, England and Wales, 2013/14. Home Office. Download at: https://www.gov.uk/government/statistics/hate-crimes-england-and-wales-2013-to-2014 Accessed: 24.02.2015

(2015) Counter-Terrorism and Security Act Chapter 6. [Online] Available at: http://www.legislation.gov.uk/ukpga/2015/6/contents/enacted

(2015) Extremism in schools: the Trojan Horse affair, Seventh Report of Session 2014-15. Report, together with formal minutes relating to the report. House of Commons Education Committee. London.

(2015) *Muslim community rejects the State's criminalisation of Islam and condemns moves to silence legitimate critique and dissent* (joint statement). Available at: https://jointmuslimstatement.wordpress.com/ Accessed: 16.03.2015

(2015) Muslim Poll, Telephone Fieldwork: 26th January – 20th February 2015. Prepared by ComRes. PDF.

5 Pillars (2014) Muslim wins court case against Transport Police for unlawful "terror" arrest [Online] Available at: http://5pillarsuk.com/video/muslim-wins-court-case-against-transport-police-forunlawful-terror-arrest/

5Pillars (2015) Poll: One in three Londoners feel "uncomfortable" about the Muslim mayor. [Online] Available at: http://5pillarsuk.com/2015/08/13/poll-one-in-three-londoners-feel-uncomfortable-about-muslim-mayor/

5Pillars (2015) Poll: Over 50% of Brits view Islam as threat to UK. [Online] Available at: http://5pillarsuk.com/2015/07/06/poll-over-50-of-brits-view-islam-as-threat-to-uk/ Accessed: 07.07.2015

5Pillarz (2014) Bolton men fined £600 for threatening to "torch" and "blow up" new mosque. [Online] Available at: http://www.5pillarz.com/2014/12/06/bolton-men-fined-only-600-for-threatening-to-torch-and-blow-up-mosque-on-facebook / Accessed: 06.12.2014

5Pillarz (2014) Man who ripped off a Muslim woman's niqab gets off lightly. [Online] Available at: http://www.5pillarz.com/2014/11/06/man-who-ripped-off-a-muslim-womans-niqab-gets-off-lightly/ Accessed: 06.11.2014

A Paper Bird (2015) Gay hanging in Iran: Atrocities and impersonations [Online] Available at: http://paper-bird.net/2015/07/20/gay-hanging-in-iran/ Accessed: 21.07.2015

Adams, D. Halal – Tell It as It Is – British National Party. [Online] Available at: http://www.bnp.org.uk/news/halal-%E2%80%94-tell-it-it Accessed: 23.10.2014

Adams, R. (2014) Inside Park View academy: Religion row school 'is victim of its success' – The Guardian. [Online] Available at: http://www.theguardian.com/education/2014/may/14/inside-park-view-academy-religion-row-school-victim-of-success

Adams, R. (2014a) Education experts voice fury over Ofsted's 'Trojan Horse' schools inquiry – The Guardian. [Online] Available at: http://www.theguardian.com/education/2014/jun/03/education-experts-ofsted-trojan-horse-birmingham-schools Accessed: 14.04.2015

Adams, R. (2014b) Jewish schools complain over 'hostile' Ofsted inspections – The Guardian. [Online] Available at: http://www.theguardian.com/education/2014/oct/14/jewish-schools-complain-ofsted-inspections Accessed: 12.08.2015

Adams, R. (2015) Trojan horse school in Birmingham to be renamed – The Guardian. [Online] Available at: http://www.theguardian.com/education/2015/mar/24/trojan-horse-school-park-view-birmingham-renamed Accessed:

24.03.2015

Afshar, H. (2008). Can I see your hair? Choice, agency and attitudes: the dilemma of faith and feminism for Muslim women who cover, *Ethnic and Racial Studies*, 31:2, 411-427

Afshar, H. (2013). The politics of fear: What does it mean to those who are otherized and feared?. *Ethnic and Racial Studies, 36*, 1, 9-27.

Ahmed, S. (2014) Why I won't be wearing the 'Poppy Hijab' – Media Diversified. [Online] Available at: http://mediadiversified.org/2014/11/05/why-i-wont-be-wearing-the-poppy-hijab/ Accessed: 07.11.2014

Al Jazeera (2014) Is the British media Islamophobic? [Online] Available at: http://www.aljazeera.com/programmes/listeningpost/2014/06/british-media-islamophobic-201461415613648985.html Accessed: 22.10.2014

Allen, C. (2014) The poppy hijab is just Islamophobia with a floral motif – The Conversation. [Online] Available at: https://theconversation.com/the-poppy-hijab-is-just-islamophobia-with-a-floral-motif-33692 Accessed: 08.11.2014

Ameli, S. R. (2011) *Why the U.S. is following xenophobia?* Captured November 6, 2011 from http://farsi.khamenei.ir/others-note?id=17680 Accessed: 06.11.2011

Ameli, S. R. Merali, A. and Shahghasemi, E. (2012). *France and the Hated Society*. Wembley: Islamic Human Rights Commission.

Ameli, S. R., & Faridi, B., & Lindahl, K., & Merali, A. (2006). *Law & British Muslims: Domination of the majority or process of balance?*. Wembley: Islamic Human Rights Commission.

Ameli, S. R., Azam, A., Merali, A., & Islamic Human Rights Commission (Great Britain). (2005). *British Muslims' expectations of the government: Secular or Islamic? What schools do British Muslims want for their children?*. Wembley: Islamic Human Rights Commission.

Ameli, S. R., Elahi, M. & Merali, A. (2004). *Social discrimination: Across the Muslim divide. British Muslims' expectations of the government*, v. 2. Wembley: Islamic Human Rights Commission.

Ameli, S. R., Merali, A. (2006). *Hijab, meaning, identity, otherization and politics: British Muslim women.* Wembley: Islamic Human Rights Commission.

Ameli, S. R., Mohseni, E. & Merali, A. (2013). *Once Upon a Hatred: Anti-muslim Experiences in the USA.* Wembley: Islamic Human Rights Commission.

Ameli, S. R., Mohseni, E., Shahghasemi, E., Rahimpour, M. (2011). *Getting the message: The recurrence of hate crimes in the UK.* Wembley: Islamic Human Rights Commission.

American Civil Liberties Union of New Jersey (2010) *ACLU Backgrounder on Body Scanners and "Virtual Strip Searches".* PDF.

Amnesty International (2012) *Europe: Choice and prejudice: A summary: Discrimination against Muslims in Europe.* https://www.amnesty.org/en/library/info/EUR01/002/2012/en Accessed: 26.04.2012

Anderson, S. (2014) VIDEO: Dramatic scenes as police come between anti-war demonstrators and EDL group in Portsmouth – Portsmouth News. [Online] Available at: http://www.portsmouth.co.uk/news/defence/video-dramatic-scenes-as-police-come-between-anti-war-demonstrators-and-edl-group-in-portsmouth-1-6229850 Referenced by Pitt, B., same date, Islamophobia Watch

Ansari, F. (2006) *British Anti-Terrorism: A Modern Day Witch-hunt.* Wembley: Islamic Human Rights Commission.

Athwal, H. And Burnett, J. (2014) Investigated or ignored? An analysis of race-related deaths since the Macpherson report. Institute of Race Relations, London.

Awan, I. (2013) *All-Party Parliamentary Group on Islamophobia.* Centre for Applied Criminology, Faculty of Education, Law and Social Sciences. Birmingham City University. PDF.

Awan, I. (2014), Operation 'Trojan Horse': Islamophobia or Extremism?. Political Insight, 5: 38–39. doi: 10.1111/2041-9066.12062

Baldwin, T. and Sherman, J. (2004) Race chief sets it out in black and white – The Times. [Online] Available at: http://www.thetimes.co.uk/tto/news/uk/article1905270.ece

Barker, A. & Lowman, E. B. (2015, inferred) Settler Colonialism – Global Social Theory. [Online] Available at: http://globalsocialtheory.org/concepts/settler-colonialism/ Accessed: 12.08.2015

Barrett, D. (2014) Theresa May: New moves towards time limits for suspects placed on police bail – The Telegraph. [Online] Available at: http://www.telegraph.co.uk/news/politics/11162998/Theresa-May-New-moves-towards-time-limits-for-suspects-placed-on-police-bail.html Accessed: 21.10.2014

BBC News (2010) Muslim woman wearing veril 'refused bus ride' in London. [Online] Available at: http://www.bbc.co.uk/news/uk-england-berkshire-10728912

BBC News (2010) Stop-and-search powers ruled illegal by European court. [Online] Available at: http://news.bbc.co.uk/1/hi/uk/8453878.stm Accessed: 26.08.2014

BBC News (2011) Birmingham Project Champion 'spy' cameras being removed. [Online] Available at: http://www.bbc.co.uk/news/uk-england-birmingham-13331161 Accessed: 01.04.2015

BBC News (2014) A terrorism trial could be heard entirely in secret for the first time in an English court. [Online] Available at: http://www.bbc.co.uk/news/uk-27704747 Accessed: 06.11.2014

BBC News (2014) Boris Johnson: Children at risk of radicalisation should be in care [Online] Available at: http://www.bbc.co.uk/news/uk-26413024

BBC News (2014) Former promising footballer fined £1,000 for

racist Facebook post. [Online] Available at:
http://www.bbc.co.uk/news/uk-scotland-tayside-central-
28354079 Referenced by Pitt, B., same date, Islamophobia Watch

BBC News (2014) Germany 'would accept UK exit from EU' to
protect migration rules [Online] Available at:
http://www.bbc.co.uk/news/uk-29874392 Accessed: 06.11.2014

BBC News (2014) Middlesbrough fan Julie Phillips banned from
every ground. [Online] Available at:
http://www.bbc.co.uk/news/uk-england-tees-30505809
Referenced by Pitt, B., same date, Islamophobia Watch

BBC News (2014) Police question Pastor James McConnell over
Islam remarks [Online] Available at:
http://www.bbc.co.uk/news/uk-northern-ireland-27732156
Accessed: 26.08.2014

BBC News (2015) Coalition row over 'hate preachers' on
university campuses [Online] Available at:
http://www.bbc.co.uk/news/uk-politics-31682016 Accessed:
02.03.2015

BBC News (2015) Muslim ex-police officer criticises Prevent
anti-terror strategy [Online] Available at:
http://www.bbc.co.uk/news/uk-31792238 Accessed:
10.03.2015

BBC News (2015) PM David Cameron defends letter to Islamic
leaders [Online] Available at: http://www.bbc.co.uk/news/uk-
30877447 Accessed: 19.01.2015

BBC News (2015) Tower Hamlets election fraud mayor Lutfur
Rahman removed from office [Online] Available at:
http://www.bbc.co.uk/news/uk-england-london-32428648
Accessed: 18.05.2015

BBC News (2015) What went wrong at Kids Company? [Online]
Available at: http://www.bbc.co.uk/news/uk-33788415

Beech, R. (2015) How obeying the law will no longer be enough
to protect you from the police – Mirror. [Online] Available at:
http://www.mirror.co.uk/usvsth3m/how-obeying-law-no-

longer-5688690

Benjamin, T. (2014) Protest held against planned Astley Bridge mosque – The Bolton News. [Online] Available at: http://www.theboltonnews.co.uk/news/11307989.Protest_held _against_planned_Astley_Bridge_mosque/ Referenced by Pitt, B., same date, Islamophobia Watch

Bennett, R. (2011) Racial integration is a 'two-way street' – The Times. [Online] Available at: http://www.thetimes.co.uk/tto/news/politics/article2903074. ece

Berger, J. (1998) Ways of Seeing in Chandler, D., *Notes on 'The Gaze'*. [Online] Available at: http://visual-memory.co.uk/daniel/Documents/gaze/gaze08.html

Bhambra, G. K. (2015) Reading across the 'Colour Line': Texts, Traditions and Academic Solidarity – The Disorder of Things. [Online] Available at: http://thedisorderofthings.com/2015/02/10/reading-across-the-colour-line-texts-traditions-and-academic-solidarity/ Accessed: 10.02.2015

Blackburn, M. (2015) Yobs spray 'die Muslims die' in graffiti attack – on Sikh temple in Thornaby – Gazette Live. [Online] Available at: http://www.gazettelive.co.uk/news/teesside-news/yobs-spray-die-muslims-die-9985403

Bodi, F. (2014) IHRC response to tackling extremism in the UK, a government report – Islamic Human Rights Commission. [Online] Available at: http://www.ihrc.org.uk/publications/reports/10904-teuk-response Accessed: 20.01.2015

Bodi, F. et al. (2001) *The Oldham Riots*. Wembley: Islamic Human Rights Commission

Boffey, D. (2014) Park View Academy hits back in Trojan horse row – The Guardian. [Online] Available at: **http://www.theguardian.com/education/2014/jun/07/park-view-trojan-horse-staff-pupils-angry** Accessed: 22.06.2014

Brighouse, T. Sir. (2014) Trojan horse affair: five lessons we must learn – The Guardian. [Online] Available at: http://www.theguardian.com/education/2014/jun/17/trojan-horse-affair-five-lessons-help-schools Accessed: 14.04.2015

British National Party. Muslim Grooming Scandal: "White Girls to Blame" Muslim public tells BBC [Online] Available at: http://www.bnp.org.uk/news/muslim-grooming-scandal-%E2%80%9Cwhite-girls-blame%E2%80%9D-muslim-public-tells-bbc Accessed: 22.10.2014

Brown, K. E. & Saeed, T. (2014): *Radicalization and counter-radicalization at British universities: Muslim encounters and alternatives*, Ethnic and Racial Studies

Brown, K. E. (2013) Gender, Prevent and British Muslims – Public Spirit. [Online] Available at: http://www.publicspirit.org.uk/gender-prevent-and-british-muslims-2/ Accessed: 06.11.2014

Cage Prisoners. *Section 44: Stop and Search Code of Practice Consultation.* PDF.

Cameron, D, PM. (2011) "PM's speech at Munich Security Conference." [Online] Available at: http://webarchive.nationalarchives.gov.uk/20130109092234/http://number10.gov.uk/news/pms-speech-at-munich-security-conference/ Speech.

Cameron, D. (2007) What I learnt from my stay with a Muslim family – The Guardian. [Online] Available at: http://www.theguardian.com/commentisfree/2007/may/13/comment.communities

Cameron, D., PM. (2015) "Extremism: PM Speech". Birmingham, UK. Speech. [Online] Available at: https://www.gov.uk/government/speeches/extremism-pm-speech Accessed: 27.07.2015

Cantle, T. (2001) Community Cohesion: A Report of the Independent Review Team. Home Office. PDF.

Carter-Esdale, O. (2015) Britain's Problem with Islam –

Huffington Post. [Online] Available at:
http://www.huffingtonpost.co.uk/oliver-carteresdale/britain-islam_b_6783436.html Accessed: 10.03.2015

Casciani, D. (2014) Analysis: The Prevent strategy and its problems – BBC News. [Online] Available at:
http://www.bbc.co.uk/news/uk-28939555 Accessed: 05.11.2014

Channel 4 (2015) Newcastle 'anti-Islam' march outnumbered by counter demo [Online] Available at:
http://www.channel4.com/news/pegida-newcastle-anti-islam-march-germany-dresden Accessed: 02.03.2015

Choudhury, T. (2007) *The Role of Muslim Identity Politics in Radicalisation (a study in progress)*. London: Department for Communities and Local Government. PDF.

Choudhury, T. and Fenwick, H. (2011). *The Impact of Counter-terrorism Measures on Muslim Communities*. Manchester: Durham University; Equality and Human Rights Commission.

Clark, L. (2014) The 'eight faces' of anti-Muslim trolls on Twitter – Wired. [Online] Available at:
http://www.wired.co.uk/news/archive/2014-07/04/anti-muslim-twitter-trolls-study Accessed: 14.07.2015

Collyer, M et al. (2011) The impact of overseas conflict on UK communities. Joseph Rowntree Foundation.

Conlan, T. (2015) Channel 4's Cathy Newman apologises for 'misunderstanding' over mosque – The Guardian. [Online] Available at:
http://www.theguardian.com/media/2015/feb/06/channel-4-cathy-newman-apologises-mosque Accessed: 09.02.2015

Coolness Of Hind (2014) Rotheram, Race and "White" Paedophilia [Online] Available at:
http://coolnessofhind.wordpress.com/2014/08/29/rotherham-race-and-white-paedophilia/ Accessed: 29.08.2014

Coolness Of Hind (2014) Rotherham, Race and "White" Paedophilia [Online] Available at:
http://coolnessofhind.wordpress.com/2014/08/29/rotherham-

race-and-white-paedophilia/ Accessed: 14.11.2014

Coolnessofhind.wordpress.com (2015) Bradford Trojan Hoax Exposed (4): Bradford Council categorised "religious conservatism" as an "issue" during Trojan Hoax affair – Coolness of Hind. [Online] Available at: https://coolnessofhind.wordpress.com/2015/09/02/bradford-trojan-hoax-exposed-4-bradford-council-categorised-religious-conservatism-as-an-issue-during-trojan-hoax-affair/

Costs of War (2014). Economic Costs Summary: $4.4 Trillion and Counting. Accessed March 10, 2015 from http://costsofwar.org/article/economic-cost-summary.

Costs of War (2015). Direct War Death in Afghanistan, Iraq, and Pakistan October 2001-April 2014. Accessed March 10, 2015 from http://www.costsofwar.org/sites/default/files/Direct%20War%20Death%20Toll%20in%20Iraq,%20Afghanistan%20and%20Pakistan%20since%202001%20to%20April%202014%206%2026.pdf

.

CPS (2014) *Hate crime and crimes against older people report.* The Crown Prosecution Service. PDF.

Cranmer, F. (2015) "Spiritual Influence" and elections updated: Lutfur Rahman found guilty of illegal electoral practices – Law & Religion UK. [Online] Available at: http://www.lawandreligionuk.com/2015/04/23/spiritual-influence-and-elections-updated-lutfur-rahman-found-guilty-of-illegal-electoral-practices/ Accessed: 18.05.2015

Creese, B. and Lader, D. Edited by Smith, K. (2014) Hate Crimes, England and Wales, 2013/14. Home Office Statistical Bulletin. https://www.gov.uk/government/organisations/home-office/about/statistics Accessed: 24.02.2015

Croft, J. (2014) Judges overturn secret terror trial ruling – Financial Times. [Online] Available at: http://www.ft.com/cms/s/0/592c21de-f225-11e3-ac7a-00144feabdc0.html#axzz34nGcNkCQ Accessed: 16.06.2014

Crowther, S. and Sankey, I. *Liberty's response to the Home Office consultation on police powers to stop and search.* Liberty, Protecting Civil Liberties and Promoting Human Rights. 2013. PDF.

Culley, J. (2014) Teacher suspended over alleged comment about Muslim student's headscarf at Sunning Hill Primary School in Daubhill – The Bolton News. [Online] Available at: http://www.theboltonnews.co.uk/news/11471668.Teacher_sus pended_over_alleged_comment_about_Muslim_student_s_hea dscarf/ Referenced by Pitt, B., same date, Islamophobia Watch

Daggett, S. (2010). *Costs of Major U.S. Wars.* CRS Report for Congress: Prepared for Members and Committees of Congress

Daily Mail (2009) 'Kills soldiers' Muslim blogger is back in job as Treasury civil servant [Online] Available at: http://www.dailymail.co.uk/news/article-1199099/Kill-soldiers-Muslim-blogger-job-Treasury-civil-servant.html Accessed: 12.08.2015

Dale, S. (2014) Watch: Peaceful vigil becomes noisy protest in Middlesbrough as UDL members arrived to 'disrupt' it – Gazette Live. [Online] Available at: http://www.gazettelive.co.uk/news/teesside-news/peaceful-vigil-became-noisy-protest-7575211 Referenced by Pitt, B., same date, Islamophobia Watch

Davies, E., Steere, T. And Duell, M. (2014) Pizza Express reveal ALL the chicken they use is halal – but they don't tell customers unless they ask staff – Daily Mail. [Online] Available at: http://www.dailymail.co.uk/news/article-2622052/Pizza-Express-reveal-chicken-use-halal-dont-tell-customers-unless-ask -staff.html Accessed: 23.10.2014

Dearden, L. (2015) David Cameron extremism speech: Read the transcript in full – The Independent. [Online] Available at: http://www.independent.co.uk/news/uk/politics/david-cameron-extremism-speech-read-the-transcript-in-full-10401948. html Accessed: 21.07.2015

Derby Telegraph (2014) Derby shopping row: Tesco defends its policy on advertising Halal meat [Online] Available at:

http://www.derbytelegraph.co.uk/Derby-shopping-row-Tesco-defends-policy/story-23005731-detail/story.html Accessed: 23.10.2014

Dixon, H. (2013) 'Imams promote grooming rings' – The Telegraph. [Online] Available at: http://www.telegraph.co.uk/news/uknews/crime/10061217/Imams-promote-grooming-rings-Muslim-leader-claims.html Accessed: 22.10.2014

Dobson, R. (2014) British Muslims face worst job discrimination of any minority group, according to research – The Independent. [Online] Available at: http://www.independent.co.uk/news/uk/home-news/british-muslims-face-worst-job-discrimination-of-any-minority-group-9893211.html Accessed: 03.12.2014

Dodd, V. (2004) 90% of whites have few or no black friends – The Guardian. [Online] Available at: http://www.theguardian.com/uk/2004/jul/19/race.world Accessed: 14.04.2015

Dodd, V. (2005) Two-thirds of Muslims consider leaving UK – The Guardian. [Online] Available at: http://www.theguardian.com/uk/2005/jul/26/polls.july7 Accessed: 14.04.2015

Dodd, V. (2013) Is child grooming and sexual abuse a race issue? – The Guardian. [Online] Available at: http://www.theguardian.com/uk/2013/may/14/child-grooming-sexual-abuse-race

Dodd, V. (2014) Threat of extremist attack in UK is escalating, say police – The Guardian. [Online] Available at: http://www.theguardian.com/uk-news/2014/oct/17/extremist-attack-threat-escalating-uk-isis-syria Accessed: 14.11.2014

Dodd, V. (2015a) Black and minority ethnic Britons 'worse off' after budget – The Guardian. [Online] Available at: http://www.theguardian.com/society/2015/jul/26/black-minority-ethnic-britons-budget-george-osborne-benefit-cuts?C

MP=EMCNEWEML6619I2 Accessed: 30.07.2015

Dodd, V. (2015b) Jihadi threat requires move into 'private space' of UK Muslims, says police chief – The Guardian. [Online] Available at:
http://www.theguardian.com/world/2015/may/24/jihadi-threat-requires-move-into-private-space-of-uk-muslims-says-police-chief?CMP=share_btn_tw Accessed: 26.05.2015

Dodd, V., Laville, S. and Pidd, H. (2014) Syria crisis: stop your sons joining war, urges Met police – The Guardian. [Online] Available at: http://www.theguardian.com/uk-news/2014/apr/23/sons-war-syria-metropolitan-police

Doward, J. & Wazir, B. (2002) British television accused of institutional racism – The Guardian. [Online] Available at: http://www.theguardian.com/media/2002/aug/25/mediaunions.broadcasting

Doyle, D. (2014) Town centre mosque burgled – Rotherham Advertiser. [Online] Available at:
http://www.rotherhamadvertiser.co.uk/news/96862/town-centre-mosque-burgled.aspx

Echo News (2014) Faith leader defends Islamic centre plan. [Online] Available at: http://www.echo-news.co.uk/news/11441496.Faith_leader_defends_Islamic_centre_plan/ Referenced by Pitt, B., same date, Islamophobia Watch

El Hamel. C. (2002). Muslim Diaspora in Western Europe: The Islamic Headscarf (Hijab), the Media and Muslims' Integration in France. *Citizenship Studies, 6, 3, 293-308.*

El-Enany, N. (2015) Why Muslims can't trust the legal system: The Lutfur Rahman judgement and institutional racism – Critical Legal Thinking. [Online] Available at: http://criticallegalthinking.com/2015/05/16/why-muslims-cant-trust-the-legal-system Accessed: 18.05.2015

Elgot, J. (2015a) Cathy Newman, Channel 4 Presenter, Apologises to Mosque, announces break from Twitter – Huffington Post. [Online] Available at:

http://www.huffingtonpost.co.uk/2015/02/12/cathy-newman-channel-4-mosque_n_6667900.html?1423738315 Accessed: 12.02.2015

Elgot, J. (2015b) Channel 4's Cathy Newman Apologises After CCTV Footage Emerges of Mosque Incident – The Huffington Post. [Online] Available at: http://www.huffingtonpost.co.uk/2015/02/05/cathy-newman-mosque_n_6620026.html Accessed: 09.02.2015

Eliassi, B. (2013). Orientalist Social Work: Cultural Otherization of Muslim Immigrants in Sweden. *Critical Social Work*, 2013 Vol. 14, No. 1.

Ellis-Petersen, H. (2015) Radicalisation play cancelled by theatre after concerns about 'extremist agenda' – The Guardian. [Online] Available at: http://www.theguardian.com/stage/2015/sep/04/islamism-play-withdrawn-by-national-youth-theatre

Emanuel, L. (2014) Man convicted over Islamophobic spitting incident in Cabot Circus, Bristol. [Online] Available at: http://www.bristolpost.co.uk/Man-convicted-Islamophobic-spitting-incident/story-25642813-detail/story.html Referenced by Pitt, B., same date, Islamophobia Watch

Erdagoz, H. (2015) The startling rise of Islamophobia in the West – Daily Sabah. [Online] Available at: http://www.dailysabah.com/opinion/2015/02/18/the-startling-rise-of-islamophobia-in-the-west Accessed: 18.03.2015

Evans, D. (2014) Bristol Muslim woman's shock at being spat at and verbally abused in Cabot Circus – Bristol Post. [Online] Available at: http://www.bristolpost.co.uk/Bristol-Muslim-woman-s-shock-spat-verbally-abused/story-21751194-detail/story.html

Evans, M. (2015) Islamic charity under spotlight after being accused of promoting extremism – The Telegraph. [Online] Available at: http://www.telegraph.co.uk/news/uknews/crime/11418680/Islamic-charity-under-spotlight-after-being-accused-of-promoting-extremism.html Accessed: 19.02.2015

Exeter Express and Echo (2015) Update 2.30pm: Parts of Exeter city centre to remain cordoned-off after suspicious packages found [Online] Available at:
http://www.exeterexpressandecho.co.uk/Update-2-30pm-Parts-Exeter-city-centre-remain/story-26797929-detail/story.html Accessed: 30.06.2015

Express & Star (2015) £100k for two marches: The cost of right-wing protests in the Black Country. [Online] Available at:
http://www.expressandstar.com/news/2015/09/21/100k-for-two-marches-the-cost-of-right-wing-black-country-protests/

Express and Star (2015) Far right marches cost West Midlands Police £415k. [Online] Available at:
http://www.expressandstar.com/news/2015/08/24/far-right-marches-cost-west-midlands-police-415k/

Express and Star (2015) Thousands wage war on planned Dudley mosque. [Online] Available at:
http://www.expressandstar.com/news/2015/05/21/thousands-wage-war-on-planned-dudley-mosque/

Fang, L. (2015) Centre for Security Policy compares Islamic religion to the Plague – The Intercept. [Online] Available at:
https://firstlook.org/theintercept/2015/06/29/star-nbcs-voice-lends-musical-talent-islamophobia-cause Accessed: 07.07.2015

Feldman, R. (2013) When maternity doesn't matter, Dispersing pregnant women seeking asylum. Maternity Action. Refugee Council. PDF.

Fenton, S. (2015a) Exeter city centre evacuated in bomb scare after discovery of two packages 'with wires coming out' – The Independent. [Online] Available at:
http://www.independent.co.uk/news/uk/crime/exeter-city-centre-evacuated-in-bomb-scare-after-discovery-of-two-packages-with-wires-coming-out-10353224.html Accessed: 30.06.2015

Fenton, S. (2015b) Tourist takes selfie in Brighton, arrested on terrorism offences – The Independent. [Online] Available at:

http://www.independent.co.uk/news/uk/crime/tourist-takes-selfie-in-brighton-arrested-on-terrorism-offences-10364287.html Accessed: 07.07.2015

Flanagan, B. (2014) We're as British as fish 'n' chips, UK Muslims tell PM – Al Arabiya. [Online] Available at: http://english.alarabiya.net/en/News/world/2014/06/16/We-re-as-British-as-fish-and-chips-UK-Muslims-tell-Cameron.html Accessed: 16.06.2014

Fraser, D. (2015) Immigration: more or less? – BBC News. [Online] Available at: http://www.bbc.co.uk/news/uk-scotland-scotland-business-31813407 Accessed: 12.03.2015

Fraser, G. (2015) The Lutfur Rahman verdict and the spectre of 'undue spiritual influence' – The Guardian. [Online] Available at: http://www.theguardian.com/commentisfree/2015/apr/29/lutfur-rahman-tower-hamlets-mayor-verdict-undue-spiritual-influence?CMP=share_btn_tw Accessed: 18.05.2015

Gainsborough Standard (2011) Man convicted of abusive behaviour. [Online] Available at: http://www.gainsboroughstandard.co.uk/news/local/man-convicted-of-abusive-behaviour-1-3383859

Gale, R. (2014) Between the city lines. In *Writing the City in British Asian Diasporas* (p. 114-133). Routledge.

Gander, K. (2015) Far right plans march against 'Jewification of Britain' in Stamford Hill – The Independent. [Online] Available at: http://www.independent.co.uk/news/uk/home-news/far-right-plans-march-against-jewification-of-britain-in-stamford-hill-10017859.html Accessed: 12.08.2015

Gani, A. (2015) Mosque 'deeply disappointed' by Cathy Newman's reaction to venue confusion – The Guardian. [Online] Available at: http://www.theguardian.com/media/2015/feb/12/mosque-deeply-disappointed-by-cathy-newmans-reaction

Gardham, D. (2009) Muslim who justified killing British troops

back at Treasury – The Telegraph. [Online] Available at:
http://www.telegraph.co.uk/news/uknews/5810703/Muslim-
who-justified-killing-British-troops-back-at-Treasury.html
Accessed: 12.08.2015

Gardner, F. (2015) Prevent strategy: Is it failing to stop
radicalisation? – BBC News. [Online] Available at:
http://www.bbc.co.uk/news/uk-31756755 Accessed:
10.03.2015

Gilby, N., Ormston R., Parfrement J. And Payne, C. (2011)
*Amplifying the Voice of Muslim Students: Findings from Literature
Review.* Department for Business and Innovation Skills, Research
paper number 55. London. PDF.

Gilligan, A. (2014) Trojan Horse: how The Guardian ignored and
misrepresented evidence of Islamisim is schools – The
Telegraph. [Online] Available at:
http://blogs.telegraph.co.uk/news/andrewgilligan/100275346
/trojan-horse-how-the-guardian-ignored-and-misrepresented-
evidence-of-islamism-in-schools/ Accessed: 16.06.2014

Gilligan, A. (2015) Islamic 'radicals' at the heart of Whitehall –
The Telegraph. [Online] Available at:
http://www.telegraph.co.uk/news/politics/11427370/Islamic-
radicals-at-the-heart-of-Whitehall.html Accessed: 12.08.2015

Gilligan, A. And Mendick, R. (2015) Extremism in Britain: Now
the crackdown is launched – The Telegraph. [Online] Available
at: http://www.telegraph.co.uk/news/uknews/terrorism-in-
the-uk/11457174/Extremism-in-Britain-Now-the-crackdown-is-
launched.html Accessed: 10.03.2015

Glazebrook, D. (2014) The use and abuse of British Muslims –
Russia Today. [Online] Available at: http://rt.com/op-
edge/211499-isis-cameron-muslims-media-abuse/ Accessed:
06.12.2014

Glazebrook, D. (2015) British Values: Real and Imagined –
Counter Punch. [Online] Available at:
http://www.counterpunch.org/2015/04/03/british-values-
real-and-imagined/ Accessed: 08.04.2015

González, J. and Torres, J. (2011) News For All the People: The Epic Story of Race and the American Media. Verso Books.

Goodfellow, M. (2015) "The Migrant Crisis" The real issue here is inconvenienced British holidaymakers – Media Diversified. [Online] Available at: http://mediadiversified.org/2015/07/30/the-migrant-crisis-the-real-issue-here-is-inconvenienced-british-holidaymakers/

Goodhart, D. (2014) Mapping Integration. Demos, London.

Gore, W. (2015) Isis video: We must report the facts – but not be the conduit for gruesome propaganda – The Independent. [Online] Available at: http://www.independent.co.uk/voices/comment/isis-video-we-must-report-the-facts—but-not-be-the-conduit-for-gruesome-propaganda-10021853.html Accessed: 04.02.2015

Government UK (2010a) Home Office Statistical Findings 1/10 (2nd edition), *Racist incidents, England and Wales, 2009/10*. Excel sheet.

Government UK (2010b) Pre-release access to: *Racist incident statistics, England and Wales, 2009/10*. PDF.

Government UK (2011a) Home Office Statistical Findings 1/11, *Racist incidents, England and Wales, 2010/11*. Excel sheet. Download at: https://www.gov.uk/government/statistics/racist-incidents-england-and-wales-2010-to-2011 Accessed: 24.02.2015

Government UK (2011b) Pre-release access to: *Racist incident statistics, England and Wales, 2010/11*. Download at: https://www.gov.uk/government/statistics/racist-incidents-england-and-wales-2010-to-2011 Accessed: 24.02.2015

Government UK (2011c) Statistical News Release: Racist Incidents, England and Wales, 2010/11. [Online] Download at: https://www.gov.uk/government/statistics/racist-incidents-england-and-wales-2010-to-2011 Accessed: 24.02.2015

Government UK (2012a) Statistics: Racist incidents, England and Wales 2011/12. Download at:

https://www.gov.uk/government/publications/racist-incidents-table-england-and-wales-2011-to-2012—2/racist-incidents-england-and-wales-2011-12 Accessed: 24.02.2015

Government UK (2012b) Pre-Release Access to: *Hate Crimes, England and Wales, 2011/12*. Download at:
http://www.homeoffice.gov.uk/publications/science-research-statistics/research-statistics/crime-research/racist-incidents-1112/ Accessed: 24.02.2015

Government UK (2012c) Pre-Release Access to: *Racist Incident Statistics, England and Wales, 2011/12*. Download at:
https://www.gov.uk/government/statistics/racist-incidents-table-england-and-wales-2011-to-2012—2 Accessed: 24.02.2015

Government UK (2012d) Statistical News Release: Hate *Crimes, England and Wales 2011/12*. Download at:
http://www.homeoffice.gov.uk/publications/science-research-statistics/research-statistics/crime-research/racist-incidents-1112/ Accessed: 24.02.2015

Government UK (2012e) Statistical News Release: Racist Incidents, England and Wales, 2011/12. Download at:
https://www.gov.uk/government/publications/racist-incidents-table-england-and-wales-2011-to-2012—2/racist-incidents-england-and-wales-2011-12 Accessed: 24.02.2015

Government UK (2012f) Statistics: Hate crimes, England and Wales 2011 to 2012 [Online] Available at:
https://www.gov.uk/government/publications/hate-crimes-england-and-wales-2011-to-2012—2/hate-crimes-england-and-wales-2011-to-2012 Accessed: 24.02.2015

Government UK (2012g) Table HC.02 Hate crimes in England and Wales by offence type, 2011/12. Download at:
http://www.homeoffice.gov.uk/publications/science-research-statistics/research-statistics/crime-research/racist-incidents-1112/ Accessed: 24.02.2015. Excel sheet.

Government UK (2013a) An Overview of Hate Crime in England and Wales – Appendix Tables. Download at:
https://www.gov.uk/government/statistics/an-overview-of-

hate-crime-in-england-and-wales Accessed: 24.02.2015

Government UK (2013b) Figure 19: Emotional impact of hate crime incident, adults aged 16 and over, 2011/12 and 2012/13 CSEW. Download at: https://www.gov.uk/government/statistics/an-overview-of-hate-crime-in-england-and-wales Accessed: 24.02.2015

Government UK (2013c) Pre-release access to: An Overview of Hate Crime in England and Wales. Download at: https://www.gov.uk/government/statistics/an-overview-of-hate-crime-in-england-and-wales Accessed: 24.02.2015

Government UK (2014a) Pre-release access to: Hate Crimes, England and Wales, 2013/14. Home Office. Download at: https://www.gov.uk/government/statistics/hate-crimes-england-and-wales-2013-to-2014 Accessed: 24.02.2015

Government UK (2014b) Statistical News Release: Hate Crimes, England and Wales, 2013/14. Home Office. https://www.gov.uk/government/statistics/hate-crimes-england-and-wales-2013-to-2014 Accessed: 24.02.2015

Government UK (2015) Half-masting of flags following the death of King Abdullah bin Abdulaziz, King of Saudi Arabia – Gov.uk. [Online] Available at: https://www.gov.uk/government/news/half-masting-of-flags-following-the-death-of-king-abdullah-bin-abdulaziz-king-of-saudi-arabia Accessed: 23.01.2015

Green, C. (2015) Wimbledon 2015: Security tightened for tennis tournament following Tunisia attack – The Independent. [Online] Available at: http://www.independent.co.uk/sport/tennis/wimbledon-2015-security-tightened-for-tennis-tournament-following-tunisia-attack-10352672.html Accessed: 07.07.2015

Grice, A. & Morris, N. (2015) Nigel Farage sparks race row by insisting discrimination in the workplace should be legalised – The Independent. [Online] Available at: http://www.independent.co.uk/news/uk/politics/nigel-farage-sparks-another-race-row-by-calling-for-end-to-out-of-dat

e-legislation-on-discrimination-in-the-workplace-
10102133.html?cmpid=facebook-post Accessed: 13.03.2015

Griffin, B. (2013) Oxford Union Debate: I Will Not Fight For
Queen and Country – Veterans for Peace. [Online] Available at:
http://veteransforpeace.org.uk/2013/i-will-not-fight-for-
queen-and-country/

Griffin, T., Aked, H., Miller D. & Marusek S. (2015) *The Henry
Jackson Society and the Degeneration of British Neoconservatism:
Liberal Interventionism, Islamophobia and the 'War on terror'*. Public
Interest Investigations, London. PDF.

Grosfoguel R., Brittain V., Wilson A., Kundnani, A. et al. (2013)
Exclusive Screening and Q&A: Zone of Non-Being
Guantanamo.
https://www.youtube.com/watch?v=7TgRXHKM2E8

Grosfoguel, R. & Mielants, E. (2006) The Long-Durée
Entanglement Between Islamophobia and Racism in the
Modern/Colonial Capitalist/Patriarchal World System: An
Introduction. *Human Architecture: Journal of the Sociology of Self-
Knowledge*, 5(1), Article 2.

Grosfoguel, R. (2012) Author Evening: Is Islamophobia a form of
racism? Wembley: Islamic Human Rights Commission
https://www.youtube.com/playlist?list=PL0BCSWzStP7Uc7aS
RLspYcXS26GLk1iaz

Grosfoguel, R. (2013) Discussion: Decolonizing Postcolonial
Studies and the Paradigms of Political-Economy. Wembley:
Islamic Human Rights Commission
https://www.youtube.com/watch?v=o0bcqBdg360

Grosfoguel, R. (2014) Discussion: Postcolonial or Decolonial?
Differences and Similarities between Postcolonial Studies and
the Decolonial Perspective. Wembley: Islamic Human Rights
Commission
https://www.youtube.com/watch?v=3WUZTFIkb_4

Groves, J. (2015) UK Muslims helping jihadis, says Cameron:
Communities must stop 'quietly condoning' barbaric ISIS, PM

warns in blunt speech – Daily Mail. [Online] Available at:
http://www.dailymail.co.uk/news/article-3130540/David-
Cameron-says-communities-stop-quietly-condoning-ISIS-blunt-
speech.html

Hafez, F. (2015) From Anti-Semitism to Islamophobia: The
European far right's strategic shift – Discover Society. [Online]
Available at: http://discoversociety.org/2015/07/01/from-anti-
semitism-to-islamophobia-the-european-far-rights-strategic-shif
t/ Accessed: 01.07.2015

Hanna, C. (2014) Northern Ireland's Muslim leaders accept
private apology from North's First Minister after defending
alleged 'anti-Islamic remarks' by Belfast preacher – Inside
Ireland.ie. [Online] Available at:
http://insideireland.ie/2014/05/29/norths-deputy-first-
minister-says-alleged-anti-islamic-remarks-by-belfast-preacher-
on-18th-may-must-be-full-investigated-by-the-psni-106278/
Accessed: 26.08.2014

Harker, J. (2012) This is how racism takes root – The Guardian.
[Online] Available at:
http://www.theguardian.com/commentisfree/2012/jul/22/ho
w-racism-takes-root

Harle, V. (2000). *The enemy with a thousand faces: The tradition of
the other in western political thought and history.* Westport, Conn:
Praeger.

Hashmat, S. (2015) Islam is defined by its followers. We
moderate Muslims must act – The Telegraph. [Online] Available
at: http://www.telegraph.co.uk/women/womens-
life/11332635/Paris-Charlie-Hebdo-massacre-We-moderate-Mu
slims-must-act.html Accessed: 09.01.2015

Hedges, P. (2015) Islamism, Radical Islam, Jihadism: The
Problem of Language and Islamophobia. Nanyang
Technological University, Singapore. PDF.

Hill, D. (2009) Boris Johnson converts to Islam – The Guardian.
[Online] Available at:
http://www.theguardian.com/uk/davehillblog/2009/sep/08/

boris-johnson-islam-east-london-mosque

Hjerm, M. (December 01, 1998). National Identities, National Pride and Xenophobia: A Comparison of Four Western Countries. *Acta Sociologica, 41, 4*, 335-347.

HM Government (2015) *Individuals at risk of being drawn into Serious and Organised Crime – a Prevent Guide.* Strategic Centre for Organised Crime, Office for Security and Counter-Terrorism. PDF.

Hooper, S. (2015a) Schoolboy accused of extremism over pro-Palestine views – Simon Hooper. [Online] Available at: http://simonhooper.com/2015/07/23/schoolboy-accused-of-extremism-over-pro-palestine-views/

Hooper, S. (2015b) Stifling freedom of expression in UK schools – Al Jazeera. [Online] Available at: http://www.aljazeera.com/indepth/features/2015/07/stifling-freedom-expression-uk-schools-150721080612049.html Accessed: 23.07.2015

Hoskote, R. (2007) Retrieving the Far West: Towards a Curatorial Representation of the House of Islam in Merali, S. (2008) *Re-Imagining Asia: A Thousand Years of Separation.* London: SAQI.

Howarth, M. (2014) The changing face of Britain: A child in Birmingham is now more likely to be a Muslim than Christian – Daily Mail. [Online] Available at: http://www.dailymail.co.uk/news/article-2755654/The-changing-face-Britain-A-child-Birmingham-likely-Muslim-Christian.html

Howse, P. (2015) Overlapping 'Trojan Horse' inquiries criticised by MPs – BBC News. [Online] Available at: http://www.bbc.co.uk/news/education-31905704 Accessed: 17.03.2015

Huffington Post (2015) Channel 4's Cathy Newman 'Ushered Out' of London Mosque during Open Day [Online] Available at: http://www.huffingtonpost.co.uk/2015/02/01/visit-my-mosque-open-day-_n_6589114.html Accessed: 10.02.2015

Hunington, S. P. (1993) The Clash of Civilisations? – Foreign Affairs. [Online] Available at: https://www.foreignaffairs.com/articles/united-states/1993-06-01/clash-civilizations

Hussain Y and Bagguley P, 'Funny looks: British Pakistanis' experiences after 7th July 2005', *Ethnic and Racial Studies*, 36.1 (2013), 28-46

Hussain, D. (2014) The Criminalisation of Islam in the British Media – Huffington Post. [Online] Available at: http://www.huffingtonpost.co.uk/dilly-hussain/islamophobia-uk-media_b_6248614.html Accessed: 03.12.2014

ICM Research (2005) Muslim Poll – July 2005. PDF.

iEngage (2009) ENGAGE Exclusive: Azad Ali cleared of wrongdoing by Civil Service investigation [Online] Available at: http://www.iengage.org.uk/archived-news/408-engage-exclusive-azad-ali-cleared-of-wrongdoing-by-civil-service-inves tigation- Accessed: 12.08.2015

Ingles, El. (2011) Our Muslim Troubles: Lesson from Northern Ireland. PDF.

Insted (2014) The Trojan Horse affair in Birmingham [Online] Available at: http://www.insted.co.uk/trojan-horse.pdf

Institute of Race Relations (2014) Investigated or ignored? [Online] Available at: http://www.irr.org.uk/news/investigated-or-ignored/

Ipsos MORI (2007) Race Relations 2006: A Research Study. Commission for Race Equality, London. PDF.

Iqbal, S. (2015) I'm a Muslim woman, Mr Cameron: here's what your radicalisation speech means to me – The Guardian. [Online] Available at: http://www.theguardian.com/commentisfree/2015/jul/24/da vid-cameron-radicalisation-speech-muslim-woman Accessed: 28.07.2015

Islamic Human Rights Commission (2005) IHRC response to: 'Preventing Extremism Together: Places of Worship'. [Online] Available at:
http://www.ihrc.org.uk/publications/briefings/6473-ihrc-response-to-preventing-extremism-together-places-of-worship-
Accessed: 20.01.2015

Islamic Human Rights Commission (2006) You ONLY have the Right to Silence. [Online] Available at:
http://www.ihrc.org.uk/publications/briefings/6420-you-only-have-the-right-to-silence Accessed: 20.01.2015

Islamic Human Rights Commission (2009a) IHRC on CST's response to its briefing. [Online] Available at:
http://www.ihrc.org.uk/publications/briefings/4274-ihrc-on-cst-s-response-to-its-briefing

Islamic Human Rights Commission (2009b) Briefing: UK / Anti-Terrorism – Whose Hearts and Minds? Contest 2 in Context. [Online] Available at:
http://www.ihrc.org.uk/publications/briefings/9085-briefing-uk-anti-terrorism-whose-hearts-and-minds-contest-2-in-context
Accessed: 20.01.2015

Islamic Human Rights Commission (2009c) Preventing Violent Extremism; Response by the Islamic Human Rights Commission to UK Government consultation. [Online] Available at:
http://www.ihrc.org.uk/publications/briefings/9108-preventing-violent-extremism-response-by-the-islamic-human-rights-commission-to-uk-government-consultation-september-2009 Accessed: 20.01.2015

Islamic Human Rights Commission (2010a) IHRC objects to the use of nude body scanners – Open Letter to UK government. [Online] Available at:
http://www.ihrc.org.uk/publications/briefings/9378-ihrc-objects-to-the-use-of-nude-body-scanners-oen-letter-to-uk-government Accessed: 20.01.2015

Islamic Human Rights Commission (2010b) Alert: UK – Oppose Full Body Scanners at UK airports. [Online] Available at:

http://www.ihrc.org.uk/activities/alerts/9379-alert-uk-oppose-full-body-scanners-at-uk-airports Accessed: 20.01.2015

Islamic Human Rights Commission (2010c) Alert: UK – Response to consultation paper on the use of body scanners in an aviation security environment. [Online] Available at: http://www.ihrc.org.uk/activities/alerts/9383-alert-uk-response-to-consultation-paper-on-code-of-practice-for-the-acce ptable-use-of-advanced-imaging-technology-in-an-aviation-security-environment Accessed: 20.01.2015

Islamic Human Rights Commission (2011) Schedule 7: New figures released by Home Office for 2010/11 Overview. [Online] Available at: http://www.ihrc.org.uk/publications/briefings/9897-schedule-7-new-figures-released-by-home-office-for-2010-11-ove rview Accessed: 20.01.2015

Islamic Human Rights Commission (2012) Response to Home Office Consultation Paper: REVIEW OF THE OPERATION OF SCHEDULE 7. [Online] Available at: http://www.ihrc.org.uk/publications/briefings/10372-response-to-home-office-consultation-paper-review-of-the-oper ation-of-schedule-7 Accessed: 20.01.2015

Islamic Human Rights Commission (2013a) Press release: IHRC victory on 'strip-search' body scanners. [Online] Available at: http://www.ihrc.org.uk/activities/press-releases/10411-press-release-ihrc-victory-on-strip-search-body-scanners Accessed: 20.01.2015

Islamic Human Rights Commission (2013b) British Muslims – 'The Suspect Community'? [Online] Available at: http://www.ihrc.org.uk/publications/briefings/10686-british-muslims-the-suspect-community Accessed: 20.01.2015

Islamic Human Rights Commission (2013c) The amendments to Schedule 7 Terrorism Act 2000. [Online] Available at: http://www.ihrc.org.uk/publications/briefings/10778-schedule-7-amends-2013 Accessed: 20.01.2015

Islamic Human Rights Commission (2014a) Legal challenge

mounted against UK anti-terror law. [Online] Available at: http://www.ihrc.org.uk/news/ihrc-in-media/11259-legal-challenge-mounted-against-uk-anti-terror-law Accessed: 27.01.2015

Islamic Human Rights Commission (2014b) Press release: Police anti terror drive destined to fail. [Online] Available at: http://www.ihrc.org.uk/activities/press-releases/11276-press-release-police-anti-terror-drive-destined-to-fail Accessed: 27.01.2015

Islamic Human Rights Commission (2014c) Press release: Anti-terror bill is a recipe for more alienation . [Online] Available at: http://www.ihrc.org.uk/activities/press-releases/11283-press-release-anti-terror-bill-is-a-recipe-for-more-alienation Accessed: 27.01.2015

Islamic Human Rights Commission (2015a) Press release: IHRC to end participation in anti-terror laws consultations. [Online] Available at: http://www.ihrc.org.uk/activities/press-releases/11331-press-release-ihrc-to-end-participation-in-anti-ter ror-laws-consultations Accessed: 27.01.2015

Islamic Human Rights Commission (2015b) Event Report: 'Preventing Violent Extremism?' Conference. [Online] Available at: http://www.ihrc.org.uk/news/event-reports/11499-event-report-preventing-violent-extremism-conference-

Islamic Human Rights Commission (21 July 2015) Press release – UK: British government is in denial over extremism. [Online] Available at: http://ihrc.org.uk/activities/press-releases/11493-press-release-uk-british-government-is-in-denial-over-extremis m

ITV News (2014) Vandals forced Cardiff mosque to shut after robbery. [Online] Available at: http://www.itv.com/news/wales/update/2014-09-16/cardiff-mosque-forced-to-shut-after-being-smashed-up/

Izaakson, J. (2015) Lutfur Rahman Verdict: An Overview – Ceasefire Magazine. [Online] Available at: https://ceasefiremagazine.co.uk/jennifer-izaakson-lutfur-rahman-verdict/ Accessed: 18.05.2015

Jacobs, J. B., & Potter, K. (1998). *Hate crimes: Criminal law & identity politics*. New York: Oxford University Press.

Jamal, A. A., & Naber, N. C. (2008). *Race and Arab Americans before and after 9/11: From invisible citizens to visible subjects*. Syracuse, N.Y: Syracuse University Press.

James Carr, Dr. (2014) *Experiences of Anti-Muslim Racism in Ireland*. Ireland: Hate and Hostility Research Group. PDF.

Johnson, B. (2014) The children taught at home about murder and bombings – The Telegraph. [Online] Available at: http://www.telegraph.co.uk/news/politics/10671841/The-children-taught-at-home-about-murder-and-bombings.html

Johnston, I. (2015) 'Mix-up, not sexism' as Channel 4 presenter Cathy Newman is turned away from a mosque on 'Visit My Mosque Day' – The Independent. [Online] Available at: http://www.independent.co.uk/news/uk/home-news/mixup-not-sexism-as-channel-4-presenter-cathy-newman-is-turned-away-from-a-mosque-on-visit-my-mosque-day-10016835.html Accessed: 09.02.2015

Jones, O. (2015) Government policy will seal the mouths of Muslim pupils – The Guardian. [Online] Available at: http://www.theguardian.com/commentisfree/2015/jul/01/muslim-children-enemy-radicalisation Accessed: 01.07.2015

Joseph, S. and D'Harlingue (2012) The Wall Street Journal's Muslims: Representing Islam in American Print News Media. *Islamophobia Studies Journal*, 1(1), 131-162.

Kaballo, A. (2013) The scandal of stop and search – Respect Party. [Online] Available at: http://www.respectparty.org/2013/09/26/the-scandal-of-stop-and-search-2/ Accessed: 21.01.2015

Kapoor, N. (2015) Deport, Deprive, Extradite: On the removal of rights in terrorising times – Discover Society. [Online] Available at: http://discoversociety.org/2015/07/01/deport-deprive-extradite-on-the-removal-of-rights-in-terrorising-times/

Accessed: 01.07.2015

Kassimeris, G and Jackson, L. (2012) *British Muslims and the discourse of dysfunction: community cohesion and counterterrorism in the West Midlands*, Critical Studies on Terrorism, 5:2, 179-196, DOI: : 10.1080/17539153.2012.684970

Kerbaj, R. and Griffiths, S. (2015) 100 Islamist teachers face ban – The Sunday Times. [Online] Available at: http://www.thesundaytimes.co.uk/sto/news/uk_news/Educ ation/article1540185.ece

Kerner (1967) Report of the National Advisory Commission on Civil Disorders.

Khalek, R. (2015) "American Sniper" spawns death threats against Arabs and Muslims – The Electronic Intifada. [Online] Available at: https://electronicintifada.net/blogs/rania-khalek/american-sniper-spawns-death-threats-against-arabs-an d-muslims

Khan, MG. (2014) Trojan Horse – conjuring the sale, the witch and the grand inquisitor – Open Democracy. [Online] Available at: https://www.opendemocracy.net/ourkingdom/mg-khan/trojan-horse-%E2%80%93-conjuring-slave-witch-and-gra nd-inquisitor Accessed: 21.11.2014

Khattab, N., & Johnston, R. (2014) Ethno-religious identities and persisting penalties in the UK labor market. The Social Science Journal, http://dx.doi.org/10.1016/j.soscij.2014.10.007

Khiabany, G. (2010) Muslim Women and Veiled Threats: From 'Civilising Mission' to 'Clash of Civilisations'. In *Pointing the Finger: Islam and Muslims in the Contemporary UK Media.* Edited by Petley, J., Richardson, R. and Richardson J. London: One World Publications.

Khiabany, G.(2012) Terror, Culture and Anti-Muslim Racism. In *Media and Terrorism: Global Perspectives.* Edited by Freedman, D. and Thussu, D. London: Sage

Kilpatrick, C. (2015) Muslim woman racially abused and assaulted by motorist as she walked along a Portadown road –

Belfast Live. [Online] Available at:
http://www.belfastlive.co.uk/news/belfast-news/muslim-woman-racially-abused-assaulted-9540394 Accessed: 30.06.2015

Klug, B. (2015) The limits of analogy? Comparing Islamophobia and Antisemitism – Discover Society. [Online] Available at:
http://discoversociety.org/2015/07/01/the-limits-of-analogy-comparing-islamophobia-and-antisemitism/ Accessed:
01.07.2015

Kraemerei (1998) This is Men and Women Speaking.

Kumar, A. (2014) Tower Hamlets: The Last Outpost of the Raj Falls – Ceasefire Magazine. [Online] Available at:
https://ceasefiremagazine.co.uk/tower-hamlets-outpost-raj-falls/ Accessed: 18.05.2015

Kumaravadivelu, B. (2008). *Cultural globalization and language education.* New Haven: Yale University Press.

Kundnani, A. (2001) "From Oldham to Bradford: the violence of the violated." *Race and Class* 43 (2): 105-131.

Kundnani, A. (2005) The politics of a phoney Britishness – Arun Kundnani. [Online] Available at:
http://www.kundnani.org/2005/01/21/the-politics-of-a-phoney-britishness/ Accessed: 16.04.2015

Kundnani, A. (2007) *The End of Tolerance: Racism in 21st Century Britain.* London: Pluto Press.

Kundnani, A. (2009) *Spooked! How not to prevent violent extremism.* London: International Race Relations. PDF.

Kundnani, A. (2012a) Multiculturalism *and its discontents: Left, Right and liberal.* European Journal of Cultural Studies, 15 (2) 155-166, Sage Publications.

Kundnani, A. (2012b) *Blind Spot? Security Narratives and Far-Right Violence in Europe.* The Netherlands: International Centre for Counter-Terrorism – The Hague. PDF.

Kundnani, A. (2015) Counter-terrorism policy and re-analysing extremism – International Race Relations. [Online] Available at: http://www.irr.org.uk/news/counter-terrorism-policy-and-re-analysing-extremism/ Accesed: 19.02.2015

Kunst, J. R., Tajamal, H., Sam, D. L. & Ulleberg, P. (2012) Coping with Islamophobia: The effects of religious stigma on Muslim minorities' identity formation. International Journal of Intercultural Relations 36 (2012) pages 518-532

Lambert, R. Dr., and Githens-Mazer, J. (2010) *Islamophobia and Anti-Muslim Hate Crime, UK Case Studies 2010*, London: European Muslim Research Centre and University of Exeter

Lancashire Telegraph (2014) Racist Darwen teen jailed for throwing pot noodle at Asian boys walking home from mosque. [Online] Available at: http://www.lancashiretelegraph.co.uk/news/11535633.Racist_Darwen_teen_jailed_for_throwing_pot_noodle_at_Asian_boys_walking_home_from_Mosque/ Referenced by Pitt, B., same date, Islamophobia Watch

Laville, S. (2014) Secret terror trial is threat to open justice, human rights campaigners warn – The Guardian. [Online] Available at: http://www.theguardian.com/law/2014/jun/04/uk-secret-terrorism-trial-legal-justice-human-rights Accessed: 09.06.2014

Law, I (2007) Research Findings, The Racism Reduction Agenda. Centre for Ethnicity and Racism Studies. Leeds.

Law, I., Simms, J., & Sirriyeh, A. (2013). Challenging Racist Violence and Racist Hostility in 'Post-Racial' Times: Research and Action in Leeds, UK, 2006–2012. *Social Inclusion, 1*(1), 13-20.

Lawrence, M. (2015) British democracy is nearing a crisis point – New Statesman. [Online] Available at: http://www.newstatesman.com/politics/2015/04/british-democracy-nearing-crisis-point Accessed: 16.04.2015

Lea, J. (2003) From Brixton to Bradford: Ideology and Discourse on Race and Urban Violence in the United Kingdom – John Lea's Website. [Online] Available at:

http://www.bunker8.pwp.blueyonder.co.uk/misc/riots.htm
Accessed: 12.08.2015

Leech, R. (2014) My brother wanted to be a jihadi – and society
is creating many more like him – The Guardian. [Online]
Available at:
http://www.theguardian.com/commentisfree/2014/oct/22/br
other-jihadi-terrorist-society-extremism?CMP=twt_gu Accessed:
22.10.2014

Leicester Mercury (2014) No-go areas in Leicester for Muslin
women wearing niqab [Online] Available at:
http://www.leicestermercury.co.uk/areas-Leicester-Muslim-
women-wearing-niqab/story-21342283-detail/story.html
Referenced by Pitt, B., same date, Islamophobia Watch

Lentin, A. (2015) What does race do? Ethnic and Racial Studies,
38:8, 1401-1406. London: Routledge.

Levy, G. (2013) The man who hated Britain: Red Ed's pledge to
bring back socialism is a homage to his Marxist father. So what
did Miliband Snr really believe in? The answer should disturb
everyone who loves this country – Daily Mail. [Online]
Available at: http://www.dailymail.co.uk/news/article-
2435751/Red-Eds-pledge-bring-socialism-homage-Marxist-fath
er-Ralph-Miliband-says-GEOFFREY-LEVY.html Accessed:
12.08.2015

Lewis, P. (2010) Birmingham stops camera surveillance in
Muslim areas – The Guardian. [Online] Available at:
http://www.theguardian.com/uk/2010/jun/17/birmingham-
stops-spy-cameras-project Accessed: 01.04.2015

Liberty (2010) Chief Constable Slams Birmingham Surveillance
Scheme [Online] Available at: https://www.liberty-human-
rights.org.uk/news/press-releases/chief-constable-slams-birmi
ngham-surveillance-scheme Accessed: 01.04.2015

Lindisfarne, N. And Neale, J. (2015) Gang Abuse in Oxford –
Sexism, Class, Violence. [Online] Available at:
https://sexismclassviolence.wordpress.com/2015/03/12/gang
-abuse-in-oxford/ Accessed: 31.03.2015

Lindley, D. (2015) University of Birmingham: A Hotspot for Fascists – Slaney Street. [Online] Available at: http://www.slaneystreet.com/2015/03/16/university-of-birmingham-a-hotspot-for-fascists/ Accessed: 17.03.2015

Lips, L. (2010) Azad Ali and Man Made Law – Harry's place. [Online] Available at: http://hurryupharry.org/2010/01/28/azad-ali-and-man-made-law/ Accessed: 12.08.2015

Longhi, S. & Platt, L. (2008) Pay Gaps Across Equalities Areas. Equality and Human Rights Commission, Manchester.

MacAskill, E. (2015) MI5 chief seeks new powers after Paris magazine attack – The Guardian. [Online] Available at: http://www.theguardian.com/uk-news/2015/jan/08/mi5-chief-charlie-hebdo-attack-paris-andrew-parker Accessed: 09.01.2015

Macpherson, J. (2014) Mosque damaged after nearby arson attack on caravan – Accrington Observer. [Online] Available at: http://www.accringtonobserver.co.uk/news/local-news/mosque-damaged-after-nearby-arson-8301836 Referenced by Pitt, B., same date, Islamophobia Watch

Macpherson, W., Sir (1999) The Stephen Lawrence Inquiry. Report of an inquiry. Presented to Parliament. PDF.

Mailk, n. (2014) The Sun's 'Unite against Isis' campaign is a proxy for anti-Muslim bigotry – The Guardian. [Online] Available at: http://www.theguardian.com/commentisfree/2014/oct/08/sun-unite-against-isis-muslim-bigotry Accessed: 24.07.2015

Majeed, A. (2010) Policing, Protest and Conflict: A Report into the Policing of the London Gaza Demonstrations in 2008 – 2009. Wembley: Islamic Human Rights Commission

Manning, A. (2011) The successes and failures of multiculturalism – Policy Network. [Online] Available at: http://www.policy-network.net/pno_detail.aspx?ID=4084&title=The-successes-and

-failures-of-multiculturalism Accessed: 12.08.2015

Mansfield, R. (2014) National Front try to disrupt Islamic Society peaceful march in Newport – South Wales Argus. [Online] Available at:
http://www.southwalesargus.co.uk/news/11605343.National_Front_try_to_disrupt_Islamic_Society_peaceful_march_in_New port/ Referenced by Pitt, B., same date, Islamophobia Watch

Marshall, T. (2015) Muslim mother 'attached for wearing hijab' as she went to collect children from London primary school – Evening Standard. [Online] Available at:
http://www.standard.co.uk/news/crime/muslim-mother-attacked-by-group-of-women-for-wearing-hijab-as-she-went-to-collect-children-from-london-primary-school-10300208.html Accessed: 24.07.2015

Martz, R. B. (2009). Hate crimes. In Greene, H. T., & Gabbidon, S. L. *Encyclopedia of race and crime*. Los Angeles: SAGE, pp 339-342.

Mason, R. (2015) Nigel Farage: British Muslim 'fifth column' fuels fear of immigration – The Guardian. [Online] Available at:
http://www.theguardian.com/politics/2015/mar/12/nigel-farage-british-muslim-fifth-column-fuels-immigration-fear-ukip Accessed: 12.03.2015

McCarthy, N. (2013) Bring back the Project Champion spy cameras in Birmingham, says city's Muslim MP – Birmingham Mail. [Online] Available at:
http://www.birminghammail.co.uk/news/local-news/bring-back-project-champion-spy-1343736 Accessed: 01.04.2015

McDonald, H. (2014a) Racism in Northern Ireland: 'They called our children monkeys' – The Guardian. [Online] Available at:
http://www.theguardian.com/uk-news/2014/jun/12/racism-northern-ireland-couple-tell-abuse-belfast Accessed: 16.06.2014

McDonald, H. (2014b) Belfast preacher who denounced Islam as evil issues apology – The Guardian. [Online] Available at:
http://www.theguardian.com/uk-news/2014/jun/06/belfast-preacher-islam-evil-apology Accessed: 26.08.2014

McElroy, D. (2014) Ireland 'leads the world in Islamic values as Muslim states lag' – The Telegraph. [Online] Available at: http://www.telegraph.co.uk/news/worldnews/europe/ireland/10888707/Ireland-leads-the-world-in-Islamic-values-as-Muslim-states-lag.html Accessed: 16.06.2014

McGovern, M., Prof., and Angela Tobin. *Countering Terror or Counter-Productive? Comparing Irish and British Muslim Experiences in Counter-insurgency Law and Policy.* Lancashire: Edge Hill University, 2010. PDF.

McMohan, V. (2014) Stormont urged to fund Nothern Ireland's first mosque – Irish Mirror. [Online] Available at: http://www.irishmirror.ie/news/irish-news/politics/stormont-urged-fund-northern-irelands-3676062 Accessed: 26.08.2014

Meer, N. & Spaeti, C. (2015) Focus: Islamophobia and contemporary 'Europe' – Discover Society. [Online] Available at: http://discoversociety.org/2015/07/01/focus-islamophobia-and-contemporary-europe/?utm_content=bufferb89c9&utm_medium=social&utm_source=twitter.com&utm_campaign=buffer Accessed: 01.07.2015

Merali, A. (2002) They hate women, don't they? – The Guardian. [Online] Available at: http://www.theguardian.com/world/2002/jun/21/gender.september11

Merali, A. (2013) Schools, Lies and Muslimness – Islamic Human Rights Commission. [Online] Available at: http://ihrc.org.uk/news/comment/10808-schools-lies-and-muslimness Accessed: 14.04.2015

Merali, A. (2014) Presentation at 'Institutional Islamophobia: A conference to examine state racism and social engineering of the Muslim community', *Mapping Anti-Muslim Experiences – the Domination Hate Model of Intercultural Relations,* https://www.youtube.com/watch?v=Rn0paU0EMz4

Metropolitan Police. Communities Together [Online] Available at: http://content.met.police.uk/Site/communitiestogether

Accessed: 31.08.2015

Midgley, N. (2010) BBC would 'rather read a little Muslim boy's script', claims Lynda La Plante – The Telegraph. [Online] Available at: http://www.telegraph.co.uk/culture/tvandradio/6920052/BBC-would-rather-read-a-little-Muslim-boys-script-claims-Lynda-La-Plante.html

Minhas, R. (2011) Presentation at: 'NATT Conference', *Stephen Lawrence Education Standard.*

Mirza, H. (2014) Neither male nor white: Are Muslim girls in danger of slipping through the cracks of the 'Trojan horse' fiasco? – Goldsmiths University. [Online] Available at: http://www.gold.ac.uk/academics/heidimirzamuslimgirls.php Accessed: 08.11.2014

Modood, T. (2015) Islamophobia and the struggle for recognition – Discover Society. [Online] Available at: http://discoversociety.org/2015/07/01/islamophobia-and-the-struggle-for-recognition/ Accessed: 01.07.2015

Mohamed, L. ed. (2015 ongoing) The Prevent Diaries – Islamic Human Rights Commission. [Online] Available at: http://www.ihrc.org.uk/activities/projects/11495-the-prevent-diaries

Mohammed, J and Siddiqui, A. Dr. *The Prevent Strategy: A Cradle to Grave Police-State.* London: CAGE, 2013. PDF.

Morris, N. (2014) War in Iraq: Rushanara Ali MP steps down from Labour front bench in protest at military action – The Independent. [Online] Available at: http://www.independent.co.uk/news/uk/politics/war-in-iraq-rushanara-ali-mp-steps-down-from-labour-front-bench-in-protest-at-military-action-9758967.html Accessed: 29.09.2014

Mukadam, M. & Scott-Baumann, A. with Chowdhary, A. & Contractor, S. (2010) *The training and development of Muslim Faith Leaders: Current practice and future possibilities.* The Department for Communities and Local Government. London.

Mulvey, L. (1975) Visual Pleasure and Narrative Cinema. [Online] Available at: http://imlportfolio.usc.edu/ctcs505/mulveyVisualPleasureNarrativeCinema.pdf

Muslim Advocates (2011). *Losing liberty: The state of freedom 10 years after the Patriot Act*. Accessed February 29, 2015 from: http://d3n8a8pro7vhmx.cloudfront.net/muslimadvocates/pages/47/attachments/original/Losing_Liberty_The_State_of_Freedom_10_Years_After_the_PATRIOT_Act.pdf?1330650785

Muslim Council of Britain (2015) Letter to Secretary of State for Communities and Local Government [Online] Available at: http://www.mcb.org.uk/lettertossclg/. Accessed: 19.01.2015

Muslim Reverie (2013) Beyond "equal representation": some thoughts on racebending villains of color in white-dominated sci-fo and comic book films [Online] Available at: https://muslimreverie.wordpress.com/tag/ras-al-ghul/

Neckles, L. (Equanomics UK), Samota, N. (CRJ UK) and Blake, M. (BTEG) *Stop and search overall engagement report*. 2013. PDF.

New Statesman (2011) Full transcript | David Cameron | Speech on radicalisation and Islamic extremism | Munich | 5 February 2011 [Online] Available at: http://www.newstatesman.com/blogs/the-staggers/2011/02/terrorism-islam-ideology

Newham Monitoring Project (2013) NMP publishes its submission to Home Office on stop and search [Online] Available at: http://www.nmp.org.uk/2013/09/27/nmp-publishes-its-submission-to-home-office-on-stop-and-search/ Accessed: 20.01.2015

Newman, M. (2015) Surveillance state: Preventing far right extremism? Schools in EDL and BNP heartland only monitoring ethnic minority pupils – The Bureau of Investigative Journalism. [Online] Available at: http://www.thebureauinvestigates.com/2015/03/31/prevent-policy-schools-barnsley-edl-bnp-heartland/ Accessed: 14.04.2015

NUS Connect (2015) Why I won't be working with Prevent (and how you can avoid it, too) [Online] Available at: http://www.nusconnect.org.uk/articles/why-i-won-t-be-working-with-prevent-and-how-you-can-avoid-it-too

Nye, C. (2013) 'Disgusting' Islamophobic DVDs sent to London mosques – BBC News. [Online] Available at: http://www.bbc.co.uk/news/uk-england-london-23808038 Accessed 29.08.2014

OnIslam(2014) UK Anti-terror Laws Stir Muslim Ire [Online] Available at: http://www.onislam.net/english/news/europe/479783-uk-anti-terror-laws-stir-muslim-ire.html Accessed: 27.01.2015

Palmer, A. (2014) We can't avoid the threat of Islam – The Telegraph. [Online] Available at: http://www.telegraph.co.uk/news/uknews/immigration/108 82891/We-cant-avoid-the-threat-of-Islamism.html Accessed: 08.06.2014

Parker, A. (2015) Terrorism, Technology and Accountability – Address by the Director General of the Security Service, Andrew Parker, to the Royal United Services Institute (RUSI) at Thames House, 8 January 2015 – Security Service MI5. [Online] Available at: https://www.mi5.gov.uk/home/about-us/who-we-are/staff-and-management/director-general/speeches-by-the-d irector-general/director-generals-speech-on-terrorism-technology-and-accountability.html Accessed: 09.01.2015

Parris, M. (2015) Hear my warning: a new prejudice is on the rise – The Spectator. [Online] Available at: http://www.spectator.co.uk/columnists/matthew-parris/9472722/anti-muslim-prejudice-is-real-and-its-scary/ Accessed: 19.03.2015

Parry, R. (2014) Britain First march through Rotherham – The Star. [Online] Available at: http://www.thestar.co.uk/news/local/britain-first-march-through-rotherham-1-6877971

Perry, B. (2001). *In the name of hate: Understanding hate crimes.*

New York: Routledge.

Phillips, C. (2011) *Institutional racism and ethnic inequalities: an expanded multilevel framework. Journal of social policy*, 40 (01). pp. 173-192.

Pitt, B. (2014) Douglas Murray links up with Christian fundamentalist homophobe to smear Newham –mega-mosque' supporters – Islamophobia Watch. [Online] Available at: http://www.islamophobiawatch.co.uk/douglas-murray-links-up-with-christian-fundamentalist-homophobe-to-smear-newham-mega-mosque-supporters/

Pitt, B. (2014) Happy new year from the EDL – Islamophobia Watch. [Online] Available at: http://www.islamophobiawatch.co.uk/happy-new-year-from-the-edl/

Pitt, B. (2014) Luton Islamic Centre exposes EDL lies – Islamophobia Watch. [Online] Available at: http://www.islamophobiawatch.co.uk/luton-islamic-centre-exposes-edl-lies/

Pitt, B. (2014) Muslim school protesters march through Portsmouth – Islamophobia Watch. [Online] Available at: http://www.islamophobiawatch.co.uk/muslim-school-protesters-march-through-portsmouth/

Pitt, B. (2014) The EDL goes to Downing Street – Islamophobia Watch. [Online] Available at: http://www.islamophobiawatch.co.uk/the-edl-goes-to-downing-street/

Pitt, B. (2014a) Police investigate racist attack at Warrington mosque – Islamophobia Watch. [Online] Available at: http://www.islamophobiawatch.co.uk/police-investigate-racist-attack-at-warrington-mosque/

Pitt, B. (2014b) BNP links up with Infidels and NF in Bolton anti-mosque campaign – Islamophobia Watch. [Online] Available at: http://www.islamophobiawatch.co.uk/bnp-links-up-with-infidels-and-nf-in-bolton-anti-mosque-campaign/

Pitt, B. (2014c) Torygraph discovers 'jihad on dogs' –
Islamophobia Watch [Online] Available at:
http://www.islamophobiawatch.co.uk/torygraph-discovers-
jihad-on-dogs/

Pitt, B. (2014d) UKIP councillor brands Jaloos 'call to war', links
to Facebook page proposing 'cull' of Muslims – Islamophobia
Watch. [Online] Available at:
http://www.islamophobiawatch.co.uk/ukip-councillor-brands-
jaloos-call-to-war-links-to-facebook-page-proposing-cull-of-mus
lims/

Pitt, B. (2014e) Britain First continues campaign of harassment –
Islamophobia Watch. [Online] Available at:
http://www.islamophobiawatch.co.uk/britain-first-continues-
campaign-of-harassment/

Pitt, B. (2014f) Fascists unite to oppose mosque in New
Addington – Islamophobia Watch. [Online] Available at:
http://www.islamophobiawatch.co.uk/fascists-unite-to-
oppose-mosque-in-new-addington/

Pitt, B. (2014g) Demonstrate against South East Alliance in
Cricklewood – Islamophobia Watch. [Online] Available at:
http://www.islamophobiawatch.co.uk/demonstrate-against-
south-east-alliance-in-cricklewood/

Pitt, B. (2014h) Man charged over 'racist' mosque attack –
Islamophobia Watch. [Online] Available at:
http://www.islamophobiawatch.co.uk/man-charged-over-
racist-mosque-attack/#more-36083 Accessed: 29.08.2014

Pitt, B. (2014i) Another flop for the fascists in Cricklewood –
Islamophobia Watch. [Online] Available at:
http://www.islamophobiawatch.co.uk/another-flop-for-the-
fascists-in-cricklewood/ Accessed: 30.08.2014

Pitt, B. (2014k) Five convicted over EDL Thatcham protest –
Islamophobia Watch. [Online] Available at:
http://www.islamophobiawatch.co.uk/five-convicted-over-
edl-thatcham-protest/

Pitt, B. (2014l) 'Muslim men are raping women' – investment banker caught on camera launching racist rant on train – Islamophobia Watch. [Online] Available at: http://www.islamophobiawatch.co.uk/muslim-men-are-raping-women-investment-banker-caught-on-camera-launching-racist-rant-on-train/

Pitt, B. (2014m) More anti-Muslim bigotry from Sun columnist Katie Hopkins – Islamophobia Watch. [Online] Available at: http://www.islamophobiawatch.co.uk/more-anti-muslim-bigotry-from-sun-columnist-katie-hopkins/

Pitt, B. (2014n) Blackburn man speaking to police told onlookers he would burn down their mosque – Islamophobia Watch. [Online] Available at: http://www.islamophobiawatch.co.uk/blackburn-man-speaking-to-police-told-onlookers-he-would-burn-down-their-mosque/

Pitt, B. (2014o) 'Bigot' Eric King who was spared jail for Islam hate mail says he will continue to share his views online – Islamophobia Watch. [Online] Available at: http://www.islamophobiawatch.co.uk/bigot-eric-king-who-was-spared-jail-for-islam-hate-mail-says-he-will-continue-to-share-his-views-online/

Pitt. B (2014j) Another flop for the fascists in Cricklewood – Islamophobia Watch. [Online] Available at: http://www.islamophobiawatch.co.uk/another-flop-for-the-fascists-in-cricklewood/ Accessed: 14.11.2014

Pocklington, D. (2015) "Spiritual Influence" and elections – Law & Religion UK. [Online] Available at: http://www.lawandreligionuk.com/2015/02/11/spiritual-influence-and-elections/ Accessed: 18.0.2015

Poole, E. (2011) *Change and Continuity in the Representation of British Muslims Before and After 9/11: The UK Context.* Global Media Journal – Canadian Edition, 4(2), 49-62.

Porter, G. & Cortbus, C. (2015) White supremacists linked to Mold Tesco stab fanatic Zack Davies training far-right activists at Welsh boot camps – Daily Post. [Online] Available at: http://www.dailypost.co.uk/news/north-wales-news/zack-davies-nactional-action-mold-9879273

Powell, M. (2015) Welcome to East London: Muslim gang slashes tyres of immigration-riad van before officers showered with eggs from high-rise – Daily Mail. [Online] Available at: http://www.dailymail.co.uk/news/article-3174610/Welcome-East-London-Muslim-gang-slashes-tyres-immigration-raid-van-officers-showered-eggs-high-rise.html Accessed: 28.07.2015

Proctor, I. (2014) 'Muslim men are raping women' – investment banker caught on camera launching racist rant on train – Mirror. [Online] Available at: http://www.mirror.co.uk/news/uk-news/muslim-men-raping-women-investment-4437818 Referenced by Pitt, B., same date, Islamophobia Watch

Publications.parliament.uk (2006) Young Black People and the Criminal Justice System. House of Commons. Transcript of oral evidence.

Quaker Peace and Social Witness (2014) The new tide of militarisation. [Online] Available at: http://old.quaker.org.uk/files/Militarisation-briefing-web.pdf

Quartermaine, A. (2014) *Conversations with... Mona Siddiqui.* Exchanges: the Warwick Research Journal. Volume 1, Issue 2.

Quinn, B. (2015) City of London police put Occupy London on counter-terrorism presentation with al-Qaida – The Guardian. [Online] Available at: http://www.theguardian.com/uk-news/2015/jul/19/occupy-london-counter-terrorism-presentati on-al-qaida

Rayburn, N. R., Earleywine, M., & Davison, G. C. (2003). Base rates of hate crime victimization among college students. *Journal of Interpersonal Violence*, 18, 10, 1209-1221.

Razack, S.H. (2008). Casting Out: The Eviction of Muslims from Western Law and Politics. Toronto: University of Toronto Press

Read, J. G. (2008).Muslims inAmerica. *Contexts: Understanding People in Their SocialWorlds*, 7(4), 39-43.

Report of the Zahid Mubarek Inquiry Volume 1. (2006) London: The Stationary Office. PDF

Report of the Zahid Mubarek Inquiry Volume 2. (2006) London: The Stationary Office. PDF

Rev Billings, A., Dr. & Holden, A., Dr. (2008) Interfaith Interventions and Cohesive Communities, The effectiveness of interfaith activity in towns marked by enclavisation and parallel lives. The Burnley Project, Lancaster University. PDF

Richardson, H. (2015) Teachers 'fear extremism debates in class' – BBC News. [Online] Available at: http://www.bbc.co.uk/news/education-32162012

Robertson, G. (2014) Council bans Scottish Defence League city march because of 'high chance of violence risking public safety' – Daily Record. [Online] Available at: http://www.dailyrecord.co.uk/news/scottish-news/council-bans-scottish-defence-league-4644436

Robinson, M. (2014) Katie Hopkins faces Twitter outrage after series of anti-Muslim and anti-Palestinian messages are sent from her account – Daily Mail. [Online] Available at: http://www.dailymail.co.uk/news/article-2829730/Calls-arrest-Katie-Hopkins-inciting-racial-hatred-series-anti-Muslim-anti-Palestinian-Tweets-sent-account.html Accessed: 14.11.2014

Rogers, J. F. (2015) The majority of votes doubt that Islam is compatible with British values – The Telegraph. [Online] Available at: http://www.telegraph.co.uk/news/general-election-2015/politics-blog/11503493/The-majority-of-voters-doubt-that-Islam-is-compatible-with-British-values.html Accessed: 12.08.2015

Ryan, G. (2014) Northern Irish Muslims win apology – Church Times. [Online] Available at: http://www.churchtimes.co.uk/articles/2014/6-june/news/uk/northern-irish-muslims-win-apology Accessed: 26.08.2014

Sabin, L. (2015) Government accused of acting like 'far right' as

Eric Pickles says Muslims have 'more work to do' – The Independent. [Online] Available at: http://www.independent.co.uk/news/uk/government-accused-of-acting-like-far-right-as-eric-pickles-says-muslims-have-more-work-to-do-9986996.html Accessed: 19.01.2015

Sacc.org.uk (2015) NUS votes to oppose Prevent – Scotland Against Criminalising Communities. [Online] Available at: http://www.sacc.org.uk/news/2015/nus-votes-oppose-prevent

Santi Rozario (2012) Islamic marriage: A haven in an uncertain world, Culture and Religion: An Interdisciplinary Journal, 13:2, 159-175

Sayyid, S. (2010). Do Post-Racials Dream of White Sheep? Tolerace Working Paper, University of Leeds: Leeds cited in Sian, K below.

Sayyid, S., Law, I. & Sian, K. (2010) Analysis of integration policies and public State-endorsed institutions at national/regional levels: Equality and Human Rights Commission (EHRC). Centre for Ethnicity and Racism Studies, University of Leeds (CERS/ULeeds) PDF.

Scaife, R. (2014) Report on our first testing – University of Nottingham. [Online] Available at: http://blogs.nottingham.ac.uk/biasandblame/2014/08/08/report-on-our-first-testing/ Accessed: 06.02.2015

Schreiber, M. P. (2014). *South Asian Muslim health outcomes in Great Britain: The National Health Service and the British national imaginary*. Religious Studies Honors Projects.

Scott, S. (2015) Cadet units in state schools to increase five-fold with £50 million budget boost – Schools Week. [Online] Available at: http://schoolsweek.co.uk/cadet-units-in-state-schools-to-increase-five-fold-with-50-million-budget-boost/

Sian, K. (2013) *Spies, surveillance and stakeouts: monitoring Muslim moves in British state schools*, Race Ethnicity and Education. PDF

Sian, K. Dr. (2012a) The Grooming We Can't Hide From – The

Platform. Available at: http://www.the-platform.org.uk/2012/06/20/the-grooming-we-cant-hide-from/ Accessed: 01.04.2015

Sian, K. Dr. (2012b). Gurdwaras, Guns and Grudges. Available at:
http://www.theplatform.org.uk/2012/08/15/gurdwarasguns-and-grudges/ Accessed 05.03.2013

Siddique, H. (2014) David Cameron risks row by posing with blacked-up morris dancers – The Guardian. [Online] Available at: http://www.theguardian.com/stage/2014/oct/13/david-cameron-risks-row-posing-blacked-up-morris-dancers Accessed: 05.11.2014

Slater, C. (2014) Man, 34, arrested over arson attack on minibus at Manchester mosque – Manchester Evening News. [Online] Available at:
http://www.manchestereveningnews.co.uk/news/greater-manchester-news/man-34-arrested-over-arson-7820031

Sleigh, S & Randhawa, K. (2015) Hampstead primary school pupils is deemed at risk of Islamist radicalisation – Evening Standard. [Online] Available at:
http://www.standard.co.uk/news/london/hampstead-primary-school-pupil-is-deemed-at-risk-of-islamist-radicalisation-10410122.html Accessed: 24.07.2015

Smith, M. (2014) Rotherham taxi drivers face 'daily' racist abuse – The Star [Online] Available at:
http://www.thestar.co.uk/news/rotherham-taxi-drivers-face-daily-racist-abuse-1-6927524 Referenced by Pitt, B., same date, Islamophobia Watch

Smith, M. (2015) Cathy Newman turned away from mosque on #VisitMyMosque day – The Guardian. [Online] Available at:
http://www.theguardian.com/media/2015/feb/02/cathy-newman-turned-away-from-mosque-on-visitmymosque-day Accessed: 09.02.2015

Sommers, J. (2015a) Channel 4 Regrets Letting Ex-CIA Agent Claim Baghdad Massacre Would Have Been 'Ideal' –

Huffington Post. [Online] Available at:
http://www.huffingtonpost.co.uk/2015/01/22/channel-4-news-michael-scheuer_n_6523262.html Accessed: 10.02.2015

Sommers, J. (2015b) 7/7 Bombings anniversary poll shows more than half of Britons see Muslims as a threat – Huffington post. [Online] Available at:
http://www.huffingtonpost.co.uk/2015/07/03/77-bombings-muslims-islam-britain-poll_n_7694452.html Accessed: 07.07.2015

Stacey, M., Carbone-Lopez, K., & Rosenfeld, R. (2011). Demographic change and ethnically motivated crime: The impact of immigration on anti-Hispanic hate crime in the United States. *Journal of Contemporary Criminal Justice*, 27, 3, 278-298.

Stahl, A. (2015) The Fear of Homegrown Terror is Breeding Repression in the UK – Truthout. [Online] Available at:
http://www.truth-out.org/news/item/29566-the-fear-of-homegrown-terror-is-breeding-repression-in-the-uk Accessed: 12.03.2015

Staub, E. (2005). The Origins and Evolution of Hate, With Notes on Prevention. Sternberg, Robert J. (Ed), (2005). *The psychology of hate.*, (pp. 51-66). Washington, DC, US: American Psychological Association, x, 263 pp.

Stone, J. (2015) Boris Johnson accuses Muslim Council of Britain of 'claiming porn-freak jihadists for mainstream Islam' – The Independent. [Online] Available at:
http://www.independent.co.uk/news/uk/politics/boris-johnson-accuses-muslim-council-of-britain-of-claiming-pornfreak-jihadists-for-mainstream-islam-10079496.html

Suleiman, Y, Prof. (2013) *Narratives of Conversion to Islam in Britain Female Perspectives.* University of Cambridge, in association with The New Muslims Project, Markfield

SWNS (2014) Former BBC presenter rants about 'Rotherham p*kis', denounces 'horrific Muslim infiltration of Britain' [Online] Available at: http://swns.com/news/former-bbc-presenter-posts-foul-mouthed-facebook-rant-about-rotherham-pkis-62838/ Referenced by Pitt, B., same date, Islamophobia Watch. Accessed: 29.08.2014

Syal, R. (2014) Michael Fallon withdraws 'careless' immigration remark – The Guardian. [Online] Available at: http://www.theguardian.com/politics/2014/oct/27/michael-fallon-withdraws-careless-immigration-remark-swamped Accessed: 27.10.2014

Tadeo, M. (2014) 'I didn't mean to insult Muslim community': Northern Ireland First Minister Peter Robinson claims Islam comments 'were misinterpreted' – The Independent. [Online] Available at: http://www.independent.co.uk/news/uk/politics/i-didnt-mean-to-insult-muslim-community-northern-irelands-peter-robi nson-claims-islam-comments-were-misinterpreted-9455207.html Accessed: 26.08.2014

Taylor, D. (2015) Trojan horse row: governor banned from involvement with schools – The Guardian. [Online] Available at: http://www.theguardian.com/education/2015/sep/07/trojan-horse-governor-banned-schools-birmingham

Taylor, M. (2015) Racist and anti-immigration views held by children revealed in schools study – The Guardian. [Online] Available at: http://www.theguardian.com/education/2015/may/19/most-children-think-immigrants-are-stealing-jobs-schools-study-sho ws?CMP=share_btn_tw Accessed: 20.05.2015

The Crown Prosecution Service (2014) Conviction rate for hate crime at all-time high [Online] Available at: http://www.cps.gov.uk/news/latest_news/conviction_rate_fo r_hate_crime_at_all-time_high/ Accessed: 24.02.2015

The Crown Prosecution Service. Racist and Religious Crime – CPS Guidance [Online] Available at: http://www.cps.gov.uk/legal/p_to_r/racist_and_religious_cri me/#a10 Accessed: 24.02.2015

The Guardian (2005) Britain 'sleepwalking to segregation'.

[Online] Available at:
http://www.theguardian.com/world/2005/sep/19/race.social
exclusion

The Guardian (2006) Full text: David Cameron's speech to CSJ
Kids symposium [Online] Available at:
http://www.theguardian.com/politics/2006/jul/10/conservati
ves.law

The Guardian (2014a) Channel 4's Muslim call to prayer is top
in viewer complaints tally [Online] Available at:
http://www.theguardian.com/media/2014/may/08/channel-
4-muslim-prayer-ramadan-top-complaint-2013 Accessed:
23.10.2014

The Guardian (2014b) Ofsted credibility at stake over 'Trojan
House' schools inquiry [Online] Available at:
http://www.theguardian.com/education/2014/jun/03/ofsted-
credibility-at-stake-trojan-horse Accessed: 14.04.2015

The Guardian (2014c) Rights and wrongs of the Trojan horse
schools affair in Birmingham [Online] Available at:
http://www.theguardian.com/education/2014/jul/28/rights-
and-wrongs-trojan-horse-birmingham

The Guardian (2015a) Groundless anti-terror laws must go
[Online] Available at:
http://www.theguardian.com/politics/2015/feb/05/groundle
ss-antiterror-laws-must-go

The Guardian (2015b) Woman arrested at Heathrow on
suspicion of terrorism offences [Online] Available at:
http://www.theguardian.com/uk-news/2015/feb/18/woman-
arrested-heathrow-suspected-terrorism-offences Accessed:
19.02.2015

The Guardian (2015c) Lutfur Rahman ruling is a democratic
outrage [Online] Available at:
http://www.theguardian.com/politics/2015/apr/26/lutfur-
rahman-ruling-democratic-outrage?CMP=share_btn_tw
Accessed: 18.05.2015

The Guardian (2015d) The Guardian view on the fall of Kids Company: a social policy morality tale [Online] Available at: http://www.theguardian.com/commentisfree/2015/aug/05/the-guardian-view-on-the-fall-of-kids-company-a-social-policy-morality-tale

The Independent (2015) PREVENT will have a chilling effect on open debate, free speech and political dissent. [Online] Available at: http://www.independent.co.uk/voices/letters/prevent-will-have-a-chilling-effect-on-open-debate-free-speech-and-political-dissent-10381491.html

The Telegraph (2014) A challenge beyond political squabbling [Online] Available at: http://www.telegraph.co.uk/education/10885511/A-challenge-beyond-political-squabbling.html Accessed: 09.06.2014

The Telegraph (2015) Radical preacher at Islamic charity event promotes extremism [Online] Available at: http://www.telegraph.co.uk/news/uknews/crime/11419088/Radical-preacher-at-Islamic-charity-event-promotes-extremism.html Accessed: 19.02.2015

The Voice (2015) Manchester Uni Maps Inequalities Across England And Wales [Online] Available at: http://www.voice-online.co.uk/article/manchester-uni-maps-inequalities-across-england-and-wales Accessed: 09.01.2015

Thornton, S., QPM. (2010) Project Champion Review. Thames Valley Police. PDF. Available at: http://www.statewatch.org/news/2010/oct/uk-project-champion-police-report.pdf Accessed: 01.04.2015

Topkara, E. B. (2015) Keep calm: not a terrorist – Discover Society. [Online] Available at: http://discoversociety.org/2015/07/01/keep-calm-not-a-terrorist/ Accessed: 01.07.2015

Turner, B. (2007) 'The Enclave Society: Towards a Sociology of Immobility', European Journal of Social Theory, 10 (2):287–303

Tyrer, David (2011): "Flooding the Embankments: Race, biopolitics and sovereignty", in: Sayyid, Salman / Vakil, AbdoolKarim (eds), *Thinking through Islamophobia: Global Perspectives.* London: Hurst, pp. 93-110

University College Union (2015) Campaigning against the counter-terrorism and security bill (paragraphs 3.1-3.3), Motion 62 – Composite: prevent duty and anti-terrorism. Section 7 of the NEC's report to Congress. UCU Congress. [Online] Available at:
http://www.ucu.org.uk/index.cfm?articleid=7523#62

Urbs.London (2015) Religious Faith in London: Muslims [Online] Available at: http://urbs.london/religous-faith-in-london-muslims/ Accessed: 30.07.2015

Virasami, J. (2015) On racism and prejudice: being black and brown in Britain – Occupy.com. [Online] Available at:
http://www.occupy.com/article/racism-and-prejudice-being-black-and-brown-britain Accessed: 29.01.2015

Warner, J .A (2009) Anti-Immigrant nativism. In Greene, H. T., and Gabbidon, S. L., *Encyclopaedia of race and crime.* Los Angeles: Sage, 18-22.

Waters, A. M. (2013) As the niqab controversy shows, not all women are feminists – National Secular Society. [Online] Available at: http://www.secularism.org.uk/blog/2013/09/as-the-niqab-controversy-shows-not-all-women-are-feminists Accessed: 22.09.2014

Wearing, D. (2015) If extremists are those who 'don't identify with Britain', then I'm one of them – The Independent. [Online] Available at:
http://www.independent.co.uk/voices/comment/if-extremists-are-those-who-dont-identify-with-britain-then-im-one-of-them-10404346.html Accessed: 28.07.2015

Webber, G. (2014) Going Undercover: Human Rights and the Niqab – Huffington Post. [Online] Available at:
http://www.huffingtonpost.co.uk/gabriel-webber/niqab_b_5547281.html Accessed: 21.10.2014

Wigan Today (2014) Online hate campaign forces garage owner to hit back [Online] Available at: http://www.wigantoday.net/news/local/online-hate-campaign-forces-garage-owner-to-hit-back-1-7017584 Referenced by Pitt, B. 22.12.2014 Islamophobia Watch

Williams, N. (2012) Hate crime factsheet – CIVITAS. Available at: http://www.civitas.org.uk/crime/ Accessed: 24.02.2015

Williams, Y. R. (2001). Permission to Hate: Delaware, Lynching, and the Culture of Violence in America. *Journal of Black Studies, 32*, 1, 3-29.

Wilson, T. (2014) Piccadilly Gardens race attack: Muslim student's headscarf torn off as she's branded 'terrorist p*ki'- Mancunian Matters. [Online] Available at: http://www.mancunianmatters.co.uk/content/051171523-piccadilly-gardens-race-attack-muslim-students-headscarf-torn-shes-branded Referenced by Pitt, B., same date, Islamophobia Watch

Withnall, A. (2014) Baroness Warsi resigns over Gaza conflict saying she 'can no longer support Government policy' – The Independent. [Online] Available at: http://www.independent.co.uk/news/uk/politics/baroness-warsi-resigns-over-gaza-conflict-saying-she-can-no-longer-support-government-policy-9648529.html Accessed: 05.08.2014

Woolf, N. (2015) American Sniper: anti-Muslim threats skyrocket in wake of film's release – The Guardian. [Online] Available at: http://www.theguardian.com/film/2015/jan/24/american-sniper-anti-muslim-threats-skyrocket

World Bulletin (2014a) Islamophobia no obstacle for British Muslim women – World Bulletin. [Online] Available at: http://www.worldbulletin.net/muslim-world/142896/islamophobia-no-obstacle-for-british-muslim-women Accessed: 21.08.2014

World Bulletin (2014b) Although it is unlikely the movement will be banned in the UK, it is highly speculated that restrictions will be put on the group especially by the Charity Commission – World Bulletin. [Online] Available at: http://www.worldbulletin.net/haber/144406/uk-to-place-curbs-on-muslim-brotherhood Accessed: 14.11.2014

World Bulletin (2014c) A senior adviser in the UK Home Office said one particular group would like to implement death camps in the UK for everyone not seen as "white British" – World Bulletin. [Online] Available at: http://www.worldbulletin.net/haber/144664/rise-in-far-right-extremism-alarming-the-uk Accessed: 14.11.2014

World Bulletin (2014d) Metropolitan Police figures have shown offences have increased from 344 to 570 in the last year – World Bulletin. [Online] Available at: http://www.worldbulletin.net/haber/145517/islamophobic-attacks-increase-65-in-london Accessed: 14.11.2014

World Bulletin (2014e) Islamic Charity and human rights campaigners accuse British government of anti-Muslim bias – World Bulletin. [Online] Available at: http://www.worldbulletin.net/haber/146830/uk-muslims-criticize-pms-charity-commission-proposals Accessed: 14.11.2014

World Bulletin (2014f) UK Muslim group threatens govt with legal action – World Bulletin. [Online] Available at: http://www.worldbulletin.net/haber/146882/uk-muslim-group-threatens-govt-with-legal-action Accessed: 14.11.2014

World Bulletin (2014g) Anti-terror powers allowing police to stop individuals at UK ports for up to nine hours are challenged in Supreme Court – World Bulletin. [Online] Available at: http://www.worldbulletin.net/haber/148251/legal-challenge-mounted-against-uk-anti-terror-law Accessed: 14.11.2014

Yazdiha, H. (2013) *Law as Movement Strategy: How the Islamophobia Movement Institutionalizes Fear Through Legislation*, Social Movement Studies: Journal of Social, Cultural and Political Protest. PDF.

York, C. (2014) Britain First are still using fake stories to peddle their 'message' – Huffington Post. [Online] Available at: http://www.huffingtonpost.co.uk/2014/12/01/britain-first-_n_6248286.html

Yorkshire Evening Post (2014) Jail for Leeds thug who threw can of alcohol over Muslim woman [Online] Available at: http://www.yorkshireeveningpost.co.uk/news/latest-news/top-stories/jail-for-leeds-thug-who-threw-can-of-alcohol-over-muslim-woman-1-6990672 Referenced by Pitt, B., same date, Islamophobia Watch

Yorkshire Standard (2014) 19-year-old released on bail after alleged Koran-burning video. [Online] Available at: http://www.yorkshirestandard.co.uk/news/19-year-old-released-on-bail-after-alleged-koran-burning-video-9133/ Referenced by Pitt, B., same date, Islamophobia Watch

Yorkshire Standard (2014) Britain First advises supporters to avoid Bradford, Dewsbury and all of East London. [Online] Available at: http://www.yorkshirestandard.co.uk/news/britain-first-advises-supporters-to-avoid-bradford-dewsbury-and-east-lond on-8855/ Referenced by Pitt, B., same date, Islamophobia Watch

YouGov (2004) Survey for Commission for Racial Equality. PDF.

YouGov (March, 2015)

Zahedi, A. (2011). Muslim American Women in the Post-11 September Era. *International Feminist Journal of Politics, 13,* 2, 183-203.

Zempi, I. & Chakraborti, N. (2014) Islamophobia, Victimisation and the Veil. Palgrave Pivot.